In a cultural history which considers the transformation of south Indian institutions under British colonial rule in the nineteenth century, Pamela Price focuses on the two former 'little kingdoms' of Ramnad and Sivagangai which came under colonial governance as revenue estates. She demonstrates how rivalries among the royal families and major zamindari temples, and the disintegration of indigenous institutions of rule, contributed to the development of nationalist ideologies and new political identities among the people of southern Tamil country. The author also shows how religious symbols and practices going back to the seventeenth century were reformulated and acquired a new significance in the colonial context. Arguing for a reappraisal of the relationship of Hinduism to politics, Price finds that these symbols and practices continue to inform popular expectation of political leadership today.

UNIVERSITY OF CAMBRIDGE ORIENTAL PUBLICATIONS 51

KINGSHIP AND POLITICAL PRACTICE IN COLONIAL INDIA

A series list is shown at the back of the book

Kingship and political practice in colonial India

PAMELA G. PRICE
University of Oslo

CAMBRIDGE
UNIVERSITY PRESS

CAMBRIDGE UNIVERSITY PRESS
Cambridge, New York, Melbourne, Madrid, Cape Town, Singapore, São Paulo

Cambridge University Press
The Edinburgh Building, Cambridge CB2 8RU, UK

Published in the United States of America by Cambridge University Press, New York

www.cambridge.org
Information on this title: www.cambridge.org/9780521552479

First published 1996
This digitally printed version 2008

A catalogue record for this publication is available from the British Library

Library of Congress Cataloguing in Publication data

Price, Pamela G.
Kingship and political practice in colonial India / Pamela G. Price.
     p.   cm. – (University of Cambridge oriental publications: 51)
Includes bibliographical references.
ISBN 0 521 55247 8 (hc)
1. Tamil Nadu (India) – Politics and government. 2. Ramanathapuram (India) – Politics and
government. 3. Civakaṅkai (India) – Politics and government. 4. India – History – British
occupation, 1765–1947. I. Title. II. Series: University of Cambridge oriental publications:
no. 51.
DS485.M28P74 1996
954.03 – dc20   95–17917 CIP

ISBN 978-0-521-55247-9 hardback
ISBN 978-0-521-05229-0 paperback

TO RALPH B. PRICE AND MARGARET R. PRICE

IN MEMORIAM

CONTENTS

ILLUSTRATIONS

Plates

Figures

Map

ACKNOWLEDGEMENTS

In the course of the long gestation period of this work, I have probably accumulated more than the usual debts of gratitude. For the most part I have referred to individual assistance in footnotes. Here I will take the opportunity to make some special mentions.

Robert Frykenberg and George Hart were sources of inspiration at the University of Wisconsin-Madison. The initial manuscript took form while I was living in Berkeley, California, where I regularly met up with Thomas Metcalf, Gene Irschick, David Gilmartin, Sandy Freitag, Emily Hodges and Jim Ryan, among others. Since then David and Sandy have stayed close to the progress of this study.

In Madras, C. Bhadrinath (former Commissioner of the Tamil Nadu Archives), Balachandran (formerly of the Department of Politics and Public Administration, University of Madras), and M. Raja (former Second Assistant Registrar of the High Court) greatly facilitated research which I carried out in the mid 1970s. I am grateful to the administration of the Tamil Nadu Archives and the High Court of Madras for giving me access to the necessary documents. Dick and Joanne Waghorne and Richard and Nancy Newell were ever-generous hosts in Madras, sharing their lives in south India with me.

Other scholars, students and friends in Tamil Nadu have provided valuable assistance and support. I am especially grateful to Vijaya and Saraswathi Venugopal of Madurai Kamaraj University for sharing their wide knowledge with me over many years. The late K. Paramasivam encouraged my interest in Tamil nationalist ideology. Maravar royal kin and persons associated with the royal houses of Ramnad and Sivagangai were generous with their time and patient with my questions. Of special significance were two brothers of the last Zamindar of Ramnad, Mangalanatha Dorai and Kasinath Dorai, and J. Rengaswamy Iyer, school teacher and former tutor of a Sivagangai zamindar. Jon David and Allen Eisendrath were good companions in the field, while Ed Gargan was convinced that I could not fail.

Colleagues at the University of Oslo, in particular Helge Pharo and Bjørn Qviller, have kept the faith, while contact with Hans Blomkvist of the

University of Uppsala has strengthened my confidence in the study of the *longue durée* in Indian political development.

Important in the development of this work has been contact with scholars who have worked on south India, including David Ludden, Carol Breckenridge, Arjun Appadurai, Burton Stein, David Shulman, Nick Dirks, Joanne Waghorne, Cindy Talbot, Chris Baker, Stu Blackburn and Norman Cutler. To be a part of the scholarly exploration of culture and politics in south India has been an experience of continuous intellectual stimulation. I hope this book can play a part in the renewed debate about kingship which I expect to follow from the appearance of Joanne Waghorne's *The Raja's Magic Clothes: Re-Visioning Kingship and Divinity in England's India* (University Park: The Pennsylvania State University Press, 1994). I received a copy of the book while this manuscript was in production.

I am grateful to David Gilmartin, Gunnel Cederlöf, Bjørn Qviller and Sumathi Ramaswamy for reading and commenting on the penultimate version of this work. I remain responsible for the contents.

At the University of Oslo, Tormud Klemsdal, Department of Geography, kindly drew the map and Ståle Skogstad, AV-Centre, gave photographic assistance.

Research and writing for the project were funded by: a Fulbright-Hayes Dissertation Fellowship, the Graduate School of the University of Wisconsin-Madison, a National Endowment for the Humanities Summer Stipend, the Department of History at the University of Oslo, the Norwegian Council for Research, the Institute for Comparative Cultural Studies in Oslo and the Swedish Collegium for Advanced Studies in the Social Sciences in Uppsala.

Chapters 3 and 6 are revised and expanded versions of the following articles: 'Raja-dharma in 19th Century South India: Land, Litigation and Largess in Ramnad Zamindari', *Contributions to Indian Sociology, N.S.*, vol. 13, no. 2, 1979, pp. 207–40, and 'Warrior caste "Raja" and Gentleman "Zamindar": One Person's Experience in the Late Nineteenth Century.' *Modern Asian Studies* vol. 17, pt. 4, 1983, pp. 563–90, published by Cambridge University Press.

Arne Wang has made much possible by sharing his home in Oslo with me. Ralph and Margaret Price, two outstanding teachers, were the first to talk with me about history, culture and politics.

THE TRANSLITERATION OF TAMIL WORDS

The system of transliteration of the *Madras University Tamil Lexicon* is the one generally used in this study. I have departed from this system, however, in cases where a technical word has a commonly accepted form in English usage: viz. dharma, nattamgar, pandaram, ambalagar, dharmakarta. In transliterating the names of persons, places, clans, castes and titles I have employed both conventional usage, (for example, Vellalar, Ahambadiya, Brahmin) and the usage of the documentary source (namely newspapers, letters in the files of the Board of Revenue, or diaries).

Non-English words are italicised and, where appropriate, given diacritical markings the first time they appear in the text.

GLOSSARY

abhishekam	consecration by means of pouring particular liquids
agraharam	in Sivagangai and Ramnad, a village in which Brahmins are the dominant landholders
Ahambadiya	a warrior caste allied with the Maravars, providing persons to serve on palace staffs
alangaram	decoration
antastu	an absolute status associated with wealth
arzi	an official letter or petition
betel	a nut from a palm tree which is chewed
bhajans	devotional songs
Brahmin	from the varna with the highest ritual purity, often a priest or learned in Sanskrit texts
caushauyum	a cloth given in temple ritual to signify authority
chakra	a metal plate with geometric lines used in ritual
chattiram	a house of rest and nourishment for pilgrims
Chola	a medieval kingdom (AD 900–1200) based in the Kaveri river valley
darshanan	an auspicious sight
devadasi	a woman married to a god in a temple, participating in ritual, dancing
devi	female deity
devastanam	a place or establishment of the gods
dharma	correct moral, social, political, cosmic order
dharmakarta	the protector of a temple
dharmasanam	a gift of religious charity
durbar	a public ordering of the principal domains of a kingdom with an exchange of honours between the heads of domains and the raja
ghee	clarified butter
guru	religious preceptor
guru puja	worship for a guru on a day marking his death
hundi	a draft on cash resources, a promissory note

Istimirar sanad	the grant (and its terms) of a zamindari under the colonial regime
jati	caste or subcaste
kattalai	an endowment to a temple
kaul	a lease
koyil	a temple
Kshatriya	coming from the second varna of the fourfold caste system; warriors
kulaguru	a guru whose spiritual lineage provides the religious preceptor for a family
kulatevam	the deity who protects a lineage
kumbabhishekam	a purification ceremony for a temple
Mahabharata	an ancient epic poem known throughout India
maidan	a field for military exercises; a field
mandapam	an open pavilion where rituals are performed
mantra	sacred verse; powerful verse or prayer
mariyatai	honour; marks of honour given in a ritual performance; respects
math	an institution of worship, learning and administration
lakh	one hundred thousand
Navaratri	a festival celebrating Devi, the great Goddess who is sakti
palaiyakkarar	the military chief of a domain
palaiyam	a military domain, a little kingdom
pandaram	a temple administrator
Pandyan	an early medieval kingdom based on the Vaigai river with Madurai city as its capital
parivattam	a cloth tied around the head as an honour indicating ruling authority
peshkash	tribute
pitam	a throne
prasadam	leavings from a god's meal, distributed to worshipers
puja	worship
raj	ruling regime
raja	a king
Rama	the royal hero of the epic poem, *Ramayana*, a god
Ramayana	an all-India epic poem
rani	a queen
sakti	the energy and power in the cosmos
samastanam	a kingdom; a zamindari kingdom
sanad	a grant of land giving the terms of the grant
sastras	sacred Sanskrit texts
Siva	great ascetic god of destruction
sri	royal prosperity, virtues and beauty

stanikar   a temple officer with administrative and ritual re-
                    sponsibilities
Sudra   from the fourth varna category; the servant of the
                    three higher varnas
taluk   a revenue division
tank   a pond or lake for storing water
ulluppai   offerings brought to the palace during certain festival
                    times
vallal   a man of largess, of generosity
vijaya dasami   the tenth, victorious day of the Navaratri festival
Vishnu   the great god of preservation and wealth
zamindari   a landed domain granted by a ruler; a domain made
                    into a revenue estate in the Permanent Settlement of
                    1801–3
zamindar   the holder of the title to a zamindari
zamindarni   a female zamindar
zenana   the section of a house where the women live in
                    seclusion or semi-seclusion

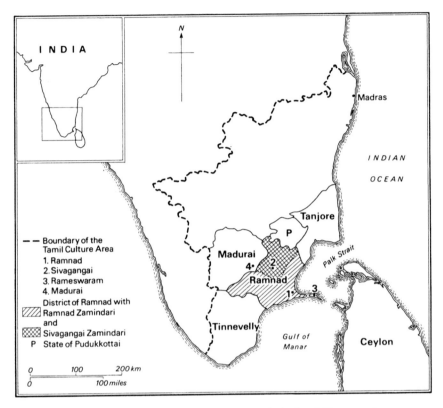

Map 1 The Ramnad district showing Ramnad Zamindari and Sivagangai Zamindari.

Introduction

Calls for the destruction of mosques and threats of rioting in western and northern India in the early 1990s almost took attention away from a bizarre political development in south India, beyond the usual breeding grounds of Hindu nationalism. At the end of the twentieth century, worship of the person of the leader, long associated with electoral politics in Tamil Nadu, has reached new extremes. Historical experience has resulted in the highlighting in Tamil Nadu of political practices which are present, but less pronounced, in other parts of India.

'Oh, Mother, you are the goddess we worship. Welcome! Welcome!' proclaimed a billboard greeting Chief Minister Jayalalitha on a campaign route.[1] A journalist continues:

To celebrate her birthday ... women embarked on long prilgrimages bearing pots of milk to offer temple gods in her name ... The adulation [of Jayalalitha] knows few bounds: trucks sponsored by her party roam the villages, tattooing likenesses of her face and torso on the arms and chests of believers. Wherever she goes, men prostrate themselves at her feet.[2]

Jayalalitha Jayaram, the former companion of Tamil Nadu's Chief Minister M. G. Ramachandran, became Chief Minister herself in 1991, approximately four years after his death. She and MGR, as he is known, had played a romantic couple in Tamil films in earlier years, though MGR was the greater star. MGR had developed a powerful personal following in the 1950s, embodying the ideals of Tamil nationalism in the films in which he starred. He was later able to turn this following, organised into fan clubs, into a formidable tool in his electoral campaigns, splitting from the Dravida Munnetra Kazhagam (DMK) and forming his own party, the AIADMK (All-India Anna DMK).[3] In the course of these campaigns and during his years as Chief Minister (1977–87), MGR's personal following developed into a widespread movement of adoration and worship. Since his death it

---

[1] Molly Moore, 'Queen Bee: She is India's Most Powerful Woman, Sweet as Honey but with a Sting', Washington Post Foreign Service, 16 October 1993. I thank Robert Hardgrave for making this article available to me.
[2] *Ibid.*
[3] DMK designates the Federation for the Progress of Dravidians.

has seemed likely that he will join the pantheon of popular heroes of Tamil culture and that shrines built to honour him will continue to appear.[4]

MGR had given Jayalalitha a post in his government, but he was careful to prevent her and other subordinates from receiving the kind of media coverage which would allow them to compete with his glamorous image. There was little to suggest that Jayalalitha would emerge eventually as the heir to MGR's charisma. In 1991, however, she portrayed herself in campaign posters as the person to whom MGR handed over royal symbols of rule. After her election, towns honoured her with presentations of swords and crowns.[5] By 1993 Chief Minister Jayalalitha had emerged with her own cult of adoration.

India has witnessed the worship of political figures before. The popular identification of Mohandas Gandhi as Mahatma or 'great soul' was an indication of the devotion which ordinary people showed him as he travelled through villages and towns in the cause of the Indian nationalist movement.[6] Newspaper stories told of the many miracles attributed to Gandhi's unusual powers. The following songs suggest special qualities which rural south Indians could find in the figure of Gandhi:

> Laugh, laugh, laugh away,
>   The King of Heaven is coming
> He, the King of Heaven is coming,
>   Say, Bodhayya:
> The King of Heaven is coming.[7]

> Our King, he was born on a wattle-mat,
> He's not the King of the velvet bed,
> He's small and he's round and he's bright and he's
>   sacred,
> O, Mahatma, Mahatma, you're our king, and we are
>   your slaves.[8]

Gandhi appears here as a royal and divine person who will some day rule in an independent India. Jayalalitha's campaign propagandists presented her as the royal heir to MGR and her followers refer to her as a goddess. That large groups of south Indians in the twentieth century relate themselves to political leadership with symbols of royalty and divinity is the effect of long-term developments in political practice.

The study here focuses on the historical experience of an area in southern

---

[4] M. S. S. Pandian, *The Image Trap: M. G. Ramachandran in Film and Politics* (New Delhi: Sage Publications, 1992), pp. 129–30.
[5] See photographs in *The Hindu* and the *Indian Express*, 23 August 1991.
[6] Shahid Amin, 'Gandhi as Mahatma: Gorakhpur District, Eastern UP, 1921–2', in Ranajit Guha, *Subaltern Studies III: Writings on South Asian History and Society* (Delhi: Oxford University Press, 1984), pp. 1–61.
[7] Raja Rao, *Kanthapura* (Delhi: Orient Paperbacks, 1971), p. 81. Raja Rao places his village in the Western Ghats, facing the Arabian Sea, p. 7.
[8] *Ibid*, p. 203.

India, demonstrating that non-western nationalisms and the particularistic politics of corruption bear the stamp of the regions and localities of their appearance. I examine political practice and values in southern Tamil country over a period of three centuries. The work is a contribution to a new tendency in writing on non-western politics focusing on the political *longue durée.* Most of the articles in the collection *Rethinking Third World Politics,* for example, suggest that the capacity to explain political development in the twentieth century improves when one takes a long-term perspective.[9] With such a perspective, one is able not only to examine the colonial experiences of communities, but also to discuss precolonial political models and ideologies.[10]

Narratives of the fate of precolonial regimes usually focus on their military downfall: chieftain X and his army were defeated by the French on the banks of Y River, while at the foot of the Z hills the British trounced the forces of two sultans and a king. Chronologies of military defeat, however, do not reveal the fate of structures and ideologies which had contributed to the functioning of old regimes. Understanding political society under colonial rule involves investigating the encounter between the new regime and institutions which had contributed to the formation of precolonial political cultures.[11] One finds that the decentralised, segmented nature of precolonial polities and societies allowed for the survival of important models and symbols for the reproduction of aspects of the political cultures of old regimes.[12]

In the narrative and analysis presented here I show that political values and conceptions derived from precolonial polities in the Tamil country continued to be transmitted in political practice, dulling the impact of colonial rule. These models and symbols changed at different rates, and

---

[9] See James Manor, ed., *Rethinking Third World Politics* (London: Longman, 1991), especially Jean-François Bayart, 'Finishing with the Idea of the Third World: The Concept of the Political Trajectory', pp. 51–71. My earlier efforts in this direction are 'Kingly Models in Indian Political Behavior: Culture as a Medium of History', in *Asian Survey*, vol. 29, no. 6, 1989, pp. 559–72; 'Using Cultural History in Development Studies', in *Forum for utviklingsstudier*, No. 2, 1989, pp. 147–58; and 'Democracy and Ethnic Conflict in India: Precolonial Legacies in Tamil Nadu', in *Asian Survey*, vol. 33, no. 5, 1993, pp. 493–506.

[10] Other recent works showing a similar interest are Douglas Haynes, *Rhetoric and Ritual in Colonial India: The Shaping of a Public Culture in Surat City, 1852–1928* (Berkeley: University of California Press, 1991); Sandria B. Freitag, *Collective Action and Community: Public Arenas and the Emergence of Communalism in North India* (Berkeley: University of California Press, 1989); and David Gilmartin, *Empire and Islam: Punjab and the Making of Pakistan* (Berkeley: University of California Press, 1988).

[11] Two studies which do this in Indian history are Thomas R. Metcalf, *Land, Landlords and the British Raj: Northern India in the Nineteenth Century* (Berkeley: University of California Press, 1979) and Arjun Appadurai, *Worship and Conflict under Colonial Rule: A South Indian Case* (Cambridge: Cambridge University Press, 1981).

[12] Recent works illustrating this point are Andrew Apter, *Black Critics and Kings: The Hermeneutics of Power in Yoruba Society* (Chicago: University of Chicago Press, 1992) and Shelly Errington, *Meaning and Power in a Southeast Asian Realm* (Princeton: Princeton University Press, 1989).

patterns of political behaviour altered, but innovations generally took place within certain parameters. These parameters were determined, in part, by the presuppositions of actors as to what constituted appropriate political action. Aspects of precolonial political cosmologies continued to inform actors' ideas of political legitimacy, the nature of power and authority, and the content of honour and political status.

Scholars of political behaviour achieve better explanatory results when they take actors' conceptions of power into consideration.[13] In adopting this method I find that the perception of honour and status as subjective reflections of objective powers is analytically inadequate. Entering into the political universe of late precolonial Tamil country and exploring the fate of precolonial symbols and values involves considering honour and status as independent, not dependent, elements in political calculations. It is necessary not only to contextualise culturally concepts of power, but also concepts of honour and status.

In discussing political practice from the late seventeenth century to the late twentieth century, I focus on a particular dynamic. This dynamic is competition among political elites involving issues of honour and status. In different historical periods the requirements for participation in this competition altered, but a preoccupation with personal honour and status in political domains has been consistent. Some of the reasons for this consistency in political action lie in the decentralised character of political society in precolonial Tamil country and in the ways in which Tamil communities interacted with institutions of British colonial rule. Aspects of precolonial political culture continued to evolve, surviving colonial rule and persisting into post-independence Tamil Nadu.

In making this argument I enter into debates in the field of South Asian studies concerning, in particular, the relationship of worship to political symbolism and action, the fate of monarchical institutions under colonial rule and the emergence of public spheres in India. A focus on the adjustment of monarchical institutions to colonial rule highlights the extent to which what we now call Hinduism served (and to an extent still serves) as ideologies of ruling administration in segmented domains. The 'embedded' nature of symbols of worship with notions of power, honour and authority helped to mitigate the potential of colonial hegemony for radical disruption in local political cultures. I argue here then that kingly culture still makes its mark in Tamil political discourse. In the course of discussing changes in monarchical structures and ideologies I find that the particularistic politics of localities were not radically discontinuous with the more universalist concerns and actions in civic arenas under colonial rule.

As public spheres emerged in the nineteenth century, the politics of

---

[13] An early statement of this methodology is the article by Benedict Anderson, 'The Idea of Power in Javanese Culture', in Claire Holt (ed.) with B. Anderson and J. Seigel, *Culture and Politics in Indonesia* (Ithaca: Cornell University Press, 1972), pp. 1–69.

particularism fed the strategies of those who would bridge the gap between unitary and segmented governing structures, achieving influence in both domains. This work thus takes issue with some of the conclusions of Douglas Haynes in his study of public culture and a civic arena in western India.[14] My argument also joins the debate raised by the *Subaltern* series concerning the autonomy of non-elite political cultures.[15] The implications of this study suggest that the potential for subaltern autonomy in Tamil country has been seriously compromised by the participation of subalterns in local institutions of worship and rule.

Precolonial Hindu culture was organised at least as much around institutions of kingship as it was around institutions of caste.[16] Because of the continuing special status and authority of royal institutions in the post-conquest period, the nature of their adaptation to colonial rule had a significance which far outweighed the relatively small number of persons involved.[17] Competition for royal honour and status occurred according to both old and new rules and had a destructive impact on the symbolic relationships which had informed precolonial political visions.[18] Cultural borrowing occurred as new relationships formed, using old and new symbols and meanings. In the midst of political transformation there was continuous preoccupation with the special status of the head of a domain. Such a focus both supports and is a function of widespread social and political segmentation, where personal rule characterises the structure of authority in a broad range of social, economic and political domain segments.[19] Monarchical political values, altered and evolved, have lived on in Tamil Nadu, in old and new institutions, informing notions of personal value and authority among Tamils.

Any evaluation of the effects of British colonial hegemony must include analysis of interactions 'interior' to Indian society. Patterns of interaction in competition were determined at least as much by evolving indigenous models as they were by concepts and institutions of the British empire.

---

[14] Haynes, *Rhetoric and Ritual in Colonial India*.

[15] See the various volumes in the series of collected essays, *Subaltern Studies: Writings on South Asian History and Society*, published in Delhi by Oxford University Press.

[16] Ronald Inden discusses this issue in 'Orientalist Constructions of India', in *Modern Asian Studies*, vol. 20, no. 3, pp. 401–46. From the point of view of cultural anthropology see Gloria Goodwin Raheja, 'India: Caste, Kingship and Dominance Reconsidered', in *Annual Review of Anthropology*, 1988, vol. 17, pp. 497–522.

[17] For a general discussion of the social significance of sacred kings see Marshal Sahlins, 'Other Times, Other Customs: The Anthropology of History', *American Anthropologist*, vol. 85, no. 3, 1983, pp. 517–44.

[18] This argument differs from Anil Seal's discussion of competition in his *Emergence of Indian Nationalism* (Cambridge: Cambridge University Press, 1968) in that the focus of the dynamic I discuss is found in political engagements among Indians, not in their relationship to the colonial regime.

[19] Rajnarayan Chandavarkar, 'Industrialization in India before 1947: Conventional Approaches and Alternative Perspectives', *Modern Asian Studies*, vol. 19, no. 3, 1985, pp. 623–8, suggests that industrial production according to local models can have elements of segmentation.

British colonial rule clearly accentuated and accelerated local processes of conflict and competition, and colonial institutions became arenas for major encounters among Indians. However, despite the role of colonial rule in the dislocation of procolonial institutions, the dynamic of political interaction was, in major ways, culturally south Indian. Evidence for this assertion comes from the focus here on discrete actions – the agency – of persons meeting historical contingencies with the use of both indigenous and colonial categories and concepts, with the manipulation of indigenous and colonial institutions and ideologies to achieve personally constructed goals.[20]

This work provides a counter-argument to Nicholas Dirks, who produced an important study of precolonial political culture in *The Hollow Crown: The Ethnohistory of an Indian Kingdom*.[21] Dirks argues for the total collapse under colonial rule of those political structures and processes which could have supported the continuing evolution of a vital royal culture. He finds colonial rule putting south Indian kingship in a 'deep freeze', creating a festishised obsession with symbols of past glory in a theatre state with an empty stage.[22] Elsewhere he argues that former little kings carried out their royal activities in 'the vortex of a cultural lag'.[23] The analysis here of political change in Maravar country, an area contiguous to Dirks' little kingdom of Pudukkottai, shows, however, powerful processes for the continuing evolution of royal symbols and values under colonial rule. Examining these processes helps us to explain the nature of the charisma of major Tamil politicians of the twentieth century.

This is not to assert that precolonial monarchical cosmologies survived intact the establishment of a modern, centralised state apparatus and the development of nationalist visions. These developments occurred amid the disintegration, to greater and lesser degrees, of institutional relationships which had supported precolonial political culture. Deformation took place above village level in the formulation of new modes of association among the remaining fragments of former systems of rule. The activities of imperial integration which occurred in the nineteenth century created new connections among heads of indigenous domains of authority and control at the same time as these heads entered into innovative ties with the imperial overlord. The new world view of nineteenth-century South Asian elites developed contemporaneously with the fragmentation – not destruction – of precolonial political visions.

---

[20] For a discussion of 'interest' as a dynamic element of human practice in the context of schemes of cultural categories, see Marshal Sahlins, *Islands of History* (Chicago: University of Chicago Press, 1985), pp. 145–51.

[21] Published in Cambridge by Cambridge University Press, 1987.

[22] See, for example, *Ibid.*, pp. 333, 355–7, 369, 397 and 402.

[23] Nicholas B. Dirks, 'From Little King to Landlord: Property, Law and the Gift under the Madras Permanent Settlement', *Comparative Studies in Society and History*, vol. 28, no. 2, 1986, p. 332.

Historians have usually interpreted the political behaviour of royal Indians in the nineteenth century as inappropriate. Legally, under direct British rule in south India, these figures were holders of estates called *zamindaris*. Their administrative title was *zamindar*, 'land-holder' in Persian. The efforts of these persons to present themselves as particularly important often appear today as – at best – colourful and somewhat comic. Alternatively, scholars and critics dismiss zamindari scenarios as futile and pathetic or the product of decadence and oppressive intent. The particularities of zamindari history have diverted attention from the ways in which this history epitomises a major transformation in Indian politics: the adaptation of the cultures of relatively decentralised precolonial state forms, orientated towards personal rule, to the establishment of the more centralised, formally bureaucratic colonial state. This was a process which took place, in various ways, in colonial possessions around the world.

In a cultural study of the fate of former kings we find part of the pattern of the retention of the past in modern Tamil Nadu. In narrating parts of the political drama, we find the practice through which the meaning of major symbols was altered. Focusing on a sub-region, Maravar country, I examine the fragmentation and continuing evolution of precolonial political cosmologies through description and analysis of major events in monarchical politics in the colonial period.

Sivagangai and Ramnad were contiguous little kingdoms in the eighteenth century, both ruled by Maravar warriors of the high-ranking Sembinattu clan. Maravars are mentioned in ancient Tamil Sangam poetry (written in about the first to third centuries, AD) as particularly terrifying fighters. By at least the sixteenth century the core area of their domination comprised a dry and flat coastal plain in south-east Tamil country which stretches out, south of the green and lush delta of Tanjore, towards the island of Sri Lanka.

Maravar country was intimidating to outsiders not only because of its fierce dominant clans, but because the territory itself resembled the *palai* region, one of the five indigenous ecological categories of ancient Tamil poetry.[24] Forested and filled with wild animals, oven-warm in the blazing sun of summer, to outsiders Maravar country called up the stereotypic emotions of the palai: thoughts of separation from loved ones, fear, anxiety and sorrow. With such an inhospitable resource base, Maravar country did not serve as an early target for the development of intensely stratified, highly ritually elaborated social formations. These were a function of the river-fed nuclear areas which gave rise to the great dynasties of medieval

---

[24] David Shulman, 'The Crossing of the Wilderness: Landscape and Myth in the Tamil Story of Rama', *Acta Orientalia*, vol. 42, 1981, pp. 21–54, and Xavier S. Thani Nayagam, *Landscapes and Poetry: A Study of Nature in Classical Tamil Poetry* (London: Asia Publishing House, 1966), p. 83.

Tamil society.[25] By the end of the seventeenth century, however, a powerful kingdom, Ramanathapuram (referred to here by its English designation, Ramnad), had emerged in Maravar country. In a process of political fragmentation which took place throughout south Indian in the eighteenth century, Sivagangai broke off to have a short existence as an independent kingdom. As the British expanded and consolidated their rule, forming the Presidency of Madras, both kingdoms became zamindaris, revenue estates, under the Permanent Settlement of 1801.[26]

The first chapter of this study outlines major features of precolonial Tamil polity and explains recurring tensions in elite political practice in Maravar country. I then turn to the evolution in dynastic competition which took place in the nineteenth century in the form of zamindari litigation in the law courts of the colonial legal system. Later chapters examine other monarchical institutions in the two former kingdoms, discussing the relationship between the ruling houses and important institutions of worship, and analysing major ritual performances and the career of a king.

The conclusion takes several themes from nineteenth century political development in Maravar country and traces their expression in political practice in twentieth century Tamil country, today's Tamil Nadu.[27]

---

[25] Burton Stein, 'Integration of the Agrarian System of South India', in R. E. Frykenberg (ed.), *Land Control and Social Structure in Indian History* (Madison: University of Wisconsin, 1969), pp. 175–216.

[26] Ramnad Zamindari was approximately 2,000 square miles in area and included about 2,167 villages. Sivagangai was approximately 1,200 square miles with about 2,058 villages. Cultivable area in Ramnad Zamindari was 538,000 acres, a quarter or more of which was waste throughout the nineteenth century. We know that Sivagangai had better resources in water, but figures of cultivable land and waste were not available.

[27] The discussion of the 'zamindari system' here retreats from the usual focus on the aims of British administration in setting up the Permanent Settlement. Within forty years of the Settlement in Madras Presidency, zamindari tenure had become associated in the official mind with disinterest in management, improvidence, financially suicidal litigation, burdensome debt and bankruptcy. Thousands of villages were lost from entitled families and only administrative indulgence saved the rest during the remaining decades of the century. By the end of the nineteenth century in Madras, Bernard Cohn reports that 804 zamindars held 40 per cent of the land. The remaining 60 per cent was in *ryotwari* tenure, held theoretically by about three million cultivators with individual titles to their plots. Bernard S. Cohn, 'Recruitment of Elites in India under British Rule', in Leonard Plotnicov and Arthur Tuden (eds.), *Essays in Comparative Social Stratification* (Pittsburgh: University of Pittsburgh, 1970), p. 132.

1
Honour, status and state formation in seventeenth- and eighteenth-century Maravar country

In outlining major features of precolonial politics in Maravar country, the main focus here is on the nature and goals of elite conflict. Examining recurring tensions in political culture and contradictions in principles of political practice, this chapter discusses elements of precolonial polity which had an impact on the development of elite engagement after colonial pacification.

In becoming acquainted with the major features of politics and worship in Maravar country one has to abandon stereotypes of an India of Brahminical dominance, obsession with ritual purity, rigid social orders and agriculture carried out with untouchable labour. This is a more fitting illustration of the highly stratified communities of wet land agriculture in the major river valleys of Tamil country. These lush, socially elaborate areas of rice cultivation were bounded geographically by socially simpler plains. The latter were peopled by cattle and sheep herders, thieving warriors and tribes. Settled agriculture developed more slowly among the dry land groups. It seems possible that the ideas of transcendent purity, divine authority and ritual rule, which characterised the institutions of kings and Brahmins of the richer stratified settlements, also emerged here later than in the valley communities.[1]

Poor soils and little rain did not completely isolate Maravar country from the elegance and oppression of sophisticated wet land living. Here, even if conventional ideas of status were less firmly anchored (than in the Tanjore delta) in notions of caste rank and ritual purity, in medieval times the area had a reasonable sprinkling of settlements which were integrated into the cultural geography of, not only Tamil country, but the South Asian subcontinent.

Maravar country was a dry plains area, inhabited by notoriously fierce and independent clans. Popular worship among these groups included blood sacrifices intended to propitiate minor gods and spirits. This worship

---

[1] The most explicit statement of this view is Susan Bayly, *Saints, Goddesses and Kings: Muslims and Christians in South Indian Society, 1700–1900* (Cambridge: Cambridge University Press, 1989), pp. 19–70. See also Christopher Baker, *An Indian Rural Economy, 1880–1955: The Tamil countryside* (Delhi: Oxford University Press, 1984), pp. 19–97.

was in stark contrast to the clean-caste worship, with flowers and fruits, of a transcendent Vishnu or Siva in river valley temples in Tanjore. By the seventeenth century, however, the warriors and agriculturalists of Maravar country were incorporated into the same political universe as that of river valley folk. This is partly because the plains people became active participants in a political culture with notions of power, status and authority which became widespread in the Tamil country between the fourteenth and sixteenth centuries. By the fifteenth century the area had also linked up with subcontinental traditions. A major pilgrimage site was Rameswaram Temple, found on Rameswaram Island, separated from the mainland by a narrow passage.[2] The temple marks the place where Rama, the hero of the epic *Ramayana*, worshipped the god Siva on the way back from his battle with the demon Ravana, lord of the island of Lanka. The title of the king of the Ramnad Kingdom of Maravar country, Setupati, reflects the privilege and responsibility of protecting the site.[3] Pilgrims from all parts of the subcontinent have been attracted to Rameswaram since at least the sixteenth century.[4]

That Maravar country, even as a dry area, should play an important role in subcontinental traditions, is mainly due to its coastline of about 120 miles, which stretches out towards the island of Sri Lanka, twenty-one miles away from the furthest point of Rameswaram Island. The waters of the Gulf of Manar and Palk Bay provided coral, *chank* (conch shells) and, especially, pearls, which had attracted merchants to the area from ancient times. The closeness of the area's ports to the more fertile lands of Sri Lanka drew the attention of monarchs ambitious for conquest of the island, as well as persons of less militant mercantile designs.

Mainland Maravar country was well integrated into regional Tamil cultural geography. It constituted the south-eastern section of the territory of Pandyamandalam, named for early medieval kings who ruled from Madurai town, on the Vaigai river.[5] Temple inscriptions found in Maravar

---

[2] James Burgess and S. M. Natesa Sastri, *Tamil and Sanskrit Inscriptions*, Archæological Survey of Southern India, vol. IV (Madras: The Government Press, 1886), pp. 56–7.

[3] Setupati means Lord of the Setu, the passageway Lord Rama used to return to the mainland from Lanka. The Setu is called Adam's Bridge in English. Agreements between the Dutch and the Setupati in the seventeenth century show that the Setupati was called 'the Tevar', a title which came to be (or was at that time) the 'caste' title used by Maravars. See S. Thananjarajasingham, *A Critical Study of Seventeenth Century Tamil Document Relation to a Commercial Treaty* (Peradeniya: The Hindu Students' Union, 1968), pp. 1 and 14. To the Dutch it appears that the Setupati was known simply as 'the Tevar': S. Arasaratnam, 'The Dutch East India Company and the Kingdom of Madurai, 1650–1700', *Tamil Culture*, vol. 10, no. 1, 1963, pp. 48–74. In the historical ballad, *Rāmayyaṉ Ammāṉai*, describing a mid-seventeenth-century invasion of Maravar country by the forces of the Nayaka of Madurai, the Setupati is known as 'the Maravar'.

[4] A. Ramaswami, *Tamil Nadu District Gazetteers: Ramanathapuram. Gazetteer of India* (Madras: The Government of Tamil Nadu, 1972), p. 946.

[5] Burton Stein, *Peasant State and Society in Medieval South India* (Delhi: Oxford University Press, 1980), map opposite page 286.

country, dating from the eleventh century, indicate the interest of Pandyan and Chola monarchs in dominating the area.[6] That temples became established in the medieval period indicates the early interest of local elites in forms of worship and political control and processes of economic development found in the river valleys.[7]

The area shared in the religio-literary traditions of the ancient and medieval periods. Nattarasankottai, six miles north-east of Sivagangai town, for example, is known as the place where the most celebrated of Tamil poets, the twelfth-century writer Kampan, is buried.[8] The birth of Masathiar, a female poet of ancient Sangam literature, is associated with Okkur, seven and a half miles north of Sivagangai,[9] while the birth of Maran Nayanar, one of the sixty-three Saivite saints appearing in the famous poem *Periapuranam*, is associated with Ilayangudi.[10] Such renowned poet-saints as the medieval Gnanasambandar, Manickavasagar and Sundarar visited sites in Maravar country and sang in praise of the god appearing there.[11]

Beginning with the period of the Vijayanagara Kingdom (fourteenth to sixteenth centuries), south India experienced an acceleration in activities of state formation which resulted in the widespread acceptance of monarchical cosmologies and the symbols and institutions which supported them. The political interests of warriors, not protection of the status of Brahmins, focused the cultural agenda.[12] With the dominance of warrior values and an increased absorption in ruling power, blood sacrifice came to have greater significance and higher status among ruling elites.[13] Inscriptional evidence indicates that Maravar country was integrated into the south Indian religio-political universe of this period.[14] As in other dry land areas, lands were increasingly brought under the control of groups which linked their status to the construction and maintenance of supra-village temples and the development of small irrigation units in tank-based, settled agriculture.[15] By

[6] V. Rangacharya, *A Topographical List of the Inscriptions of the Madras Presidency* (Madras: Government Press, 1919), vol. II, pp. 1158–97.

[7] James Heitzman discusses the political ramifications of the integration of local elites into the royal institutions of wet land agriculture in 'State Formation in South India, 850–1280', *The Indian Economic and Social History Review*, vol. 24, no. 1, 1987, pp. 57–61.

[8] Ibid., p. 923. Kamil Zvelibil reports that the poet was born in present-day Tanjore district in *Tamil Literature* vol. 10, fasc. 1 of J. Gonda, ed., *History of Indian Literature* (Weisbaden: Harrassowitz, 1974), p. 146.

[9] Ramaswami, *Ramanathapuram Gazetteer*, p. 926.

[10] *Ibid.*, p. 882.

[11] *Ibid.*, pp. 871 and 891, and Rangacharya, *A Topographical List*, p. 1176.

[12] This tendency became even stronger in the sixteenth century. See *Symbols of Substance: Court and State in Nāyaka Period Tamil Nadu* (Delhi: Oxford University Press, 1992), by Velcheru Narayana Rao, David Shulman and Sanjay Subramanyam.

[13] See, for example, Konduri Sarojini Devi, *Religion in Vijayanagar Empire* (New Delhi: Sterling Publishers Private Limited, 1990), p. 273.

[14] Rangacharya, *A Topographical List*, pp. 1159–97.

[15] David Ludden, *Peasant History in South India* (Princeton: Princeton University Press, 1985), pp. 42–67.

the eighteenth century, Maravar country was pitted with small tanks for catching rainwater which were part of systems of larger irrigation works. Because of the segmented nature of both social incorporation (of clans into castes) and political incorporation (of chieftaincies into decentralised royal domains), aspects of the area's local culture and identity survived.

Commercial expansion: introducing the Nattukkottai Chettiars

The expansion of ambition for independent royal status in Maravar country had a material basis. This basis did not necessarily influence the content of political goals so much as it provided new possibilities for their achievement. It is possible that the acceleration of state formation which saw the blossoming of chiefly pretensions to high royal status in the late precolonial period was due to new developments in commercial activities.

An extraordinary opening up of new possibilities for wealth and political negotiation came to coastal areas with the expansion of trade along the coasts of India, in the Indian Ocean and Arabian Sea and with the arrival of European traders. Arasaratnam's work on the southern coastal kingdoms of the late seventeenth century illustrates that the emergence of the Setupati as a mature participant in monarchical politics coincided with his growing involvement in, and control over, considerable actitivities of trade.[16] The Raja of Ramnad formed new alliances with Muslim traders and encouraged groups with sought-after skills to immigrate to his domain.[17]

The intertwining of Ramnad royal interests and those of merchants is found at least as early as 1660. During the time of Raja Ragunatha Setupati (1647–72), merchants of the kingdom exported cotton textiles from local weaving communities to Coromandel and Malabar ports and to Sri Lanka. This trade was facilitated by Setupati control of the channel between Rameswaram Island and the Indian mainland, through which all ships going between the two coasts had to pass.[18] While a caste of merchants, the Nattukkottai Chettiars, may have been involved in this trade, in the seventeenth and eighteenth centuries Marikkar Muslims maintained closer ties with royal kin. Marikkar boats carried royal merchandise – in particular, conch shells and pearls – to markets, bringing back horses for the Maravar army.[19] In turn, the Setupati attempted to protect Marikkar trade from Dutch incursions, with arms and agreements. Perhaps because of their support of the deposed Muthu Ramalingam Tevar at the end of the

---

[16] Arasaratnam, 'The Dutch East India Company' and his 'The Politics of Commerce in the Coastal Kingdom of Tamil Nad, 1650–1700', in *South Asia*, no. 1, 1971, pp. 1–19.

[17] Arasaratnam, 'The Politics of Commerce', and his 'A Note on Periathamby Marikkar – a 17th Century Commercial Magnate', *Tamil Culture*, vol. 11, no. 1, 1964, pp. 51-7.

[18] S. Arasaratnam, 'Commercial Policies of the Sethupathis of Ramanathapuram 1660–1690', *Proceedings of the Second International Conference Seminar of Tamil Studies* (Madras: International Association of Tamil Research, 1971), p. 251.

[19] *Ibid.*

eighteenth century, the Marikkars receded from prominence with the consolidation of British imperial rule over Maravar country.

The Nattukkottai Chettiars, also known as Nagarathars, had been involved in trade for centuries. Some writers hold that their maritime trading activities existed at least from the eighth century.[20] What is clear is that by the early seventeenth century they had emerged as itinerant merchants in salt and that, in the early ninteenth century, they were expanding their trading activities into Southeast Asia.[21] European imperial expansion and consolidation in the eighteenth century created opportunities for the broad extension of Nagarathar enterprise.

An agriculturally bleak area of north-east Sivagangai, north-western Ramnad and southern Pudukkottai state became known as Chettinad, the ancestral base of the Nattukkottai Chettiars. According to caste tales, the settlement of Chettinad followed upon continuous alterations of royal honour and support and royal persecution in other areas of south India. One story has the Nagarathars migrating to Ramnad after a Chola king massacred their women and destroyed their businesses when they refused to submit to his authority.[22] Another story finds a Pandyan king seeking the merchants' services and requesting that a Chola king send the caste to Pandyan-controlled territory, including Ramnad country.[23] However the Nagarathars may have reached Ramnad area, a local ruler is said to have granted them nine temples which are often quoted as 'caste' temples, each one corresponding to an exogamous sub-division of the community.[24] Even as their trading and moneylending firms expanded transactions over a wide geographical region, throughout Southeast Asia, and great fortunes were made, Chettinad remained the main base of Nagarathar caste organisation. From here it came to play a major role in royal finances in the colonial period.

Aspects of precolonial polities

It is not possible to analyse precolonial activities of state formation in Tamil country according to categories taken from conventional western social science. Bureaucratic and legal centralisation, marked territorial boundaries, and a monopoly of violence characterised the seventeenth- and eighteenth-century European states which Weber used as models for his

[20] M. Nadarajan, 'The Nattukkottai Chettiar Community and Southeast Asia', *Proceedings of the First International Conference Seminar of Tamil Studies* (Kuala Lumpur: International Association of Tamil Research, 1968) vol. 1, pp. 251-2.
[21] David West Rudner, *Caste and Capitalism in Colonial India: the Nattukottai Chettiars* (Berkeley: University of California Press, 1994).
[22] M. Nadarajan, 'The Nattukkottai Chettiar Community and Southeast Asia', p. 252.
[23] Edgar Thurston, *Castes and Tribes of Southern India* (New York: Johnson Reprint Corporation, 1965), vol. M to P, p. 260. Originally published in Madras, 1909.
[24] Rudner, *Caste and Capitalism*, gives an analysis of Nagarathar kinship.

famous definition.[25] During the last twenty-five years scholars of south India have achieved persuasive results by applying a model in which decentralisation rather than centralisation is the predominant feature in the organisation of the state.[26] In this model participation in palace and temple ritual performances, rather than the observance of universally applied regulations and laws, was a major support in the integration of royal polities. The boundaries of the state were fluid and shifting, local chiefs organised their own armies, and local communities processed disputes according to locally established codes.

There has been scepticism and some confusion among South Asianists about the use of the terms 'segmentary' and 'segmented' in outlining models for the precolonial state in India. This is because of Burton Stein's initial dependency on Southall's discussion of segmentary state formation among African groups with a specific segmentary lineage system.[27] Recent debate in the field of anthropology focuses on the legitimacy of applying terms developed in analysis of one ethnographic context to analysis of related phenomena elsewhere.[28] Emboldened by this debate, the word 'segmented' is employed in this study to suggest relatively decentralised systems of social and political organisation in which authority is dispersed in discrete domains. The organisation of political interaction within these domains may be modelled on those of an exemplary centre, a domain segment of special status.

It is helpful to consider, in this context, Stanley Tambiah's discussion of a model for decentralisation in state formation in Southeast Asia.[29] He draws attention to the *mandala* as an archetype for the organisation of (sacred) power in ancient and medieval South Asian society:

[T]he *mandala* ... according to a common Indo Tibetan tradition is composed of two elements − a core (*manda*) and a container or enclosing element (*la*). Mandala designs, both simple and complex, of satellites arranged around a center, occur with

---

[25] Susanne Hoeber Rudolph, 'Presidential Address: State Formation in Asia − Prolegomenon to a Comparative Study', *Journal of Asian Studies*, vol. 46, no. 4, 1987, pp. 731–46.

[26] Important contributions to this scholarship include Arjun Appadurai, 'Kings, Sects and Temples in South India, 1250–1700', in Burton Stein (ed.), *South Indian Temples: An Analytic Reconsideration* (New Delhi: Vikas Publishing House, 1978), pp. 47–73; Appadurai and Carol A Breckenridge, 'The South Indian Temple: Authority, Honor and Redistribution', in *Contributions to Indian Sociology (N.S.)*, vol. 10, no. 2, 1976, pp. 187–211; Nicholas Dirks, 'The Structure and Meaning of Political Relations in a South Indian Little Kingdom', in *Contributions to Indian Sociology (N.S.)*, vol. 13, no. 2, 1979, pp. 169–206; Dirks, 'Political Authority and Structural Change in Early South Indian History', in *Indian Economic and Social History Review*, vol. 13, no. 2, 1976, pp. 125–58; Burton Stein, *Peasant State and Society.*

[27] Stein, *Peasant State and Society*, pp. 23, 265–6.

[28] Paul Dresch, 'Segmentation: Its roots in Arabia and its flowering elsewhere', in *Cultural Anthropology*, vol. 3, no. 1, 1988, pp. 50–67.

[29] S. J. Tambiah, 'The Galactic Polity in Southeast Asia', in his *Culture, Thought and Social Action* (Cambridge, Mass.: Harvard University Press, 1985), pp. 253–87.

such insistence at various levels of Hindu Buddhist thought and practice that one is invited to probe their representational efficacy.[30]

That the mandala model was significant for medieval Tamils in certain periods is seen in their designation of the Chola domain and its major segments in terms of a mandala: Cholamandalam, Pandyamandalam, Tondaimandalam, and so on.[31]

The segments which constituted the late precolonial state were political domains of different sizes, each with a head who bore responsibility for protection of the domain. This protection involved the organisation of force, the management of major conflicts and the securing of regular worship in the temples and shrines which were important to the domain as a community of worshippers. Religious and political values and concepts together constituted ideological systems which supported the legitimacy of the head of a domain.

The heads of the major domain segments of the state took part in rituals which celebrated the superior power, honour and status of the highest-ranking ruler among them. The king and his ministers ranked above other domain heads as rulers of lesser status who shared ruling authority with the king, the chief worshipper of the realm. All domain heads engaged in ritual transactions of substances (food, cloth, jewels, etc.) with important gods and their consorts, mediated by temple priests. It was through these transactions that the gods shared their ruling authority with human rulers.

In south India ruling authority did not belong exclusively to the highest-ranking among domain heads. It was shared among gods and men in rank order. The highest ranking human ruler had the right to transact with highest honours with the highest-ranking gods. Lesser ranking heads exchanged less spectacular honours in their ritual transactions with each other and with less spectacular gods. *Mariyātai* is the word commonly used to designate these honours. It is derived from the Sanskrit *maryādā-*, with the meanings 'frontier, limit, bounds of morality and propriety, custom'.[32] In Tamil the meanings of mariyatai which were most relevant in ritual contexts were: 'courtesy, reverence, propriety of conduct', suggesting dharmic qualities.[33] The word 'dharmic' refers to the moral order of the cosmos and correct relations among human beings in a domain.

Through his exchange of honours with divinities, a ruler came to acquire a partly divine nature himself. In ritual performances organised in palaces and temples, therefore, a ruler was approached as a human with a somewhat divine nature. The highest-ranking rulers in the domains of a segmentary state were the most divine in their nature. Ritual transactions, combined

---

[30] *Ibid.*, p. 252.
[31] Stein, *Peasant State and Society*, pp. 285 and the map opposite p. 286.
[32] M. B. Emeneau and T. Burrow, *Dravidian Borrowings from Indo-Aryan* (Berkeley: University of California Press, 1962), p. 53.
[33] *Ibid.*

with success in warfare, resulted in their acquiring special status and honour compared to others.

It was the privilege and responsibility of the king to legitimise access to major resources in his kingdom. He confirmed the legitimacy of the lesser domain heads – their right to rule in preference, say, to a rival – when he invited them to his assemblies, honoured them and allowed them to honour him. Small or large domain heads allocated privileges of taking or receiving income from villages to men and women who served the realm. These included those who provided military leadership and combat service; those who organised and performed rituals in temples and ruling households; those who engaged in artistic or scholarly work to honour the ruler and his gods; and those who held village offices.

In their person kings represented the totality of their kingdoms. They were the human expression of the cosmology of their domain. Particularly in the context of notions of *dharma* (human and divine order and responsibility), any formal head of a domain bore a special relationship to the community he represented. The relationship was a significant feature of segmentary polities, a characteristic structure of authority. In these polities all heads of domains – not only chiefs, little kings and the great king – ruled, including *paterfamilias*; clan, caste and village headmen; and the administrators of temples and *maths* ('monasteries'). The exchange of honours in ritual outlined visually the administrative network of personal rule, the structure of authority.

The ruler of a large regional domain could not feasibly call all heads of domains to his assembly. Superior honour and status were acquired, there-fore, from an invitation to participate in the assemblies of the high-ranking. Around the time of the fall of the capital of the Vijayanagara Kingdom, in 1565, the ruler of the former Vijayanagara province of Madurai, Visvanatha Nayaka (c. 1529–64), selected seventy-two chiefs (*pālaiyakkārars*) of the territory as worthy of his recognition.[34] Visvanatha and the other rulers of Madurai followed the pattern of the Vijayanagara kings in periodically distributing marks of honour to the military chiefs and rulers of the area. Tirumalai Nayaka of Madurai (ruler from 1623 to 1659), for example, issued the following insignia to the Palaiyakkaran of Virukpakshi Palaiyam:

An ornament for the turban; a single-leaved ... diadem; a necklace worn by warriors; a golden bangle for the right leg; a chain of gold; a toe-ring of gold; a palanquin with a lion's face in front; an elephant with a howdah or castle; ... a horse with all its caparisons; ... a white umbrella; an ensign with the representation of a boar; a green parasol; white handkerchiefs to be waved.[35]

Such transactions in ritual ranking signified moral and political differ-ences in the identity of persons, the varying extent to which they shared authority with gods and other men in the kingdom. However, the visual

[34]   Dirks, *The Hollow Crown*, p. 49–50. *Pālaiyam* is the Tamil word for a military camp.
[35]   W. Francis, *Madras District Gazetteers: Madurai* (Madras, 1906), p. 310.

expression of domination and subordination in this hierarchical ranking did not represent an absolute status. Statuses and, thus, substantial aspects of the identification of a person could alter with the performance of service to a domain lord. In the absence of bureaucratic regulation and administration and of universal legal norms, status could not be fixed, but shifted from arena to arena. A person was ranked, not according to an absolute scale, but in relation to the changing assets and achievements of others in a specific ritual context.[36]

There were many arenas for the display and constitution of honour in a kingdom. Because absolute valuation was not possible, ritual performances existed, in a sense, as barometers – visual statements – of variable honour and status. These had to be continually defended and maintained, often with violence. Ritual emphasis on the sharing of ruling authority should not blind us to the very competitive nature of the personal relationships of governance and, thus, the fragile nature of segmented political structures. Heads of domains were engaged in intense competition – taking a variety of forms – over honour and status. Military engagements were frequent and military motifs were prominent in the religious imagery of late precolonial kingship. The segmented systems of monarchical control fragmented easily. The representation of service and sharing took place in political contexts in which heads of systems of segmentary integration continually faced the threat of dissolution. The kings of Vijayanagara had a tight hold on neither the revenues nor the ambitious lordships of constituent domains.[37] Thus emphasis on incorporation in the ritual performances of states, large and small, represented the desire of higher-ranking rulers for the solidarity of interests. This emphasis was a tacit expression of their vital need to bind refractory elements to acceptance of their authority. As David Shulman has noted, the legitimacy of precolonial Tamil kings was tenuous and continuously under attack:

The king's role is inherently agonistic, in that it pits him against an endless series of potential rivals and replacements, each with his own claim to legitimacy and equal power.[38]

Far from the idealisation of worshipful service and loyalty, rivalry and rebellion characterised political relationships. Before examining further the nature of political conflict in Tamil systems of segmented polities, it is useful

[36] Pamela Price, 'Competition and Conflict in Hindu Polity, c. 1550–1750: the Integration and Fragmentation of Tamil and Andhra Kingdoms', paper delivered to the Eighth European Conference on Modern South Asian Studies, 1983.

[37] Stein, *Vijayanagara. The New Cambridge History of India*. vol. 1.2, (Cambridge: Cambridge University Press, 1989), pp. 140–46.

[38] David Shulman, 'On South Indian Bandits and Kings', *The Indian Social and Economic Review*, vol. 17, no. 3, 1980, p. 306. This point of view argues against the interpretation of Dirks who states in *The Hollow Crown*, 'Kings are not only legitimate, they define the realm of the legitimate', p. 243, and 'The Raja, in fact, has the enunciatory function, in Foucault's terms, with respect to what order and disorder will be said to be', p. 245.

to consider the the the writing of André Wink and Dirk Kolff on elite politics in western India.[39]

Wink designates as the overwhelming principle of precolonial South Asian statecraft a ceaseless proclivity to become involved in the affairs of one's enemies or potential rivals, practising *fitna*.

Objectively *fitna* implies no more than the forging of alliances; it is thus – unlike state expansion in modern Europe – not primarily determined by the use of military power ... *Fitna* can be equated with the political expedient of *upajāpa* of the Indian *arthasastra*, comprising conciliation, gift-giving, sowing dissension among and 'winning over' of an enemy's local supporters, and involving the use of force only secondarily.[40]

Fitna also affected the politics of land controllers in localities whose 'vested rights in land' were 'shot through with conflict'. These conflicts created the opportunity for higher status rulers to influence the course of local events.[41]

Rather than having an absolutist or monopolist conception of the prerogatives of ruling authority, western Indian elites saw all politics as an occasion of the sharing of men and resources and the shifting of the balances of power among heads of fluid domains.[42] A man of high ruling status did not hope to extinguish the claims of his rivals so much as to detract from their status. In this political vision one aspired to weaken an antagonist such that he became incorporated into one's (open-ended) domain, with a demonstration that he accepted one's authority. The making of alliances and the breaking of them in an ever-shifting kaleidoscope of balancing forces was the major political activity:

The political system could not but consist of a set of allied rivals and recruiting agents, whose relations with each other and with the labour market were continually tested, negotiated over and adjusted ... Winning a war, therefore, depended very much on keeping one's men together and to induce somebody else's to change sides.[43]

Wink and Kolff discuss elite conflict in terms of continual movement in political relations: shifting, tested, negotiated alliances. Wink places much of the impetus for the nature of this development on the existence of states with imperial urges. Kolff points to the nature of the vast Indian 'military labour market' as the main variable to consider in analysing the

---

[39] André Wink, *Land and Sovereignty in India: Agrarian Society and Politics under the Eighteenth-Century Maratha Svarajya* (Cambridge: Cambridge University Press, 1986); and Dirk H. A. Kolff, *Naukar, Rajput and Sepoy: The Ethnohistory of the Military Labour Market in Hindustan, 1450–1850* (Cambridge: Cambridge University Press, 1990) and 'The End of an *Ancien Régime*: Colonial War in India, 1798–1818' in J. A. Moor and H. L. Wesseling, (eds.), *Imperialism and War: Essays on Colonial Wars in Asia and Africa*, Comparative Studies in Overseas History, 6 (Leiden: Brill, 1989), pp. 22–49.

[40] Wink, *Land and Sovereignty*, pp. 26–7.

[41] *Ibid.*, pp. 160–61.

[42] Kolff, 'The End of an *Ancien Régime*', p. 45.

[43] *Ibid.*, p. 26 and 27.

development, though he also finds a role for political culture.[44] Describing activities of fitna does not, however, locate the source of tension and the contradictions in principles of political behaviour. Further insight is possible with more precise formulations of the political preoccupations of elite figures and the nature of their relationships with their subordinates.

Honour as a preoccupation in Maravar country

In their study of the Nayaka period, from the early sixteenth to the early eighteenth centuries, Narayana Rao, Shulman and Subramanyam assert repeatedly that honour was a major concern, reflected in the poetry of the period.[45] For the most part, however, these scholars chose to focus on other themes in monarchical culture. In the exclusive forums of Nayaka courts poets drew on a range of genres, including the folk, as they wrote subtle parodies and introduced innovative themes into their representations of royalty. Discussion below of a folk poem from the seventeenth century, *Rāmayyaṉ Ammāṉai*, suggests that the common idiom of political expression was the language of honour.[46] Here, in a narrative of encounters among kings and great warriors, the poet frames the wellspring of action – its meaning and significance – entirely in terms of honour. The language of honour also pervades descriptions of Nayaka period actors' motivations and responses in J. H. Nelson's *The Madura Country: A Manual*.[47] Nelson refers continuously to his reliance on poetic sources for his study.

Telling of a war in Maravar country, *Ramayyan Ammanai* reveals the multifaceted nature of Tamil preoccupation with honour. The poem places ritual prestation, a basic marker of royal action in Tamil political culture, in a broad existential context, dealing with issues of personal worth and identity. Here the ritual arenas of temple and court prestations are inextricably tied to general cultural structures which modelled forms of formal and informal political interaction. The poem illustrates the relationship between the values a man attached to himself as a person and his rank in formal and informal hierarchies in political domains.

Research on formal ritual performances suggests that honour showed in

---

[44] Kolff, 'The End of an *Ancien Régime*', p. 23, 24, 45.

[45] *Symbols of Substance.*

[46] In 1992 folklorist Saraswathi Venugopal translated the version of the poem published by Tanjavur Saraswathi Mahal Library: *Rāmayyaṉ Ammāṉai*, edited by C. M. Ramachandran Chettiyar (Tanjavur: Tanjavur Saraswathi Mahal Library, 1978, second edition). Dr Venugopal plans to publish a revised version of the manuscript. I give the pagination of both her text and its corresponding page in the printed version. Following scholarly canons of the time, Ramachandran Chettiyar produced a 'critical edition' of the poem (with three manuscripts available to him) which was first published in 1950 under the title *Rāmaiyan Ammāṉai (Ramappayyan)*. Another version of the poem, entitled *Ramappaiyan Ammanai* and edited by S. Vaiyapuri Pillai, was published in 1951 by the University of Madras.

[47] J. H. Nelson, *The Madura Country: A Manual* (Madras: Asylum Press, 1868), pt. III, pp. 87–299. See, for example, pp. 94, 99, 102, 103, 104, 116, 125, 126 and 134.

those settings was associated with qualities of dharmic rule.[48] *Ramayyan Ammanai* shows another aspect of honour, namely political exchange in which dharmic morality was a minor issue.[49] The poem emphasises the (honorific) status a man won or lost in activities of practical politics.

In *Ramayyan Ammanai* a man's honour is the major constitution of his identity, set explosively in a context of shifting political relations. Honour both sets the frame for a man's relationships with others and is the product of specific encounters. It is a function of a man's personal control: his self-control, control over women and control of others' responses to him.

In *Ramayyan Ammanai* the making and breaking of alliances are not painless games of status competition. The poem tells of intolerable humiliation, raging anger and torturous deaths. Competition over land and demands for tribute are seamlessly interwoven into issues of dominance and subordination in interpersonal relations, framed in the language of honour.

Ramayyan Ammanai narrates events in a war which took place in 1639 when Ramayyan, the Brahmin generalissimo of the Nayaka of Madurai, led forces against the army of the Setupati of Ramnad, led by his heroic son-in-law, Vanni.[50] The historical war lasted for five months and took place in Maravar country, with the Setupati fleeing to Pambam Island, just off the mainland, only to be captured eventually and taken as prisoner to Madurai.

The poet finds motivation for the war in Ramayyan's desire to make the Setupati show honour to the Nayaka of Madurai, to make him 'bow' to the Nayaka.[51] Ramayyan tells his elder brother, 'I am going to war with the Marava [the Setupati], who has no respect for us.'[52] The Nayaka, Tirumalai, fears that Ramayyan will, like all others who challenge the Setupati, die in the attempt, but Ramayyan has succeeded in protecting the honour of Tirumalai Nayaka thus far:

> I made those who spoke ill of you surrender at the
>   entrance of Madurai.
> Did not the kings on the earth obey you and extend
>   their hands with taxes?[53]

---

[48] See, for example, Carol A. Breckenridge, 'The Śrī Mīnākṣi Sundareśvarar Temple: Worship and Endowments in South India, 1833–1925', unpublished PhD dissertation, University of Wisconsin-Madison, 1976, pp. 116 and 124 and Dirks, *The Hollow Crown*, pp. 98–106.

[49] Venugopal reports that the words commonly used for honour in the poem are: *virudu* (often associated with victory in battle: *Tamil Lexicon*, vol. VI, p. 3703), *varicai* (which has connotations of orderliness and good behaviour: *Fabricius's Dictionary*, p. 848) and *cirappu* (which has connotations of abundance and auspiciousness: *Fabricius's Dictionary*, p. 401).

[50] K. C. Kamaliah, 'Anatomy of *Rāmappaiyaṇ Ammāṇai*', in the *Journal of Tamil Studies*, no. 7, 1975, p. 48. Kamaliah appears to have used the version of the poem edited by Vaiyapuri Pillai, which differs in wording but appears not to be substantially different from Ramachandra Chettiar's text. Because of the language of the poem, Venugopal is in agreement with Kamaliah that the poem is from the seventeenth century (personal communication).

[51] Venugopal translation, *Ramayyan Ammanai*, p. 3; printed text, p. 14.

[52] *Ibid.*, p. 9; printed text, p. 19.

[53] *Ibid.*, pp. 4–5; printed text, p. 15.

Ramayyan feels that his own honour – a function of his fame as a great swordsman – is threatened as long as the Marava remains insubordinate, and he boasts of the feats of destruction and humiliation he will perform.

The conventional interpretation of the motivation of Tirumalai Nayaka in this war is that he wanted to assist a challenger to the Setupati, the latter's illegitimate brother Tambi, in a succession struggle.[54] This is the type of alliance-making and undermining involvement in the affairs of others which Wink and Kolff describe in their work. The language of *Ramayyan Ammanai* paints this activity of fitna as an enterprise to which the main actors stake their identity. Not only will some of them die, rather than show submission to their rivals, but they speak of the need to prevail as the ultimate endeavour. For example, the Setupati, Cadaikkan, says about Ramayyan, who has entered Maravar country with his army:

> Does he not know the might of Cadaikkan?
> Does he not know what will happen?
> Who can defeat me?
> I am not Cadaikkan and I am not a brave man if I do
>   not pluck out the eyes of the Brahmin who has come ...
> I am not Cadaikkan and I am a coward
> If I tie a coconut to his [Brahmin] tuft and
>   do not break it into pieces
> while the great world witnesses.[55]

The high-ranking actors in the poem live in the eye of a public which is preoccupied with the results of status competition and which the poet terms 'the world'. The world appears to be constituted mainly of other high-ranking men. Its interest is focused on issues of honour versus humiliation; it praises or it blames ('speaks ill') according to success or failure in shows of strength; it laughs at humiliation. A man will, above all, avoid being the subject of laughter and being talked ill of by the world.[56] The poet has Cadaikkan finish the above speech in this way:

> Cadaikkan's eyes became red and he spoke with rage:
> 'Will I bow to the Brahmin and pay tribute out of fear?
> Other kings will laugh at me and will talk ill of me!'[57]

The ritual results of status competition in this poem are bowing, gifting and offering tribute, but the actions which result in the ritual are killing, dishonouring ('snatching titles') and looting. We see in the story of the Maravar lords, Alagan and Kamaran, the terrible fate that can await high-status men who choose to fight rather than submit to a great general.

[54] Kamaliah, 'Anatomy', p. 30, and Nelson, *The Madura Country*, pt. II, p. 128–9.
[55] Venugopal translation, *Ramayyan Ammanai*, p. 15; printed text, pp. 24–25.
[56] The nature of this 'public' is discussed in Pamela G. Price, 'Acting in Public versus Forming a Public: Conflict Processing and Political Mobilization in Nineteenth Century South India', in *South Asia*, N.S., vol. 14, no. 1, pp. 91–121.
[57] Venugopal translation, *Ramayyan Ammanai*, p. 16; printed text, pp. 25–6.

Captured by Ramayyan's warriors, their skin is flayed while they cry out in pain. Ramayyan's men put their remains in baskets which the heroes' wives are forced to carry on their heads in full view of the general's court. When the Brahmin instructs his men to molest the wives, the women die on the spot rather than submit.[58]

A direct relationship exists between honour in the eyes of others and a man's existential worth and social identity. One of the scenarios which illustrates this relationship concerns Ramayyan's ordering the building of a causeway to the Setupati's refuge on Pambam Island. Ramayyan instructs the 'kings', military leaders who have joined forces with him, to carry stones along with the others. However, a group of prostitutes laugh at the high-ranking men:

> Where are your ornaments? your turbans?
> Where are your beautiful suits of clothes?
> Your fine speech? and swords?
> Did tiger Ramayyan make you carry stones?

The men protest to Ramayyan:

> You made the prostitutes laugh at us;
> We are like deers that were shot at with arrows,
> We are going to stab ourselves to death.[59]

Rammayan consoles the men and honours them, distributing betel leaves and nuts and presenting them with gifts.

Rammayan must console with gifting all of those who feel insulted in the course of carrying stones for the causeway. Gifting is an integral part of the action of the poem. High-ranking men honour their allies and subordinates with gifts in a range of situations: to indicate that one recognises a person as the supreme leader of a military endeavour;[60] before a hero sets out to meet a military challenge;[61] after a successful military encounter;[62] to encourage allies and subordinates to heroic efforts;[63] as a prelude to negotiations[64] and concluding negotiations.[65] Before the war, Ramayyan goes to the Minakshi Temple and tells the goddess that he will give her two crowns, one of diamonds and one of gold, if she blesses his army with victory.

Actors in the poem associate 'bowing' in honour with the successful show of force, resulting in fear in a would-be subordinate. However, some people are more worthy of fear than others. One will die first, before bowing to those whom one deems to be unworthy. Even if one subordinates oneself

[58] *Ibid.*, p. 47; printed text, p. 56.
[59] *Ibid.*, p. 50; printed text, p. 59.
[60] *Ibid.*, p. 13; printed text, p. 22.
[61] *Ibid.*, pp. 7 and 41; printed text, pp. 17–18 and 49–50.
[62] *Ibid.*, pp. 33, 42 and 44; printed text, pp. 41–2, 51, and 53.
[63] *Ibid.*, pp. 56 and 67; printed text, pp. 64–5 and 75.
[64] *Ibid.*, pp. 73 and 76–7; printed text, pp. 82 and 84–5.
[65] *Ibid.*, p. 82; printed text, p. 89.

because of fear, the subordination signals recognition of superior qualities in the honoured person. At the end of the poem, the poet narrates as emotionally complex the negotiations between the Setupati and Ramayyan and, later, the Setupati and Tirumalai Nayaka.

Carrying a plate bearing silver and golden flowers and other gifts, a surrendering Cadaikkan approaches Ramayyan who receives him 'in court'. The Setupati places the gifts before the great warrior and bows. Ramayyan is still outraged by the insulting words which Cadaikkan and his generalissimo have spoken about him in the course of the war. In his rage the Brahmin makes it impossible for Cadaikkan to have an honourable surrender. Ramayyan removes his turban, loosens his Brahmin tuft, and orders Cadaikkan, 'Take the coconut and tie it to my tuft.' Insulted, the Setupati bows again and answers:

> I have surrendered to you;
> > that is why you speak this way.
> If my nephew [son-in-law] Vanni were alive,
> > he would tie the coconut to your tuft
> > and break it![66]

Ramayyan replies angrily, 'You do not worship my feet and obey', and tells his men to bind Cadaikkan with ropes for the trip back to Madurai.

In Madurai Tirumalai Nayaka also challenges Cadaikkan:

> Hey Cadaikkan, could there be a
> Marava who does not bow to me?'

The proud Cadaikkan answers again:

> My lord, listen to my appeal!
> If my nephew Vanni were alive now,
> I would not bow to you.[67]

As a result of this challenge, Tirumalai puts Cadaikkan, chained, in prison. In conventional historical accounts Cadaikkan was released by Tirumalai as the result of negotiations by powerful groups of ascetics who came annually from different parts of India to make the pilgrimage to Rameswaram.[68] The poet of *Ramayyan Ammanai*, however, contrives a more spectacular end to the imprisonment, one which allows the Maravar ruler to show subordination to Tirumalai Nayaka with his dignity intact. A miracle takes place when Cadaikkan prays to Lord Vishnu for assistance and his bonds break. Tirumalai is impressed by this divine dispensation ('Lord Rama has shown you mercy') and decides to free Cadaikkan, presenting him with titles and gifts of jewels and silks. Cadaikkan is moved by the kind words of the

[66] *Ibid.*, pp. 76–77; printed text, pp. 84–5.
[67] *Ibid.*, p. 79; printed text, p. 87.
[68] Kamaliah, 'Anatomy of *Ramappaiyan Ammanai*', p. 46.

Nayak and is mollified. He falls at the feet of Tirumalai and offers a fitting form of subordination:

> You are my mother, father and my friend;
> I am your lover and devotee.[69]

The powerful emotions which the poet describes throughout reflect the nature of the attention which actors invest in issues of personal value and status. The poet suggests the content of this status with the treatment which he gives high-ranking persons. He honours them by either calling them 'kings' and/or describing them in the customary terms of kingship. The poet frequently entitles as king both Ramayyan and Vanni and he further conveys their special qualities among men by having the women who watch them identify them with gods, associate them with *bhoga* (enjoyment) and become sexually aroused – characteristic royal markers in Nayaka poetry:[70]

> All the women who live in Madurai,
> those who thought about Ramayyan as Devendra or
>   Vishnu,
> those who said, 'He is the king of this world.'
> ... 'he is kama himself
> ... 'He is the one with good virtues who has
> attracted the world',
> those who were longing for him and making comments,
> those who sighed
> while their saries loosened, slipping down,
> while their beautiful hair became loose,
> they pressed with their hands their breasts which
> were longing for him ... [71]

When Vanni goes in procession with his army, he attracts a similar response from women.[72] Men call out the titles of these warriors and poets sing their praises.

Lesser warrior leaders are also customarily referred to as 'kings', but what clearly indicates 'king' as a marker of high status is the treatment of European fighters who assist Ramayyan. They participate in the Tamil world of honorific behaviour, receiving gifts and bowing with folded hands.[73] They are like other warriors involved in the war:

> The fierce Yama-like Vanni [like the god of death]
>   killed the white king.
> Both troops fought fiercely.

[69] *Ibid.*, p. 81; printed text, p. 89.
[70] Narayana Rao, Shulman, Subramanyam, *Symbols of Substance*, pp. 57–67.
[71] Venugopal translation, *Ramayyan Ammanai*, pp. 11–12; printed text, p. 21.
[72] *Ibid.*, p. 19; printed text, p. 28.
[73] Ibid., pp. 55–6; printed text, p. 64.

Vanni came and stood in the battlefield and
  told the whites, 'You spoke ill of us.'[74]

The poet's continual use of 'king' to indicate men of superior rank suggests
that kingliness constitutes the honourable status towards which men strive.
That this status is fluid and subject to constant challenge is suggested by J.
H. Nelson's comments on the nature of political relations among leading
warriors in general and the palaiyakkarar chiefs in particular. Because of
sensitivity to real or unintended insults political cooperation was problematic. He commented on the difficulties faced by military leaders in the
eighteenth century:

A jealous quarrel amongst the leading chiefs, or the retirement from the scene of
action of one or two Poligars [palaiyakkarars] who fancied themselves slighted or ill-
used, would be amply sufficient to break up a force ... Consequently ... [the King]
could never for a single moment feel absolutely safe, or regard even the slightest
indications of disaffection with indifference.[75]

Nelson writes further of the lack of trust, common suspicions, 'petty feuds
and jealousies' which pervaded relations among high-ranking men.[76] Relations of honour also characterised the confederation which the palaiyakkarars formed to try to force the colonial forces out of south India in the
war of 1800–1801.[77] The army of the confederation was highly segmented in
its structure.

  Dynamic mechanisms in the cultural structures of honour and status were
principles of competition and the prevailing concept of power in the late
precolonial period.

Competition at court

Ramayyan Ammanai focuses on informal political exchanges. The section
below is concerned with ideological elements in the incorporation of actors
into formal political orders.

  In attempting to bring powerful chiefs to their service, south Indian rulers
supported practices which paradoxically undermined their status of rule. In
the ideology of monarchy lay contradictory principles which encouraged
fragmentation amidst representations of integration. Before elaborating on
this point, however, it will be useful to return to the order of the Seventy-
two Palaiyakkarars and to the first in rank in the order, the Setupati of
Ramnad. As the Nayaka kings of Madurai discovered in the course of their

---

[74] *Ibid.*, p. 60; printed text, p. 68.
[75] Nelson, *A Madura Manual*, pt. 3, p. 158.
[76] *Ibid.*, p. 290.
[77] K. Rajayyan, *South Indian Rebellion: The First War of Independence, 1800–1801* (Mysore:
    Rao and Raghavan, 1971), pp. 102, 124, 202, 205, 214, 221–2, 227, 235–6, 251 and 268.

relations with the Seventy-two Palaiyakkarars, recipients of status-marking, rank-defining insignia and titles might bite the hand that honoured them.

In deciding what rank would accrue to the heads of domains in their realm, rulers might create formal orders of membership. Visvanatha Nayaka assigned each of the Seventy-two Palaiyakkarars to the protection of one of the bastions of the great fort at Madurai in a forthright and unambiguous statement of the meaning of this particular order: membership was predicated on acceptance of the task of defending the Nayaka *raj.*

The Setupati's special rank as the first in the order of the Seventy-two Palaiyakkarars, did not, as we have seen, stem from a claim on the produce of fertile lands. Maravar country was dry and difficult. The produce of the coastal waters and Maravar country's close proximity to Sri Lanka may, however, have been a contributing factor. Other variables would also seem to have played a role in creating the Maravar's considerable military assets. He was chief of all the sub-castes of the warrior Maravar caste, which in turn had a hegemonic relationship vis-à-vis the lesser status Kallar and Ahambadiya warrior castes, to the north in present-day Pudukkottai district and to the south-west in present-day Tinnevelly district.[78] Among the other seventy-one palaiyakkarars, then, were chiefs who recognised the Setupati as their caste head. The Setupati was famous for the speed at which he could mobilise thousands of men at a call to arms. At the beginning of the eighteenth century the Maravar king could mobilise 30,000 to 40,000 men in a week.[79]

The Setupati did not come from the largest and most powerful Maravar sub-caste. The Kontaiyankottais, who settled from Maravar country west and south to the mountainous western border of Tirunelveli, were more numerous than the Sembinattu sub-caste of the Setupati and controlled villages of more fertile land. The Sembinattu population was concentrated in Maravar country, however, giving this sub-caste an advantage in military organisation.

In historical tradition, the special status of the Setupati stemmed from the association of a Sembinattu chief with the Rama story. In mythic tellings a Sembinattu chief helped Rama on his way back from Lanka and it was a Sembinattu chief who undertook to build a temple – the famous Rameswaram – at the island site where Rama worshiped Siva. Setupati patronage of the temple was an important element of dynastic status from the late sixteenth century.

In the pattern of ritual hegemony, the Setupati assembly itself exhibited

[78] William Taylor, 'Marava-Jathi-Vernanam', in *Madras Journal of Literature and Science*, vol. 4, 1836, pp. 350–60, and Dirks' discussion of the relationship between Cervaikarars, a hereditary service group, and Maravars in Tinnevelly in 'The Pasts of a Pālaiyakārar: The Ethnohistory of a South Indian Little King', the *Journal of Asian Studies*, vol. 41, no. 4, 1982, p. 661.

[79] S. Kadhirvel, *A History of the Maravas, 1700–1802* (Madurai: Madurai Publishing House, 1977), p. 48.

his gift of an icon of Durga, the tutelary goddess of warrior kings.[95] Raghunatha was privileged to initiate celebration of the festival of the Goddess, Navaratri, in a style befitting his high royal status. The Setupati was no longer expected to pay tribute to the Nayaka of Madurai, but was to honour the Nayaka as his suzerain. Tirumalai Nayaka gave Raghunatha the title 'Protector of the Queen's Tali [marriage necklace]' because his service had prevented the Nayaka, her husband, from being taken prisoner and possibly killed. The Setupati also received the personal name of the Nayaka, Tirumalai, and became henceforth known as Tirumalai Setupati.

Such transfer of a personal name suggests a double-edged flattery, closely followed as it was by the invasion of Ramnad by Tirumalai Nayaka. In formal ideological terms, in giving Raghunatha his name, the Nayaka incorporated him 'into his own sovereignty, or lordship'.[96] Considering the conflict-ridden relationship of the two royal houses, in more practical terms one can wonder if the Nayaka was implying that, if both men bore the same name/identity, attacks by one on the other would be suicidal. Or was he suggesting that, having the same name/identity of the Nayaka, the Setupati should need no more in status or rank? Tirumalai (Raghunatha) Setupati did not respond to the Nayaka invasion by strengthening the fortifications of the new kingdom, but consolidated his higher rank and status by building new temples and endowing old ones. Tirumalai's heir, however, was captured by Nayaka forces within six months of assuming the Setupati title and died in jail. He was assumed, accurately or not, to have given support to the Nayaka of Tanjore in his war against the Nayaka of Madurai. Taking warning from this affair, the next Setupati built new fortifications before attempting to throw off Nayaka ritual hegemony.[97]

Formal independence in 1702 did not result in denial by the ruling house of Ramnad of their relationship of service to the Nayaka rulers of Madurai. The rulers of Madurai had confirmed the Setupati in his superior-ranking status, legitimising his claim on enhanced honours and political authority among his rivals and subordinates and, possibly, consolidating his dynastic claim on certain privileges.[98] An eighteenth-century report of Maravar caste practices tells that when the Setupati left his palace, 'the heralds proclaim in

---

[95] Informants in Ramnad town told me that a golden image was given. Ramaswami, however, writes that the *piṭam* (upon which the icon sits and which empowers it) was given, *Tamil Nadu District Gazetteers: Ramanathapuram*, p. 84. An historical chronicle of the Madurai Nayakas reports that the founder of that dynasty, Visvanatha Nayaka, having been entitled by the King of Vijayanagar as 'Raja of the Pantiyan throne', was further honoured by being allowed to take an icon of Durga to Madurai as his tutelary deity: Dirks, *The Hollow Crown*, p. 103 and 99.

[96] Dirks, *The Hollow Crown*, p. 86 and 101–2.

[97] Kadhirvel, *A History of the Maravas*, p. 36.

[98] In this context, see Arasaratnam's discussion of Setupati privileges in activities of trade and commerce, 'The Politics of Commerce', *passim*.

panegyrics in which he is referred to as the chief of seventy-two Poligars and the Servant of Tirumalai Nayaka'.[99]

In a context where ruling status was not an exclusive quality, but widely shared, recognition of superior rank by an overlord of undeniably superior power and status was valuable to persons and lines in competition with rival claimants for the ruling title to a domain and with other dynasties for privileges of territorial domination. Thus the kings of Madurai and Tanjore retained their Nayaka title, acquired in the Vijayanagar period, even after the disintegration of the great kingdom which they had served as provincial governors. The Nayakas thus attempted to shore-up their legitimacy and to remind not only their subordinates and allies, but also their rivals of the formal source of their superior status and rank. The Nayaka of Madurai distributed insignia for establishing a minor kingdom at the same time as he announced – with his own title – that he shared in the authority of even greater kings.

The flexibility of south Indian orders of royal status and rank was such that they could survive ideological discontinuity at the top. A Muslim lord could confirm the right of a raja worshipping Siva and Vishnu to insignia which belonged to the latter's house.[100] There is no evidence of decay of institutions of 'Hindu' monarchy among the realms of the Andhra coast, subjected though they were to the overlordship of two successive Islamic dynasties.[101] The revenue administrations of these kingdoms may have developed greater extractive capacities, responding to pressures from the Muslim governments, than did the Tamil kingdoms. However, revolutions of value and institutional relationship did not occur. The persisting significance both of monarchical institutions and royal insignia and rank suggests that once the paramountcy of an overlord was established, as long as the subordinate chiefs still retained the capacity to carry out protecting activities traditionally associated with kingship, the fact that the overlord was a Muslim did not undermine the legitimacy of their rule. This phenomenon is connected to a conception of power which became closely associated with ruling authority in the Vijayanagara period and which is important for an understanding of the dynamics of late precolonial development in south India.

---

[99] Mahalingam, *Mackenzie Manuscripts*, p. 236.

[100] In 1761 the new heir to the Nuzvid raj received designation by the Subadar of the Deccan as a zamindar with a *mansab* rank and as a raja with 'the privilege of keeping Nowbut (kettle drums) and a palanquin adorned with fringes' (High Court of Madras. Defendant's Documents in Regular Appeal No. 36 of 1874. Document 1, pp. 1–2). See also Alladi Jagannatha Sastri, *A Family History of Venkatagiri Rajas* (Madras: Addison Press, 1922), pp. 4–5.

[101] Vadivelu's *The Aristocracy of Southern India*, vols. 1 and 2, suggests this in his reports of the activities of Andhra zamindaris, as does Sastri's account of the activities of the Rajas of Venkatagiri, pp. 64–93. I put the word Hindu in quotes to indicate that Hinduism as a religious category was not well-developed in precolonial south India.

Power and morality: Sakti and protection

That power was an overwhelming religious preoccupation in Tamil country is confirmed in Shulman's study of temple myths: 'In all these myths, the underlying goal is sacred power, the power that can give life and material prosperity'.[102] Reviewing the records of events in south Indian monarchical politics, we find indications that major participants acted according to a set of values of honour, status and power which, in turn, bore a close relationship to notions of energy – sakti – in worship.

While the great male divinities gave *form* to all existence, *energy* for action came from the archetypical deity, the Goddess, who was sakti, energy in the cosmos. The Goddess was known conventionally as Durga or Kali. People whose work regularly involved the pollution which comes from killing – warriors shedding blood in battle or agriculturalists destroying insects as they worked in fields – worshipped and asked for the protection of the Goddess or lesser goddesses, who were often conceptualised as her emanations. The Goddess was the only high-status, major divinity who accepted meat sacrifices. Unlike the great transcendent male deities, she was not offended or, even worse, disempowered by such an otherwise dangerously polluting sacrifice.

As mentioned above, from Vijayanagara times Navaratri was commonly the main celebration in a kingdom. The festival, which honoured the Goddess and asked for her protection for the ruling house, was also the festival which celebrated the existence of a domain as a moral community and associated it with cosmic order. Late precolonial Tamil country witnessed an expansion in the worship of the Goddess, as seen in the construction of goddess temples.[103]

Whether or not a temple was specifically a goddess temple, however, her power was a continuing theme in popular myths:

But ... power, in order to be useful to man, must be limited and channelled into proper courses. Limited in this way, power becomes auspicious and accessible ... This concept of bounded power is, as we would expect, particularly applicable to the goddess, who is so intimately linked with power.[104]

The political appropriateness of goddess worship as an object of the protection and patronage of ambitious warriors and the political appropriateness of the Navaratri festival in particular, as the choice for the ritual representation of a kingdom as a community, was due to connotations of

---

[102] Shulman, *Tamil Temple Myths: Sacrifice and Divine Marriage in the South Indian Saiva Tradition* (Princeton: Princeton University Press, 1980), p. 348.

[103] Stein, 'Devi Shrines and Folk Hinduism in Medieval Tamilnad', in Edwin Gerow and Margery D. Lang (eds.), *Studies in the Language and Culture of South Asia* (Seattle: University of Washington Press, 1973), pp. 75–90, and 'Temples in Tamil country, 1300–1750 AD', in Stein (ed.), *South Indian Temples: An Analytic Reconsideration*, pp. 11–45.

[104] Shulman, *Tamil Temple Myths*, p. 348.

sakti as a concept of power. The doctrine and practice of sakti did not, however, directly link power and personal status to caste rank. Sakti was conceptually separate from the notions of power and status in orthodox Brahmin traditions of rank.[105] Sakti, the feminine principle in cosmic creation, was relatively free-floating energy and vitality. It connoted power and status as expressed in personal achievements of strength and skill, thus implying shifting political and social relations. The orthodox Brahminical concepts of purity and personal substance presupposed an extremely stable social and political order. The late precolonial period, however, was a time of rapid alteration in political status, the status of newly proven warrior leaders and the domains they dominated. The festival of the Goddess was a successful choice for the annual celebration of the kingdom as a community because it ritually tied the shifting status of ruling lineages – a demonstration of the sakti of their leaders – to visions of the harmonious integration of the state.[106]

In understanding how a preoccupation with sakti as a concept of power could have affected perceptions of personal status the work of Susan Wadley is suggestive.[107] Wadley argues that divinity, purity, dharmic action and power are not separated rigidly in concepts of status.[108] People worship their gods, ask favours of them, fear them on occasion, because they believe that the gods are powerful. In the same way as gods are committed to aiding men and women in danger, in this ideology authoritative humans have commitments to their subordinates at times of crisis. An increase in material prosperity, when resources are used correctly, suggests that the fortunate person has both acted according to righteousness (dharma) and experienced an enhancement of his embodied powers[109] (gods are the highest embodiment of power). A person who can command considerable resources is, in substance, purer and more powerful (filled with sakti, cosmic energy) – of a different status of being – than the less capable. He has acted properly to become rich and his bodily substance has been altered through these right actions.[110]

It seems reasonable to argue that, in late precolonial political visions, a man of arms manifested his superior state of being or substance as he allocated entitlement to domains and organised institutions (assemblies of ranking or

---

[105] Marglin, 'Power, Purity and Pollution: Aspects of the Caste System Reconsidered', *Contributions to Indian Sociology (N.S.)*, vol. 11, no. 2, 1977, pp. 245–270.

[106] The dichotomy which I draw here between pollution and purity should not be exaggerated. Shulman's conclusions are useful in this context: 'I have spoken of a fundamental split in the tradition, of a clash between the longing for power and the ideal of purity ... Is not the regulation of power a sufficient guarantee of purity? Yes and no ... Impurity breaks into every life at the most crucial moments – birth and death, for a woman, puberty and childbirth. No amount of control or limitation can rule out such moments of impurity ... Impurity is dynamic, purity is static ...' *Tamil Temple Myths*, p. 348.

[107] Susan Wadley, 'Power in Hindu Ideology and Practice', in Kenneth David (ed.), *The New Wind: Changing Identities and South Asia* (The Hague: Mouton, 1977), pp. 133–57.

[108] *Ibid.*, pp. 151–2.

[109] *Ibid.*, pp. 154–5.

[110] *Ibid.*

local guards called kaval) which protected a subordinate's claim on dominion. The existence of the Navaratri festival as the main celebration of the royal domain suggests that, in south India as well as north India, a raja's very achievement and maintenance of control demonstrated greater moral worth and sakti. When a warrior competed for honour and a domain – for status, rank and territory – he was, among other things, demonstrating moral and divine power, a deserving nature. Recognition of his status in ritual represented a new identity in honour, an altered and superior nature of being. Thus a Mughal emperor, a demonstrably powerful being, could issue honours to the new heir of a 'Hindu' raj and these honours could be valued as an authoritative recognition of a legitimate claim on the privileges in a domain.

Hereditary succession: an opening for conflict

The principle of kinship was one basic to social organisation in south India, as elsewhere on the subcontinent. One entered a caste conventionally by birth from parents whose union was formed with attention to certain rules of descent; otherwise one held an illegitimate and marginal relationship to the group. In the context of political organisation as described above, principles of inherited identity collided with the principle of competition in ways injurious to the maintenance of domainal integrity.

A chief or king was a man who should have several wives and numerous offspring. He was, himself, a symbol of fertility and prosperity to his domain. Multiple alliances could serve as a resource for the integration and stability of the domain: 'Hereditary kingship is the politics of kinship, seizing upon the possibilities of the prevailing structures of descent and marriage and directing them to the needs of the state.'[111]

A chief or king entered into multiple marriages or sub-marital relationships as a way of making stable alliances with significant units of kin-linked people and/or the heads of domains. The first wife, *paṭṭa śrī* (lady of the title, *paṭṭam*), ranked first among the other women of the royal household and was chosen according to orthodox observance of the rules of descent in the ruler's sub-caste. It was most politically efficient for the ruler and the first wife to produce the male heir to the throne. Another one or more wives, ranking behind the patta sri in the hierarchy of the women's quarters, might also be selected according to orthodox observance. Further wives, however, could and did come from other sub-castes and, ranking lower than them, were wives of other castes. There were also concubines, among whose number were commonly ritual dancers or *devadasis*.[112]

[111] Thomas R. Trautman, *Dravidian Kinship* (Cambridge: Cambridge University Press, 1981), p. 357.

[112] This point comes from examination of succession litigation of Tamil and Telugu dynastic houses in the nineteenth century. See the following cases from the Judicial Committee of the Privy Council, London: Ramalakshmi and Sivanandha Perumal Sethurayer, 1872; Inderun Valungypooly Taver and Ramaswamy Pandia Talaver and Thungamma Nachiar, 1869; and

Women of different ranks and status, it appears, entered the royal household with rituals of marriage which varied with their sub-caste and caste background. Their issue, therefore, varied in relationship to the ruler in degrees of rank and legitimacy. In the absence of a male heir from the patta sri or from another woman of the raja's sub-caste, debilitating confusion and acrimony could arise during the process of selection of a legitimate heir.

Adding an element of instability to the process of selection was the flexibility which with rules of descent could be called forth in justification of a claim on the title. Legal anthropologist S. F. Moore has written on the issue of political contingencies in succession by descent:

[D]escent systems frequently have built into them legal legitimates quite separate from genealogy ... [Perhaps] all unilineal societies ... have such formal means of adjusting genealogy to convenience. The extent to which this is done in any particular society is a statistical question, which may be some index of social change or type ... The ideological model is one thing; the jural rules are another.[113]

That the process of selection to high office was sensitive to contingencies was noted by early nineteenth-century British observers in India. Even an eldest son did not succeed if he were not competent to fulfil the arduous demands of leadership.[114] A king or chief had the prerogative of choosing among his sons for his heir.[115] Rules of descent could be and were manipulated in the face of contingency. William Taylor, baffled, noticed such manipulation among Maravars: 'the law of succession [is] very peculiar, and liable to be suspended by trifling distinctions arising out of the nature of marriage relations.'[116] An example of a succession conflict in the royal house of Ramnad serves to illustrate the general point.

Kilavan Setupati (ruler from 1674 to 1710), one of the most vigorous and talented rulers of precolonial Ramnad, came to power as the winner of a succession conflict. His own death resulted in a long and complicated struggle which, as related above, resulted in the partition of Ramnad into two kingdoms (with the emergence of Sivagangai). It also resulted in the loss of a large Kallar-dominated chieftaincy to independent royal status: the emergence of Pudukkottai. Both Kilavan and his son, Bhavani, were not

Ramamani Ammal and Kulanthai Nachiar, 1871. Devadasis were women who underwent ritual marriage with a high-status god and who served as dancers and participants in temple ritual.

[113] S. F. Moore, 'Descent and Legal Position', in Laura Nader (ed.), *Law in Culture and Society* (Chicago: Aldine, 1969), pp. 387–9.

[114] High Court of Madras. Pleadings for Regular Appeal No. 36 of 1874. Judgement of J. C. Hannyngton for Original Suit No. 17 of 1871, District Court of Kistna.

[115] 'On the Subject of Interfering with the Succession of Native Princes', in Alexander Arbuthnot (ed.), *Major-General Sir Thomas Munro, Bart., K. C. P., Governor of Madras: Selections of his Minutes and Other Official Writings* (London: Kegan Paul and Co., 1881), p. 66.

[116] William Taylor, 'Marava-jatha-Vernanam', p. 353.

sons of women from the Sembinattu sub-caste and thus could not have a clearly legitimate claim on the title. Sons of a sister of a Setupati were appropriately claimants for the title since the inherited royal privilege to rule could be traced through females of the family who belonged to one of the two royal Sembinattu lines (*kiḷai*). Kilavan was the son of a Kontaiyan-kottai woman. Having no son of his own by a Sembinattu woman, he nominated his son by a non-Sembinattu woman, according to some sources. Whether Kilavan nominated Bhavani or not, the man believed himself to have a superior claim to that of a cousin who was ambitious for the title. Extended civil warfare ensued in the 1720s. Bhavani was not a popular personality and, even after gaining the title for seven years, as noted above he lost in the battle with Sasivarna and Kattaya Tevar.

It was not only the inherently manipulable nature of the rules within the ideology of kin-caste descent which was to fuel intense and common wars of succession. This manipulability existed in a context of access to rank and royal status through demonstrated superior substance – through, it would seem, demonstrated sakti. Thus, Kilavan sought to consolidate his ruler-ship, after he defeated his main rival for the throne, with the murder of the two warriors whose assistance had enabled him to take the prize. Neither one of the two is reported to have been a son of the previous Setupati, but Kilavan found their manifested power a threat. Even though Kilavan's descent was not orthodox, his reign became one of the most brilliant and popular among Maravars. His son, Bhavani, however, 'lacked tact and sagacity', and the great chiefs of the kingdom eventually rebelled, defeated and imprisoned their king.[117] The new Setupati, Kattaya Tevar, was the maternal uncle of a man who had taken the title briefly during the war of succession. This man had been nominated because he was the heir of a nephew of Kilavan.[118]

Conclusion

Contradiction among principles of political action was a creative element in patterns of state formation during the late precolonial period. In the nineteenth century, in the context of a new type of overlord, these elements of fragmenting tension would prove destructive, contributing to the frag-mentation of precolonial monarchical cosmology. The desire to reproduce royal honour and status was a dynamic element in the continuing evolution of monarchical ideology in the course of the nineteenth century.

The reason for pointing to succession conflict in particular is because

---

[117] Kadhirvel, *A History of the Maravas*, p. 59. In the course of almost twenty years of warfare following the death of Kilavan, Bhavani married a daughter of his father's chief concubine in an attempt, it would seem, to enhance his claim to the title, *A History of the Maravas*, p. 57.

[118] The nephew himself had been installed in 1710, when Bhavani proved unacceptable as the new Setupati.

conflict over inheritance and succession came to dominate nineteenth-century kingly politics. An unwillingness to accept the legitimacy of royal successors characterised royal kin, who tied up and depleted the energies and fortunes of the ruling houses of former palaiyams and little kingdoms.

In his study of medieval monarchical cosmology, David Shulman outlines political conceptions which, though literary in expression, bear a general relation to the formulations discussed above.[119] In his focus on kings, Brahmins and clowns, Shulman paints a political universe characterised by figures whose politico-cosmological identities are in continual transformation and whose cosmic statuses exist in relationship, not to an absolute ideal, but to each other. Historical chronologies detailing continuous rebellions and struggles over succession confirm Shulman's universe, in which the legitimacy of the king is continually under question and in which, in a sense, a clown can transform into a king and a king into a clown. The volatile responses to perceived insults in *Ramayyan Ammanai* suggest the intensity with which men of high rank protected their honour and status, formal and informal.

A focus on conflict and division should not blind us to an important aspect of late precolonial Tamil monarchical cosmologies. As frames for action they integrated many social and political processes and relationships into balanced and complementary oppositions in the ideology of kingship. A high-status lord attempted to bind powerful chiefs to his service in ritual which held promise of their own future lordship. The Setupati of Ramnad became independent of the suzerainty of the Nayaka of Madurai, but still sought to legitimise his status with reference to Setupati service in the Nayaka's order of the Seventy-two Palaiyakkarars. In the nineteenth century, what was once creative tension, loosely binding together actors ideologically, would accelerate processes of separation which sorely tested these balances. By the end of the nineteenth century, formal kingship had lost its capacity to represent the community of new nationhood which preoccupied urban elites.

---

[119] David Shulman, *The King and the Clown in South Indian Myth and Poetry* (Princeton: Princeton University Press, 1985).

2
Cosmological fragmentation in the public sphere

The great energy for political engagement which we saw in activities of state formation in Maravar country in the seventeenth and eighteenth centuries had implications for the establishment of British rule generally in southern Tamil country in the course of the eighteenth century. The British East India Company succeeded in pacifying the southern Tamil area only after half a century of combating warrior resistance in the 'Poligar wars'.[1] The rulers of Sivagangai and Ramnad joined in the palaiyakkarar confederacy against the British of 1800–1801. As a result, in the process of imperial consolidation, Company officials gave titles to the domains to members of the royal families whom they judged amenable to Company interests. Sivagangai and Ramnad kingdoms were incorporated into the Presidency of Madras in the Permanent Settlement of 1801–3 as revenue estates, zamindaris, with a fixed revenue demand or *peshkash*.

The policy of a Permanent Settlement had developed under long debate among Company administrators in the late eighteenth century and was justified on the grounds of agricultural improvement.[2] Deprived of their armies and presented with a fixed ('permanent') revenue demand, the warrior lords should turn their attention to the improvement of the productivity of their estates and, thus, to the increase of their personal fortunes. Theoretically, they would in the process introduce agrarian capitalism into the countryside. However, the more immediate and practical consideration of the Company in the south was the considerable political influence of former chiefs and kings and British fear of the unstable consequences of disbanding their administrations.[3]

The main work of the consolidation of British rule in nineteenth-century south India took place in the first half of the century. There were major shifts in policy during this period. The development of support for a new

---

[1] K. Rajayyan, *The Rise and Fall of the Poligars of Tamilnadu* (Madras: University of Madras, 1974), pp. 37–113.

[2] Ranajit Guha, *A Rule of Property for Bengal: An Essay on the Idea of Permanent Settlement* (Paris: Mouton, 1963), pp. 90–159.

[3] This point follows from the discussion of the circumstances of giving the title of Ramnad to the sister of a raja in *The Indian Law Reports: Madras Series*, vol. 24, 1901, 'The Ramnad Case', pp. 613–36.

revenue policy, away from the Permanent Settlement, and towards agreements with individual cultivators or *ryots* is the most famous.[4] However, the general outlines of a centralised ruling administration, based partly on models developed in late eighteenth-century Bengal, appear not to have altered greatly in this period.

Radical change in governance was clearly involved in colonial administration of conflict management. Local and regional armies were disbanded in Madras Presidency under the Permanent Settlement and the state assumed a monopoly over organised force. The establishment in 1802 of a system of centralised dispute processing with three levels of appeal was also an innovation.[5] Colonial institutions and procedures for dispute processing played a major role in the transformation of indigenous politics in the nineteenth century.

The civil law courts of the empire attracted attention and had an influence out of proportion to the numbers of suits which were ajudicated. There are several reasons for this. Colonial consolidation entailed the truncation and adaptation of formal structures of rule. However, because of prevailing characteristics of social and political segmentation, within zamindari estates and in non-zamindari areas there were smaller domains of rule – those, for example, of clan leaders, caste headmen, village officers, temple and math administrators and chief merchants. Following the dislocations of colonial pacification, however, native political life was marked by the relative absence of formal governing structures for the recognition and legitimisation of these local and supra-local authorities. Similarly, there was an absence of formal arenas for negotiation with the government by representatives of subject domains (*durbar* assemblies had previously served this function). The Anglo-Indian legal system quickly became important in providing officially recognised, formal arenas for representation, ranking and competition.

The use of the colonial courts appealed to men (and, as we shall see, women) of considerable wealth and local authority because of traditions of looking to superior lords for confirmation of ruling status and access to domain privileges. Precolonial ruling lords of high status had responsibilities for the management of major disputes, upon the request of those involved.[6] Such management was often a necessary part of the process of granting titles and honours, since conflict occurred over the sharing of privileges of lordship in domains.

We saw in the previous chapter that the representation of honour and status in public had been a major element in the politics of ritual. The

[4] A recent study of this period is Burton Stein, *Thomas Munro: The Origins of the Colonial State and his Vision of Empire* (Delhi: Oxford University Press, 1989).

[5] Chittaranjan Sinha, *The Indian Civil Judiciary in the Making, 1800–33* (New Delhi: Munshiram Manoharlal, 1969), pp. 8 and 11; J. Duncan M. Derrett, 'The Administration of Hindu Law by the British', in his *Religion, Law and the State in India* (London: Faber and Faber, 1968), p. 278.

[6] Arjun Appadurai, *Worship and Conflict*, pp. 105–38, discusses this issue.

management and the meaning of appearances in public remained a major preoccupation in indigenous politics in the nineteenth century and contributed to the considerable interest which surrounded the litigation of people of wealth and ruling status.[7] Through their legal involvements zamindari kin provided much drama and excitement for the curious. They tied up zamindari estates in almost continual litigation, as ambitious relations competed for the titles to former chieftaincies and little kingdoms. Competition in litigation processes was, however, powerfully affected by the rules for participation established by the legal officers of the Company. Participants used Anglo-Indian legal texts and procedures as tools of manipulation to achieve political ends poorly described by Anglo-Indian legal categories. However, neither litigants nor, it would seem, observers of the court dramas remained unaffected by the concepts and social categories of Anglo-Indian legal practice.

When zamindari kin competed for the title to local rule, the conflicts developed a significance and meaning beyond their localities partly because adjudication took place in the new centralised system of dispute processing. The colonial demand for the universal applicability of rules drew judicial attention away from a focus on the special meanings and incidences of succession in indigenous domains. Thus, the winners of succession disputes in colonial courts became transformed from embodiments of monarchical cosmology, exerting authority downwards in vertically-orientated chains of ritual linkages, to members of 'families' which were, in turn, members of a Presidency-wide, horizontally defined, new social class – the 'native aristocracy'.[8]

When the influential Maharaja of Bobbili made an attempt to improve the manners and morals of his fellow zamindars, he wrote a book in English, published in 1905, which he called *Advice to the Indian Aristocracy*. Here he referred to 'the present reigning noblemen' as a 'class'.[9] In the course of the nineteenth century, the experience of the ruling houses in the public sphere removed them conceptually from their original settings, giving them a new, awkward regional identity which was most easily articulated in English.

Litigation at district level took political competition beyond the realm of the estate or *samastanam* (kingdom), as it was locally known. In the high court of appeal in Madras an even wider attention focused on these elite conflicts. They constituted an element in the discourses of the emerging public sphere in the Presidency capital. Zamindari litigation was a topic of newspaper reportage, and issues and themes of zamindari litigation politics played a role in forming values and categories in the political culture of the

---

[7] For a discussion of ritual performance and the distinction between acting in public and forming a public in south India see Price, 'Acting in Public versus Forming a Public'.

[8] The term, 'aristocracy', applied to zamindars became ubiquitous. See, for example, Vadivelu, *The Aristocracy of Southern India*, vol. 1 (vol. 2 appeared in 1908).

[9] *Advice to the Indian Aristocracy* (Madras: Addison, 1905), p. xvii.

new urban-centred public life. In nineteenth-century Madras Presidency this public mainly consisted of English-language-educated males who developed an interest in issues of government policy and public welfare which extended beyond the concerns of ranking in local communities.[10]

Litigation did not encourage respect for zamindari rule. The civil courts were arenas of public representation, but the processes of representation in litigation quickly became ones over which participants had little control. As members of zamindari families engaged lawyers and testified against each other, they applied legal and social categories and acted out social dramas which made them agents of changed perceptions. The perceptions of primary concern in this chapter are of the nature and significance of caste membership and status, the political engagement of elite women and, related to both of these, south Indian kingship. The adaptation of royal succession conflicts to the rules and procedures of civil litigation involved major transformations in kingly politics. Changes occurred in perceptions of royal honour and the meaning of royal symbolism among actors in the developing 'public opinion'.[11]

The emergence of an Indian nationalist consciousness among men who participated in voluntary associations from the middle of the nineteenth century has long been a focus of scholarly discussion. Scholars of Indian nationalism, however, have not been concerned with the fate of indigenous political institutions in the perceptions of the (limited) public. It has not been an issue that elite politicians dismissed indigenous monarchy as they sought formal models for governance in the emerging nation. The acceptance of western institutions by early nationalist elites appears in conventional historiography as a natural result of western-style training and occupation. Educated in British history and political philosophy and hoping to use the rhetorical weapons of British reasoning to force concessions from colonial rulers, members of the Indian National Congress adopted western models of governance in what appears as the smooth and inevitable consequence of British rule. Thus a major shift in political conceptions appears to have taken place in a process strangely free of tension and conceptual dislocation.

A more nuanced appreciation of change in political consciousness comes with exploration of the processes through which the public came to reject indigenous models of formal rule. Benedict Anderson has argued that social and political perception altered with the introduction of printing and the appearance of newspapers in early modern societies.[12] The implications of his work suggest that the printing of legal reports and litigation procedures

---

[10] R. Suntharalingam, *Politics and Nationalist Awakening in South India, 1852–1891* (Tucson: University of Arizona Press, 1974).

[11] Suntharalingam, *Politics and Nationalist Awakening*, holds evidence that those engaged in the new politics saw themselves as forming 'public opinion', pp. 151–230.

[12] Benedict Anderson, *Imagined Communities: Reflections on the Origin and Spread of Nationalism* (London: Verso, 1983).

contributed to the creation of the public discourse in which new notions of community identity and solidarity developed among south Indians in the nineteenth century. This chapter explores the ways in which the representation of royal families in succession litigation helped to create perceptions of indigenous monarchy which discredited it in the eyes of self-conscious 'enlightened public opinion' as it developed secular, western-influenced models for government and political negotiation. Formal kingly rule was discredited, but powerful concern with public representations of high honour and ruling status would remain a staple of political fare in Tamil country.

In the first half of the nineteenth century, rural and urban elites were preoccupied politically of the implications of colonial consolidation for authoritative relations in indigenous domains.[13] From the 1840s, however, imperial policies became increasingly interesting to groups of the politically engaged.[14] For the most part, zamindari kin did not become active participants in the voluntary associations and open meetings of public life, but remained preoccupied throughout most of the nineteenth century with competition for ruling status in localities.[15] Zamindari kin were caught in the trap of their precolonial inheritance: the ambiguous legitimacy of specific kings. The political vulnerability of title-holders was only aggravated in the context of imperial rule.

At the end of the nineteenth century a Ramnad raja, Baskara Setupati, integrated an absorption of ruling honour and status with the values and interests of English language-educated elites. By that time, however, formal monarchy had lost its capacity to represent major philosophical and political principles of state formation in south India. The political initiative had been seized by, among others, the facilitators of the Anglo-Indian legal system: famous *vakils* (advocates) of the new legal profession, most of whom had made their fortunes in zamindari litigation.[16] For these leaders of public opinion Indian kingly ideology and royal authority could not define the legitimacy of the state. These elements remained, however, to

---

[13] The work of Arjun Appadurai and Carol Breckenridge illustrates this preoccupation: Appadurai, *Worship and Conflict*, pp. 105–38, and Carol A. Breckenridge, 'The Sri Minaksi Sundaresvarar Temple', pp. 141–211.

[14] R. Suntharalingam, *Politics and Nationalist Awakening*, pp. 24–57. In 1845 a public meeting to discuss the government's policy toward Christian missionary activities attracted over 200 Hindus, p. 40.

[15] Competition in maths over succession to chief administrator and in temples over honours and shares to authoritative control remained major issues in these indigenous institutions and resulted in prolonged litigation conflicts. See Appadurai, *Worship and Conflict*, pp. 161–211, Breckenridge, 'The Sri Minakshi Sundaresvarar Temple', pp. 344–457, and Richard B. Devitt, 'Succession Struggles and the State: The Development of Strategies in Tamil *Maths*', unpublished paper delivered at the Association for Asian Studies annual conference, 1981.

[16] Pamela G. Price, 'Ideology and Ethnicity under British Imperial Rule: "Brahmins", Lawyers and Kin-Caste Rules in Madras Presidency', *Modern Asian Studies*, vol. 23, pt. 1, 1989, pp. 151–78.

influence informal public behaviour. In the politics of nationalism, kingship would become a question of tacit political culture – the provision of models for discrete, appropriate actions – not consciously and formally accepted political ideology.[17]

The new rules for succession competition

Nineteenth-century zamindari succession in south India was doubly cursed. There were, in the first place, tensions inherent in the non-exclusive and achieved nature of royal status and honour, undermining the legitimacy of specific kings. Still, even if precolonial royal succession had been problematic, tending strongly towards violent solutions, it had been possible for some late precolonial Maravar rajas to have reasonably long reigns. Tirumalai Setupati ruled for twenty-six years from 1647 to 1672 and Kilavan Setupati ruled for thirty-six years from 1674 to 1710. The eighteenth-century rulers had less stable tenures, but one early eighteenth-century Setupati ruled for fifteen years (Vijaya Raghunatha, 1710–25), and two others had reigns of about twelve years (Sivakumar, c.1736–48, and Vijaya Raghuntha, c.1749–62).[18]

Under the Permanent Settlement the vulnerability inherent in Tamil kingship was compounded by the lack of respect which royal kin had for colonial bureaucratic and legal procedures, at least in questions of succession. Neither the choices of District Collectors, in those situations where they had the prerogative, nor the decisions of imperial justices, most of whom were British, impressed would-be rajas and ranis as binding.

In asking why the colonial legal system failed to encourage respect for the ajudication of zamindari succession suits we find a number of possible answers. The use of legal instruments of wills and adoption had not been common practice in monarchical politics. A dying raja might attempt to nominate his successor, but this practice does not appear to have been institutionalised.

In taking the role of a title-distributing overlord, the colonial government did not select candidates who had proven their qualities of leadership and strength. The criteria of selection were found in that Anglo-Indian amalgamation, 'Hindu Law', and these criteria appear not to have been convincing to potential contenders.[19] The winner of a succession dispute might celebrate the triumph with rituals suggesting the destruction of threats to the cosmos (a Sivagangai rani did this in 1863). The winner might respond with a grand distribution of betel and sweets, a display of dancing girls and the music of palace bands, showing largess and invoking royal

---

[17] Price, 'Kingly Models in Indian Behavior'.
[18] The Indian Law Reports: Madras Series, vol. 24, 1901, 'The Ramnad Case', p. 619, and Ramaswami, *Tamil Nadu District Gazetteers: Ramanathapuram*, pp. 82–94.
[19] Derrett, 'The Administration of Hindu Law'.

auspiciousness. (a Ramnad raja did this in 1868). But such kingly displays could not hide the fact that the title could be, and sometimes was, given to persons with no proven qualities of political judgement and skill. The successful execution of major litigation required the exercise of financial acumen and special knowledge of the workings of the legal system and of the operations of lawyers. However, estate politicians, speculators in litigation and local big men could perform these activities on behalf of someone who in actuality had poor judgement and little talent for administration. Furthermore, actual courtroom manoeuvres, the argumentation of lawyers and the testimony of witnesses described a political universe which hardly touched on the visions of majesty and power – *śrī* and sakti – which were the stuff of monarchical cosmology.[20]

The texts of legal process were, on the contrary, English translations of Brahminical codes, the products of late eighteenth-century Orientalist scholarship.[21] In establishing the imperial legal system in Bengal and Madras, Company legal officials were misleadingly convinced that 'schools' of Indian law, existing in precolonial times, had guided, among other activities, the inheritance and partition of caste families.[22] Initially, imperial officers did not realise that the subjects they called Hindus had no common legal code as such; different communities of castes and sub-castes had their own rules and had been accustomed, in most cases, to managing their disputes among themselves.

In cases of broader political significance, precolonial chiefs and kings managed disputes; however, they had functioned more in the capacity of administrators than legislators.[23] Rulers had not managed disputes with reference to codes of abstract, generalisable rules:

[T]he commands of Hindu kings were administrative, in the sense that they were addressed to specific individuals and groups, were not of general applicability, and were subject to alteration or repeal according to the pragmatic needs of kingship.[24]

Late eighteenth-century Company officials had not understood that the legal codes of orthodox religious tradition, the *Dharmasastras*, had served only as a distant model for dharma; the *sastras* were not to be closely applied to all.

---

20 Valuable discussions of sri in ideologies of rule are Alf Hiltebeitel, *The Ritual of Battle: Krishna in the Mahabharata* (Chicago: University of Chicago Press, 1976) and Bryan Pfaffenberger, *Caste in Tamil Culture: The Religious Foundations of Sudra Domination in Tamil Sri Lanka* (Syracuse: Syracuse University, 1982).

21 J. Duncan M. Derrett, 'The British as Patrons of the Sastras', in Derrett, *Religion, Law and the State in India*, pp. 225–73.

22 Marc Galanter, 'The Displacement of Traditional Law in Modern India', in *Journal of Social Issues*, vol. 14, no. 4, 1968, p. 75.

23 Appadurai takes this distinction from Robert Lingat, *The Classical Law of India* (New Delhi: Thomson Press; Berkeley: University of California Press, 1973), pp. 224–32, in his *Worship and Conflict*, p. 68.

24 Appadurai, *Worship and Conflict*, p. 68.

In the colonial legal system of the Presidency of Madras, zamindari issues of inheritance and succession were ajudicated according to translated texts which colonial officials deemed to be the 'personal' law of the Hindus, Hindu Law, as it was known. With a few important exceptions, the colonial legal system treated royal succession in Ramnad and Sivagangai as an issue in the inheritance of family property by non-royal Hindus, as this was understood by colonial legal practitioners. The decision to manage zamindari succession according to Hindu Law had radical consequences for monarchical politics. Zamindari relatives, predisposed in the first place to making challenges, had difficulty in accepting Hindu Law as a basis for the selection of a new raja. Paradoxically however, Hindu Law came to loom larger and larger in their affairs, as rounds and rounds of litigation took place. This is partly because these laws determined who could initiate litigation with a reasonable chance of winning. Even more significant than political incompetents winning the title was the public role in succession politics which Hindu Law and historical contingency gave to royal women.

In Madras Presidency Hindu Law incorporated Vijñaneśvara's commentary on the *Yājñavalkya-smṛti*, the *Rju-Mitākṣarā*, written between 1121 and 1125.[25] The Anglo-Indian legal tradition held that 'the Mitaksara school' had been dominant in south India. In this school, a father and his sons were co-owners in the father's property and were assumed to be undivided in their interest. Division came if and when a partition of the family took place.

[S]ince a son dying before partition was only a *co-owner* [author's emphasis] and not a full owner of a defined share, on his death the interest in the joint property did not pass by succession at all, but remained with those who were co-owners.[26]

Even though sons could demand a partition, the main trend in Hindu Law was toward patriarchal and patrilineal jointness.[27] In the absence of sons, a widow could inherit the property of her husband, but a grandson's claim was superior to a daughter's, following the death of the widow.[28] In this way came openings for widows (several, in the case of zamindars), daughters of widows, and the sons and daughters of daughters of widows.

The Mitaksara did not contain special rules for the succession of property with special 'prestige value', as Sontheimer phrases the case, but emphasised the importance of equal shares among all coparceners.[29] This point would prove tempting for the younger brothers and cousins of zamindari rajas.

---

[25] Günther-Dietz Sontheimer, *The Joint Hindu Family: Its Evolution as a Legal Institution* (New Delhi: Munshiram Manoharlal, 1977), p. 120.

[26] Derrett, 'The History of the Juridical Framework of the Joint Hindu Family', in *Contributions to Indian Sociology*, no. 6, 1962, p. 31.

[27] Sontheimer, *The Joint Hindu Family*, p. 177.

[28] Annasawmy Ayer, *The Sivaganga Zamindary*, Judgement of the High Court, delivered 27 October 1871, Kattama Nachchiar and four others vs. Dorasinga Tevar, pp. 100–101.

[29] Sontheimer, *The Joint Hindu Family*, p. 129.

This school of law provided no allowance for families like the royal Maravars whose practices had called for the wives of a king to became *satis*, immolated upon his death, and which had only irregularly included the adoption of heirs to thrones.[30] Argumentation regarding when a widow could adopt and whom she could adopt, as well as the inheritance by females of husband's and father's property was, therefore, novel for royal kin.

The Anglo-Indian courts recognised that zamindaris had a special character only in the sense that they did not follow the usual rules of coparcenary succession in Hindu Law. The phrase, 'in the nature of a principality', was often used in succession cases; however, it indicated nothing more in a political sense in court than that the families involved in the suits would not practice partition in inheritance. Primogeniture and impartibility would continue. Within these restrictions, the legitimacy of a claim on the inheritance would be decided according to rules of Hindu Law.

'A perfect jungle of lawsuits'

The above quote was a characterisation of the Law Members of the Privy Council in 1881 as they surveyed the litigation following the death of the *Istimirar* Zamindar of Sivagangai, the first person with whom the government made the Permanent Settlement. Ramnad litigation was a little less complicated. In both zamindaris the instabilities inherent in both royal succession and the establishment of the Anglo-India system of dispute processing were accentuated by occasional failures of royal wives to bear male offspring. In Sivagangai, for reasons originating from political conditions at the time of the granting of the *sanad* of possession, there was a relatively wide range of possibilities for potential challengers to the legitimacy of a title-holder.

In 1802 the Government of Madras gave the title to Sivagangai to Gauri Vallabha (also known as Padamattur Oyya Tevar), a younger brother in the high-ranking Padamattur line. There were no surviving heirs in the line of the founder of the kingdom. The Padamattur brothers, heirs of a small palaiyam within the kingdom, were collateral kin of the last raja. Gauri Vallabha's elder brother had been dismissed by the Government as inappropriate for the sanad (grant) on the grounds of his being aged, infirm and unintelligent.[31] On the other hand, in the new zamindar's favour was his previous support of the Company in its successful attempt to destroy a rebellious faction which had taken control of Sivagangai and fought against the Company. Gauri Vallabha, although he had seven wives and three

---

[30] Privy Council. Collector of Madurai vs. Muttu Ramalinga Setupati. 1868. Record of the Proceedings. Arzi addressed by Narayana Row, the Head of Police of the Zuft Zamindari of Ramnad, 2 April 1820, pp. 10–11.

[31] High Court of Madras. Documents in Appeal No. 21 of 1887, p. 124.

Plate 1   Zenana in Sivagangai Palace

concubines, did not leave a son to inherit the zamindari. His unfortunate brother, however, had sired three sons.

For a period of approximately thirty years, through five major rounds in court, descendents of the older brother of Gauri Vallabha convinced the courts that they – not the female descendants of Gauri Vallabha or their offspring – deserved to hold the title.[32] In 1863, thirty-four years after the death of the Istimirar Zamindar, his daughter Kathama Nachiar won the title in a Privy Council decision. The Lord Justices found that, the zamindari having been given to Gauri Vallabha, it should be considered his self-acquired property. The brother's descendents – who had argued that they were undivided from Gauri Vallabha, and therefore, coparcenary heirs of the estate – were found to have no legal claim to the estate.[33]

Ramnad succession was complicated also by the circumstances of the settlement. In 1803 the Government of Madras gave the sanad to Manga-leswari Nachiar, the sister of the former ruler. The latter, Muthu Rama-lingam Setupati, had disqualified himself by siding with rebel forces during the palaiyakkarar wars of the late eighteenth century.[34] A widow of Muthu

[32] O.S. No. 4 of 1832, O.S. No. 4 of 1833, A.S. No. 2 of 1835 (Sadr Adalat), Judgement of the Privy Council, 18 June 1844, and O.S. No. 2 of 1845, reported in Annasawmy Ayer, *The Sivaganga Zamindary*.

[33] Judgement of the Lords of the Judicial Committee of the Privy Council delivered 30 November 1863, in Annasawmy Ayer, *The Sivaganga Zamindary*.

[34] *The Indian Law Reports: Madras Series*, vol. XXIV, 1901, 'The Ramnad Case', pp. 613–36, examines the selection, discussed below.

Ramalingam and her daughter, Sivagamy, attempted from 1813 to 1829 to wrest the title from Mangaleswari Nachiar, taking their cases to the Privy Council in London.[35]

As noted above, in colonial courts zamindari estates descended according to rules of primogeniture, following the dictates of Hindu Law. The clearest succession saw the entire estate going to the eldest son. The status of daughters, sons of daughters, or grandsons of daughters, because it related to the status of the wives and concubines of a zamindar, was difficult for the court to ascertain. In Sivagangai litigation, one of Gauri Vallabha's daughters and her son; a surviving widow; three daughters together; and a daughter alone presented a series of claims before the estate went back to their line in 1863.[36] Following the first major rounds on the two estates, in which competing branches struggled with the branches descending from istimirar zamindars, the structure of inheritance still was not strong enough to inhibit discord and challenge. The next set of succession struggles, from approximately 1870 to 1881, continued to arise from the ambiguities of female descent.

Ramnad succession litigation centered more around adoption, real or forged. In Ramnad, the initial weakness in the emerging inheritance structure, – giving the estate to the sister of a deposed ruler – was compounded by the need of the sister to adopt a male heir. The lack of direct male descent was an issue which different contenders seized upon from 1804 to 1829. After 1829, adoption or attempts to prevent adoption were still major issues. The widow of a zamindar, Rani Muthu Virayi, hoped to prevent Rani Parvata Vardhani, her daughter-in-law, who had only female offspring, from adopting a male heir who could compete with Muthu Virayi's own adopted son.

The ambiguities of female inheritance continued to plague the Ramnad royal kin as, in 1858, another widowed rani and her daughter tried to win the estate from Parvata Vardhani. Two years later Vardhani's adopted son, Muthu Ramalingam, brought a case against her for the title, which she had been unwilling to relinquish.[37]

The difficulty between mother and adopted son was trifling, however, compared to the threat to the ruling house which the Collector of Madurai presented in 1849 by declaring that Parvata Vardhani's adoption of Muthu Ramalingam was invalid. The office of the Collector argued for the next nineteen years that a widow 'could not adopt without the authority of her Husband, or, failing that, of all of his relatives' and that the Ramnad estate could be escheated to the Government of Madras.[38] A Privy Council

[35] Edmund F. Moore, *Reports of Cases Heard and Determined by the Judicial Committee and the Lords of Her Majesty's Most Honourable Privy Council*, vol. 12, 1867–1869, pp. 402–3.
[36] Annasawmy Ayer, *The Sivaganga Zamindary*, contains judgements of the main Sivagangai succession litigation.
[37] Moore, *Reports and Cases*, p. 408.
[38] *Ibid.*, pp. 408–9.

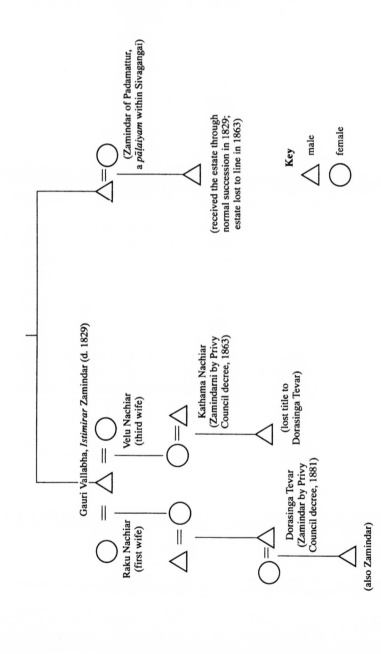

Raku Nachiar (first wife)

Gauri Vallabha, *Istimirar* Zamindar (d. 1829)

Velu Nachiar (third wife)

(Zamindar of Padamattur, a *pālaiyam* within Sivagangai)

Dorasinga Tevar (Zamindar by Privy Council decree, 1881)

Kathama Nachiar (Zamindarni by Privy Council decree, 1863)

(received the estate through normal succession in 1829; estate lost to line in 1863)

(lost title to Dorasinga Tevar)

(also Zamindar)

Key

△ male

◯ female

Fig. 1 Outline of the main points in Sivagangai succession.
Note: In the text a distinction is made between the Padamattur line and the line of the Istimirar Zamindar. Within the Istimirar Zamindar's lineage, lines traced from his wives are also mentioned.

decision in 1868 served to clear up several main points of dispute, declaring Muthu Ramalingam as the valid heir.

Ramnad was now relatively blessed, from the point of view of clear succession, with male heirs. Muthu Ramalingam was followed, in 1889, by Baskara who, in turn, had a son. In 1891, however, the liability which could follow from several male heirs, partition suits, struck when Baskara's younger brother argued unsuccessfully in the High Court that Ramnad was not 'in the nature of a principality', but ordinary coparcenary property and that he was therefore entitled to a portion of the estate.[39]

The last major dispute for the Sivagangai title illustrates the theme of weakness in the structure of inheritance due to tracing descent through women. In 1889, the line which traced itself through Ungu Muttu, Kathama Nachiar's mother, tried to retrive the estate back from the line traced through Raku, Gauri Vallabha's first wife. In 1896, the Privy Council decided against the Ungu Muthu line. Sivagangai would not bounce among the various grandsons of Gauri Vallabha as they died off one by one. Once a line continuously produced male heirs, it would retain the title.[40]

It had been uncommon for women to take formal responsibilities of rule in precolonial Maravar country. There is one example of a queen regent's ruling for a minor heir from each house during the particularly unsettling times of the late eighteenth century. The regular practice of excluding women was outlined in a petition written upon the death of the Istimirar Zamindar of Sivagangai, Gauri Vallabha. The petition was signed by uncles, brothers and husbands of Gauri Vallabha's female relatives and by several wives of the deceased raja. The statement was sent to the government to show acceptance of the succession of the Padamattur line to the Sivagangai title, bypassing any possible claims by women. The petition explained that the relations had shown their acceptance of the Padamattur heir by giving him mourning clothes, bowing and paying 'every respect to him'.[41] It then stated:

[W]hen a Zemindar dies, his son succeeds to the Government of the Zemindari ... if he has no son, his nephews are his successors; in the event of there being no nephews too, his dayadees should succeed him.[42]

(Dayadees – *tāyati* in Tamil – refers to collateral relatives.)

Gauri Vallabha's death was in 1829 and the Sivagangai royal kin had not experienced a succession for the previous three decades. As noted above, however, the Istimirar Zamindar's relations quickly discovered the potential of the courts in opening up possibilities for novel claims of succession right.

[39] *The Indian Law Reports: Madras Series*, vol. XXIV, 1901, 'The Ramnad Case', pp. 613–36.
[40] Judgement of the Lords of the Judicial Committee of the Privy Council, 27 June 1896, reported in Annasawmy Ayer, *The Sivaganga Zamindary*.
[41] High Court of Madras. Documents in Appeal No. 21 of 1887, Exhibit V, p. 141.
[42] *Ibid.*

Several justices indicated that they were aware that they were making decisions contrary to caste usage. As late as 1870 a High Court Judge, summing up a case which involved discussing points from Sanskrit authorities (Dayabhaga, Mitaksara, Smriti Chandrika and others), made a comment regarding the 'grotesque absurdity' of this exercise.[43] However, even if some judges were dissatisfied with applying Hindu Law, they found it difficult to make a place for caste or family usage because usage was difficult to prove. The unanimity among kin which the Padamattur petition expressed in 1829 was extremely rare. As later material will illustrate, from the point of view of royal kin, legal procedures were tools of competition to be manipulated, not possibilities of uncovering the abstract right of a particular claim. Perjury was, thus, a responsible tactic, not the obscuration of an absolute right to rule. As a result, the testimony of witnesses and the statements of litigants were wildly contradictory on, among other topics, caste usage.

In making their decisions through its court system, the Government of Madras was in a sense following the precolonial pattern of a powerful overlord (occasionally) selecting the ruler of a tributary state. However, the winner of a suit was not selected because the imperial government wanted a weaker or stonger ruler on the throne or because he represented a powerful faction which needed to be appeased. Winners of litigation were picked, against local practice, on the basis of criteria which spoke little to local exigencies, but served the wider needs of government from a British imperial vision: the need for a standardised law to ensure, theoretically, that justice would be given fairly to all on an equal basis. While this concept served both the demands of the novel bureaucracy developing in south India and justification for colonial rule, it was bizarre to south Indian localities. Through the door of standardised law women had a chance to enter into estate governance.

Relations of the zamindar, both close and distant, did not necessarily live in independent royal splendour. The Ramnad and Sivagangai estates were not strewn with grand palaces of wealthy cousins. Smaller chiefly domains were encompassed within the larger zamindari domains. As far as it is possible to tell, however, the highest number of villages held in those smaller domains was somewhere between thirty and forty (the number of villages in Ramnad estate as a whole was over 2000).[44] With the exception of the occasional brother or cousin who became the manager of a zamindari, the disparity between the power, status and wealth of a zamindar and a good portion of his or her near kin could be vast.

---

[43] Annasawmy Ayer, *The Sivaganga Zamindary*, p. 114.
[44] Boards Proceedings (hereafter BP) of 26 March 1874 in Boards Proceedings for March, 1874, vol. 3, no. 680 from W. M. McQuae, Collector of Madura, to J. Grose, Secretary of the Court of Wards, 30 August, 1873, no. 26, Enclosure no. 1, p. 2087 (Tamil Nadu Archives, hereafter TNA).

Close zamindari relations, by practice and/or law, were often in a dependent position vis-à-vis the zamindar. The wives of a deceased zamindar and their children were owed maintenance. The palace establishment held a number of 'hangers-on',[45] including relatives, who were dependent on royal largess. It is misleading, however, to speak only of dependent kin; in several cases it is apparent that dependent kin, in turn, maintained a residential establishment. The zamindar expressed his munificence and royal magnificence in maintaining a large palace establishment. Royal relations, on a smaller scale, similarly attempted to display royal generosity and a capacity for protection. Zamindars, though, were not particularly interested in supporting the distant establishments of their kin for successive generations and, on occasion, stopped support altogether. In fact, the life of dependent zamindari kin could be financially hazardous, as zamindars ceased maintenance or retrieved from politically uninteresting or antagonistic kinsmen the villages granted by ruling forebears. The relative and sometimes objective penury of zamindari relations and the insecurity of dependency contributed to a situation whereby a zamindar found himself or herself continuously fighting off relatives who attempted to acquire the comforts and status of rule for themselves and their heirs.

The insecurity which could exist for royal kin, dependent on the largess of a zamindar, is illustrated by the case of the relations of Sivagamy Nachiar, an early contender for the Ramnad title.

Sivagamy was the daughter of the deposed Muthu Ramalingam Setupati (she challenged the adoption of Rani Mangaleswari's grandson in the 1820s). At the time of the issuing of the Istimirar sanad, the Government of Madras was concerned about the proper maintenance of Muthu Ramalingam and his many wives and children. It was politically expedient to make arrangements for their care, as remaining supporters could create difficulty for both the new rani and the government, if they decided that the former ruler and his family were treated without honour. In 1803, the government announced that it would pay a pension to the family out of customs duties and salt revenues which it received from Ramnad Zamindari. When the East India Company gave up these sources of revenue, the Raja of Ramnad should assume the charges of maintenance.[46] Muthu Ramalingam and nine of his wives and concubines moved to Madras, while the other eight wives moved to Ramnad, where they stayed in the palace. The government paid 1,200 rupees per month for the Ramnad members and 1,000 rupees for the family in Madras.[47] At Ramnad, as the Collector of Madura later wrote, the wives of Muthu Ramalingam 'ran afoul' of Rani Mangaleswari Nachiar, the Istimirar Zamindarni, who wrote to the

---

[45] These 'hangers-on' – despised as sycophants by officials of the government – were a palace phenomenon from the time of the Istimirar Zamindar to the end of the nineteenth century.
[46] Madura District Records, vol. 4682, 24 July 1934, pp. 421–2 (TNA).
[47] Madura District Records, vol. 4577, 26 August 1829, p. 240 (TNA).

Collector suggesting that he cut off their pensions. The women petitioned for the stipend, which was paid out of zamindari funds which were kept at the Collectorate treasury. They argued that this allowance, always inadequate, had been further strained by the arrival in Ramnad of the Madras party after the death of Muthu Ramalingam.

In 1829, the complete list of dependants included more than sixty people: two sons, two daughters, two wives, fifteen concubines, a Brahmin eunuch, ten watchers, five maids, seven slaves, a *chunam* (aromatic powder) bearer, a washerwoman, two barbers and, among others, '2 Tavers, a Pillay, and a Naicker'.[48] The original arrangement – that the dependants should be paid out of zamindari-derived revenue – was not followed by Ramnad zamindars. In 1829, for example, the Raja presented the Collector of Madura with a bill for 15,000 rupees for the family expenses, refusing to bear further responsibility. In 1834, the Rani of Ramnad, Muthu Virayi Nachiar, and the Government of Madras were still bickering over who was going to pay the pensions of the surviving wives and children.[49]

The desire for material security and the influence which wealth could give was only part of the motivation for engaging in succession litigation. We find as further incitements the powerful desire for high honour and ruling status, including the capacity to show largess.

Below the themes of relative kin penury, the desire for royal honour and the emergence of unlikely rulers are united in a case study of a succession conflict. This was a conflict between two lines tracing their descent through two wives of Gauri Vallabha, the Istimirar Zamindar of Sivagangai.

The case of Dorasinga Tevar vs. Ranee Kattama Nachchiar and four others

Succession litigation was perhaps the most expensive way in which zamindari kin carried out competition for honour and status. Ramnad Zamindari survived its litigation only to be undermined as an entity at the end of the nineteenth century by the attempts of Baskara Setupati to expand the political possibilities for a zamindar king. By the middle of the century, Sivagangai was devastated by the complicated conflicts of its warring lines. Kathama Nachiar won the throne, but lost financial control of her domain. Monarchical politics in Sivagangai provided openings for speculators in litigation and local big men to make substantial inroads into the royal domain.

Seven years after Kathama Nachiar won Sivagangai back from the Padamattur line, she was faced with a contender from that large and hungry group consisting of Gauri Vallabha's other descendents. Kathama Nachiar's opponent this time was an illiterate man with mediocre ambition,

[48] Madura District Records, vol. 4677, 26 August 1929, pp. 240–44 (TNA).
[49] Madura District Records, vol. 4682, 24 July 1934, pp. 421–4 (TNA) and the Boards of Consultations (hereafter BC), back nos. 72–3, dated 16 October 1924 (TNA).

someone who, on his own, would have been incapable of prosecuting a complex litigation to the Privy Council.[50] Dorasinga Tevar was not acting alone, but was the means through which a powerful local figure succeeded in wrecking the fortunes of Kathama Nachiar's family and acquiring considerable influence in the second largest zamindari in the Tamil-speaking area of Madras Presidency.

Kathama Nachiar's success in her long efforts at litigation were due in part to the help she received from George Frederick Fischer. Fischer, a cotton merchant, had gained considerable experience in Maravar zamindari politics through involvement in the affairs of Rani Parvata Vadhani Nachiar in Ramnad. He succeeded as well in making himself a valuable support to Kathama Nachiar during her succession struggle, and was rewarded in 1864 with a ten-year lease for the entire zamindari. Fischer was to pay the Rani a *lakh* of rupees (100,000) a year and to assume a number of her debts – as well as obligations of maintenance toward her dependants – and he was to take responsibility for the peshkash (the 'tribute' or tax which the zamindar owed the government each year). After Fischer's death in 1867, Kathama affirmed the agreement with his son, Robert, who inherited the lease. Robert Fischer made over the unexpired part of the lease the following year to Venkatasami Naik for the sum of four lakhs of rupees.[51]

Venkatasami Naik, 'able, ambitious, and arrogant',[52] was Sheristadar (Chief Secretary) in the Madurai Collectorate and 'a very influencial and powerful man in the district'.[53] Rani Kathama Nachiar, however, objected to the transfer of the zamindari and refused to give her consent. She brought a court suit against Venkatasami to block him. The Civil Court decided that the royal contract with the Fischers was of a personal nature and that it was not assignable to others; however, the Rani lost her case on appeal.[54] Venkatasami took up the Sivagangai lease. In doing so, however, he was forced to relinquish his important post in government service. The judicial commentator observed:

It is thus clear that, since the aforesaid assignment of December 1868, the relations between Kathama Nachiar and Venkatasami Naik ... were considerably strained and there is therefore nothing surprising if he were then in a mood to take hold of any instrument to wreak his vengeance on the proud Zamindarni who dared defying him.[55]

It was about this time that Dorasinga Tevar was introduced to Venkatasami.

---

[50] Subordinate Judge C. Gopalan Nair gave an extremely lengthy summary of details concerning this litigation, quoted in Annasawmy Ayer, *The Sivaganga Zamindary*, pp. 417–96.
[51] *Ibid.*, p. 425.
[52] *Ibid.*, p. 434.
[53] *Ibid.*, p. 426.
[54] *Ibid.*, p. 425.
[55] *Ibid.*, p. 426.

Dorasinga Tevar was the son of Gauri Vallabha's first wife's daughter. He was an indigent zamindari relation, living off his sister, Pitchama Nachiar, and his father-in-law. Pitchama was a former zamindari rani, the widow of the last of the Padamattur line to have title to Sivagangai. After the Sivagangai title was lost to Kathama Nachiar, Pitchama was not in a strong position financially. In the meantime Dorasinga had discovered that he could make a reasonable claim to the zamindari in court and had found a patron in Ponnusami Tevar, the brother of the Raja of Ramnad and the powerful Manager of that zamindari. Ponnusami joined with Ramasami Chettiar – a Nagarathar merchant banker rich in liquid capital and possessing knowledge of the intricacies of zamindari litigation – in a plan to conduct Dorasinga's case for him. Their payment was to have been declaration of Dorasinga's reversionary rights in their favour.

Kathama diverted Ponnusami's interest by marrying her son to his daughter. Pitchama, on the other hand, was interested in supporting the claims of her brother. Two of her confidants, knowing the family affairs, took Dorasinga to Madurai to meet a new and more willing patron, Venkatasami Naik.[56]

Venkatasami procured a house for Dorasinga, opposite his own in Madurai, and attended to his physical comforts. He arranged that only he or his supporters should see or speak with Dorasinga. Venkatasami conducted the suits, appointing and paying the barristers and vakils and financing the entire effort of winning the case. Judge Gopalan noted:

Dorasinga remained passive and was quite satisfied to draw his pension and leave everything to Venkatasami Naik ... [The latter] may occasionally have consulted Dorasinga for appearance sake, but [Dorasinga] would not have dared to contradict him ... [I]t is clear that Dorasinga neither knew nor cared to know what Venkatasami was doing in his name.[57]

From the time that Dorasinga began his dependency on Venkatasami Naik, in 1868, to the time of his patron's death, in 1878, the two men entered into a series of agreements whereby Venkatasami, had he lived, could have taken control of the major part of the resources of the zamindari. In 1868, Dorasinga Tevar signed an agreement promising to make over a chiefly domain within the zamindari to Venkatasami, should he win the title.[58] At that same time it was also agreed that Venkatasami would have power of attorney as Dorasinga's agent. A bond for 40,000 rupees was executed which was to be repaid with interest when the suit was won. In the same year Dorasinga confirmed the assignment of the unexpired portion of Robert Fischer's lease to his patron, for which the latter was to pay the hapless royal 4,000 rupees a year until the suit was concluded. On this same

[56] *Ibid.*
[57] *Ibid.*, p. 427.
[58] *Ibid.*

occasion Venkatasami received another lease for ten years, which was to begin upon the expiration of the Fischer lease. This agreement did not include the Tirupattur Taluk (revenue division), which was given to Pitchama Nachiar. In 1870 another loan was made for 150,000 rupees.[59] In 1877, Dorasinga designated Venkatasami:

... agent for the management of the Zemindari, with almost absolute power, for a term of 10 years with a remuneration of ten per cent, on its gross collections, amounting to Rs. 7,54,547 and odd a year ... [60]

Two months later he granted him one of the most valuable taluks in the zamindari, worth about 20 lakhs, giving a net income of about 35,000 rupees a year. Venkatasami was to pay only 2,000 rupees a year for rent.[61] Venkatasami died in 1878, less than a year after Dorasinga Tevar won the title. His family never gained possession of the taluk; though, the zamindar did repay his loan with interest. A considerable legal tangle emerged from the various agreements.

Dorasinga Tevar was described by a contemporary judge as a 'pauper' and 'needy'.[62] He was not a completely senseless puppet in Venkatasami's hands, being 'canny ... pretty shrewd in everyday matters and small business transactions'.[63] He appears to have feared his patron.[64] One may ask why Dorasinga pursued the title, if he were willing to give up practically all of his financial powers in the zamindari and much of the income. He gave the answer to this question during the course of the litigation:

If I succeed, he [Venkatasami Naik] will have a claim to everything and be my chief officer. I don't know what I have agreed to give him. I have promised him a lease and that he may conduct everything and that I shall be content if I sit on the Zemindar's seat as Maharaja.[65]

(The throne, not the crown, was a major symbol of kingly status and authority in India.)[66] Dorasinga's simple words articulated a preoccupation with royal honour and status which characterised zamindari kin.

Dorasinga did not protect his economic powers as a zamindar; however, he did protect his access to high honours. In his last lease with Venkatasami Naik, he stipulated:

Because I, the said Dorasinga Thevar Avergal, am the trustee for the proper management of all the Devasthanams [temples] and other charities in the said Taluk [being given to Venkatasami], and for the proper supervision of all the villages and

[59] *Ibid.*, p. 428.
[60] *Ibid.*, p. 429.
[61] *Ibid.*, p. 440.
[62] *Ibid.*, pp. 426–7.
[63] *Ibid.*, p. 427.
[64] *Ibid.*, p. 433.
[65] *Ibid.*, p. 432.
[66] B. Puttaiya, 'A Note on the Mysore Throne' in *The Quarterly Journal of the Mythic Society*, vol. 11, April 1921, no. 3, p. 261.

lands which are set apart for those charities, therefore you, Venkatasami Naiker Avergal, shall not concern yourself about those matters alone within your sub-division.[67]

Dorasinga would secure the royal privilege of protecting worship, earning kingly honours in temple ritual.

Dorasinga Tevar's successful pursuit of the Sivagangai title brings out several points about estate politics. The network of intermarried relatives around the office of zamindari was dense. Dorasinga's sister was an active representative of the Padamattur claim to the zamindari and, when Dorasinga Tevar won the case, the line through Pitchama Nachiar enlarged their share of the zamindari domain.

Succession conflicts were not isolated from extra-kin concerns. The title to Sivagangai Zamindari gave access to considerable resources in terms of cash, land, labour, ruling honour and status. The most powerful and ambitious men in the locality were, therefore, intensely interested in the transition of control from one party to another. Ponnusami Tever, Venkatasami Naik and Ramasami Chettiar represented three major sources of influence and power in the Ramnad-Madurai area: high office in a large zamindari establishment, high office in government service, and successful merchant banking. When a weak, ignorant or poor individual was involved in a major zamindari transaction, the potential existed for a skilful manipulator with access to cash to establish claims on zamindari resources.

The politics of perjury: kingship and caste

Imperial justices gave oral evidence low priority in making their decisions and they complained about the regular use of alleged or forged legal instruments in court. Tension existed between the mainly British justices of the higher courts and the litigants and their lawyers over the issue of perjury. The excerpt from an 1845 judgement, a product of the prolonged struggle between the two main contending lines in Sivagangai, gives a clear illustration of judicial irritation. The justice ironically recalls an allegedly important series of events which he argued were fabricated with little subtlety:

But again, if the dramatic scene of the division [of the estate], as described by the Plaintiff's witnesses ... be considered – the discussion before the palace, [divulging] all the family matters, the retirement of Velu Nachchiar within the palace, while the subordinate actors are performing their parts, her reappearance at the dénouement, and the *finale* of the two documents, the one delivered by her to one brother, and the other to the other – it would be doing injustice to both parties to ascribe to either a greater degree of credibility than to the other.

Having expressed this opinion of the utter incredibility of the oral evidence

[67] High Court of Madras. Select Documents in Appeal No. 7 of 1894, Exhibit A, p. 5.

generally, it would be superfluous to enter into a minute examination and comparison of its individual parts and to point out each particular contradiction or inconsistency, as the Plaintiff has sought to do in her Motions ... and the Defendant in his ... Both had an easy task.[68]

Britons conceptualised the legitimacy of their rule in India partly in terms of the Anglicised legal system they maintained. A common sentiment, voiced towards the end of the nineteenth century was that of James Fitzsimmons Stephen:

Under the old despotic systems the place of law was taken by a number of vague and fluctuating customs, liable to be infringed at every moment by the arbitrary fancies of the ruler.[69]

Britons needed the legal system in part to confirm for themselves and, as they would have it, their subjects the superiority of their rule in providing institutions for the application of a type of reasoning, which they assumed to be independent, to issues of human rights which they assumed to be universal. The Justices of the Privy Council, however, periodically expressed the fear that, unless colonial judges developed a method for dealing with perjured evidence, they would become victims of their own prejudice. As they argued in 1871:

Their Lordships [of the Judicial Committee of the Privy Council] are led ... to state, as has often been stated before by this Committee, that the ordinary legal and reasonable presumptions of facts must not be lost sight of in the trial of Indian cases, however untrustworthy much of the evidence submitted to these Courts may commonly be ... [E]vidence in a particular case must not be rejected from a general distrust of native testimony, nor perjury widely imputed without some grave grounds to support the imputation.[70]

The Justices then made an attempt to support their vision of the proper functioning of the courts: 'Such a rejection [of native testimony], if sanctioned would virtually submit the decision of the rights of others to the suspicions and not to the deliberate judgement of their appointed judges.'[71] The Justices suggested a guideline: 'Nor must an entire history be thrown aside because the evidence, or some of the evidence, of some of the witnesses is incredible or untrustworthy.'[72] Perjury in court highlighted the contradiction between Indian litigants and colonial judges, whose ideological function in the colonial government was mocked by the persistent fabrications.

---

[68] Annasawmy Ayer, *The Sivaganga Zamindary*, p. 29.
[69] Leslie Stephen's *Life of Sir James Fitzjames Stephen* (New York, 1895), p. 285, quoted in Lloyd I. Rudolph and Susanne Hoeber Rudolph, *The Modernity of Tradition: Political Development in India* (Chicago; The University of Chicago Press, 1967), p. 253.
[70] Privy Council. Ramamani vs. Kulanthai, 1871, Decision of the Judicial Committee of the Privy Council.
[71] *Ibid.*
[72] *Ibid.*

With rampant resort to perjury, the type of argumentation which zamindari litigants and their lawyers offered in the civil courts indicates that they did not take seriously the proposition that judicial reasoning would disclose the 'rights' of one litigant over the other. Arguments in court were rhetorical displays, constructed to overpower the opposition even if this process resulted in sometimes remarkable fabrications of royal history, practice and kin relationships, and the misrepresentation of kingly values and symbols. Litigation in colonial dispute management was alien to the political culture of the zamindari domain and litigants used the legal instruments and concepts which the system employed as blunt-edged tools of non-violent combat. In this sense, succession remained an activity calling for the demonstration of superior political skill. Victory still represented an achieved status, even if the outcome was preceded by Anglo-Indian judicial reasoning.

With ample recourse to perjury, litigants strove to convince the justices that (1) a certain kin relationship existed, (2) such a relationship was legitimate and (3) such a legitimate relationship implied a legitimate claim on zamindari property. The competition among kin was complicated by the court practice of referring to the need to conform to actual caste usage, at the same time as justices demanded evidence of usage which was generally impossible to collect and present.

Participants in the litigation of Ramnad and Sivagangai zamindaris often took the perjurous position of arguing a claim on the basis of caste ranking in Hindu Law, when such a ranking had not characterised Maravar usage. In the course of discussions of caste usage, argumentation became further complicated with discussions concerning Maravar caste status. One implication of this discourse was that competition for zamindari titles became tied to wider issues current in developing public spheres in India in general and south India in particular. These issues included redefinitions of caste membership, the status of castes in relation to each other and competition among castes and sub-castes for status.[73]

Anglo-Indian courts accepted orthodox Brahminical definitions of caste ranking, with Brahmins being the highest ranking, purest *varna* (larger caste category); Kshatriyas (warriors) next; Vaisyas (merchants and land-holders), third; and Sudras (servants of the above), the lowest. The top three varnas were twice-born, meaning that they could undertake training in the sastras, the sacred texts of orthodoxy, and undergo a ceremony to enable them to wear the sacred thread. This, in turn, would allow them to practice 'pure' sastric rituals in their homes. In south India it was not necessarily possible to say to which varna a caste belonged or what status a caste or subcaste should have within a varna. The courts recognised as holding high caste status those castes whose customs most closely followed Brahminical usage.

[73] Price, 'Acting in Public versus Forming a Public', discusses these issues further.

From the early decades of the nineteenth century the policy of the government regarding caste status attracted intense and increasing interest, in and out of the courts of law. William McCormack commented on the phenomenon:

[The interest] proceeded not only out of sentimental attachment to own caste name but also out of imputing to the legal judgement the status of an authoritative government decision both on the social rank and also on the ceremonial privileges of the caste.[74]

The Government of Madras recognised fairly early that the fourfold division did not describe south Indian society adequately, in that in this part of the subcontinent the Kshatriya, Vaisya and Sudra distinctions had never become fully developed. Keeping the general Brahminical model of caste, however, the government decided that in Tamil country the population of caste Hindus consisted of Brahmins and Sudras. Castes which were wealthy and powerful presented problems of classification, however, because Sudra caste status was widely recognised as demeaning. In his manual of Madurai district, J. H. Nelson reported in 1868 that 'ordinary' people did not use the term 'Sudra' and added, 'In fact the term Sudra would appear to be used by Brahmans alone in speaking contemptuously of persons of low condition.'[75]

Dominant castes like the land-controlling Vellalar, whose practices were compatible with Brahminic ideas of purity, were considered high-ranking Sudras in the government system; although, when government census officers placed Vellalars in the 'Sat Sudra or Good Sudra' category in its 1901 Census, Vellalar castemen petitioned the government, protesting this designation and saying that their reputation had suffered as a result.[76] Vellalars identified with ruling authority and were the lords in the predominantly wet land villages which they controlled. This stance is clear in the complaint in the Vellalar petition that, 'the very idea of service is, as it needs be, revolting to the Vellala, whose profession teaches him perfect independence, and dependence, if it be, upon the sovereign alone for the protection of his proper interest'.[77]

The Maravars presented even more vexing problems of classification. Their practices of drinking alcoholic beverages, eating meat, performing blood sacrifices and allowing remarriage for widows were polluting from the orthodox Brahminical point of view. In terms of common patterns of legitimate marriage in south India, Maravars were anomalous in allowing a man to marry his father's sister's daughter, while the prevailing pattern was

[74] William C. McCormack, 'Caste and the British Administration of Hindu Law', in the *Journal of Asian and African Studies*, no. 1, pt. 1, 1966, pp. 28–9.
[75] J. H. Nelson, *The Madurai Country*, pp. 12–13.
[76] Edgar Thurston, *Castes and Tribes of Southern India*, vol. 7, quoted in Pfaffenberger, *Caste in Tamil Culture*, p. 33.
[77] Thurston, *Castes and Tribes*, vol. 7, pp. 366–7.

for mother's brother's daughter marriages.[78] On the other hand, not only were the rajas of the two largest Tamil zamindaries Maravars, but the heads of other smaller zamindaries were as well. Maravars were warriors with a tradition of lordship and protection in village localities. It complicated the case of Maravar caste status under the British scheme that the Maravar system of village protection carried associations with cattle-lifting and thieving. The colonial government took an extremely dim view of these practices. In the 1890s British officers collected evidence from Tinnevelly district showing that Maravars composed 10 per cent of the population, but committed 70 per cent of rural crime or dacoity.[79] Colonial authorities included Maravars among the castes stigmatised by the passing of the Criminal Tribes Act of 1911.

Sometimes in zamindari litigation legal officers described Maravars as Kshatriyas, but more often they were classified as Sudras. Disagreement existed concerning their status within the Sudra class. Opponents of the royal Maravars used this ambiguity to their advantage. In the course of the nineteenth century, in their conflicted relationship with temple priests and temple administrators, the Setupatis had to respond to the occasional charge that they were not ritually pure enough to receive the high honours and special privileges which they claimed as their right. The earliest example comes from 1834 when the Pandaram (chief administrator) of Rameswaram Temple argued that 'it is inconsistent that Zemindars who use animal food should be allowed any interference in bestowing the Kashayom or red cloth [a high honour] for the nomination of the Pundaroms of the pure Sheva Cast [sic] ...'[80]

It is unlikely that this insult in the first half of the nineteenth century reflected the way ordinary villagers experienced Maravar status in Maravar country. Long into the twentieth century Maravar lords of villages maintained their pride in coming from the community of the Setupati and the Raja of Sivagangai. Kingship was more relevant in determining local social and political status than eating meat. By the end of the nineteenth century, however, some groups in the populations of former warriors had developed a desire for higher caste status. The colonial ethnographer Thurston reported in 1909 that a Tamil proverb existed to the effect that 'a Kallan may come to be a Maravan. By respectability he may develope [sic] into an Agamudaiyan, and, by slow degrees, become a Vellala, from which he may rise to be a

[78] Louis Dumont, 'Hierarchy and Marriage Alliance in South Indian Kinship', *Occasional Papers of the Royal Anthropological Institute of Great Britain and Ireland*, no. 12, 1957, pp. 13 and 16. Maravar caste customs are discussed in Thurston, *Castes and Tribes*, vol. 5, pp. 22–48.
[79] Eugene F. Irschick, *Tamil Revivalism in the 1930s* (Madras: Cre-A, 1986), p. 200.
[80] Madura District Records, vol. 4682, 1 January 1834, To the President and Members of the Board of Revenue from J. C. Wraughten, Acting Principal Collector, p. 15. Here pure 'Sheva Caste' appears to be a reference to Vellalars, since the Pandarams bear the title Pillai.

Mudaliar.'[81] As new types of horizontal mobilisation drew groups into the realm of Indian-style public spheres, imperial ideologies and classifications became increasingly important in setting caste ranks and defining conceptions of caste status. The royal Maravars lost status among some groups because they belonged to the Maravar caste. The politics of perjury in zamindari litigation played a role in this process of conceptual change.

The rhetoric of civil litigation contributed to the coupling of the status of a particular royal house with the status of the caste of its members. As a consequence of the use of Hindu Law in litigation, classification of the royal Maravars by caste became part of the argumentation regarding the relationship between legitimate bonds of kin and rights to the estate. A debate involving Rani Muthu Virayi, the widow of Raja Annasami Setupati, and her widowed daughter-in-law, Rani Parvata Vardhani, illustrates this point. The debate took place between 1844 and 1846 and was published in the proceedings of the High Court and the Privy Council in connection with the famous Ramnad Adoption Case, the attempt by the Collector of Madurai to resume Ramnad by escheat. The Privy Council decision came down in 1868.

The relationship between the two ranis had become strained by 1843, as Muthu Virayi attempted to prevent Parvata Vardhani from taking control of Ramnad in the capacity of Guardian of her minor daughter. In 1844 Muthu Virayi's lawyers argued on her behalf that her own husband had no right to adopt Ramasami, Vardhani's husband, because Ramasami was Muthu Virayi's brother. Parvata Vardhani and her daughter, thus, had no right to the zamindari because the adoption of the deceased zamindar by his sister and his sister's husband was not legitimate according to Hindu Law.[82] In a Supplemental Plaint Muthu Virayi's lawyer argued that, according to Hindu Law, a man could adopt a son only by a woman whom he could legitimately have married.[83] Annasami could not legitimately marry his mother-in-law, who was both his wife's mother and his adopted son's mother. In the Supplemental Answer, Vardhani's lawyer stated that Maravars, though 'Sudras' and bound to conform to the rules of the Dharmasastras, 'never conform to the duties imposed by Hindu Law'.[84] The Supplemental Answer went on to list several Maravar practices which were not given in Hindu Law, including widow remarriage, and added that 'The provisions of Hindu Law are not therefore essential to their caste aucharums [customs].'

The Supplemental Answer for Vardhani, however, made a distinction between the Maravar caste and its kings, saying that, as royal Maravars, Vardhani's ancestors and those of Muthu Virayi had conformed to the rule

---

[81] Thurston, *Castes and Tribes*, vol. I, p. 7.
[82] Privy Council. The Collector of Madurai vs. Muttu Ramalinga Setupati, 1868. Case for the Appellant, p. 3.
[83] *Ibid.*, Supplemental Plaint in Record of Proceedings, p. 31.
[84] *Ibid.*, p. 33.

of Hindu Law 'hereditarily and without deviation'.[85] The Supplemental Answer asserted that Muthu Virayi's husband had adopted Ramasami in conformity to the Sastras: the zamindar could have married Ramasami's mother because the 'gotras' (lines) of his own father and his wife (the sister of the adopted) were different. The Answer quoted examples of south Indian Brahmins who had adopted their brothers-in-law, as well as sastric sources.

In the Supplemental Reply, filed in 1845, Muthu Virayi's lawyer took strong offence to the statement that Maravars did not follow Hindu Law:

The answer thus containing expressions which are dishonest, and which have reference to circumstances that have never taken place, is not fit even to be retained in the records. The Marava caste, to which both parties belong, ranks as an important one in the fourth class [Sudras], and from that fact of their being Setupatis, they are held in such great esteem as to be respected by the kings of all the countries with marks of honour. A fact which has been expressed by the Sadr Court, by remarking at large in their decree passed in Sadr Appeal No. 18 of 1814, respecting the right of Ramnad zemindary, that the provisions of Hindu law are chiefly binding upon this Marava caste and that their proceedings are consistent with the provisions of said law.[86]

The Reply went on to say that in 1835 the Sadr Adalat had also found that Sivagangai Maravars followed Hindu Law. Sama Row, Muthu Virayi's lawyer, argued that Maravars *and* their rajas were Sudras who followed Hindu Law.

Parvata Vardhani and her lawyer carried the debate further by filing a Supplemental Rejoinder the next year. In rebuttal to Muthu Virayi they pointed out that her mother-in-law's sister had married a man and borne children by him, only to remarry, at her husband's death, the husband of another sister, getting issue by him.[87] Parvata Vardhani still maintained, however, that her ancestors and those of Muthu Virayi had followed Hindu Law.

As part of their strategy for kingly legitimation, precolonial rajas of Ramnad had claimed in inscriptions to follow the law of Manu, a famous orthodox code; however, it was a Maravar royal norm before the Permanent Settlement that the son of the sister of a king should inherit the kingdom, in the absence of a male heir.[88] Such a norm, among others, was not according to the dictates of Hindu Law.

This exchange constituted a debate about the constituents of south Indian royalty, but it was entirely framed within official colonial categories. In the course of this debate a process of cultural translation took place – a

[85] *Ibid.*
[86] *Ibid.*, Supplemental Reply in Record of Proceedings, p. 38.
[87] *Ibid.*, Supplement Rejoinder in Record of Proceedings, p. 41.
[88] *Ibid.*, Record of the Proceedings. Arzi addressed by Narayana Tow, the Head of Police to the Zuft Zemindari of Ramnad, 2 April 1820, pp. 10–11. This was the result of a survey he undertook as to the inheritance rights of a zamindar. Because kilai (line) membership was traced through females, a sister's son would be in the same kilai as the dead raja.

reinterpretation of historical experience. Such translations in a public arena informed the sociological and political visions of 'native public opinion'. Litigation resulted in a process of cosmological fragmentation, a desacralisation of kingship, in the public sphere. The indignities only continued.

The politics of perjury: royal wives and 'concubines'

In the proceedings of the litigation discussed above, Parvata Vardhani misrepresented kingly marriage by saying that only the first wife of a king was legitimately married: her Supplemental Rejoinder claimed that other women were 'kept mistresses' and had no rights to inheritance from the Raja.[89] The Rani in this case was trying to discredit two ex-wives of Raja Annasami who had joined with Muthu Virayi against the adoption of Ramasami and who claimed to be heirs of Annasami. Ten years later Vardhani charged that Annasami's sixth wife had also been a concubine and that this woman's mother and grandmother had been concubines.[90] In their intense competition, royal widows and their kin, with the assistance of lawyers, entered into a discursive process which dishonoured major symbols of royal power and auspiciousness: the wives of a king and the devadasis who danced in major temples and at palace events.

Royal litigants and their allies played on the misapprehensions of British judges in concocting perjurous tales. They played a role in disassociating zamindars from precolonial monarchical cosmology. The convention of rhetorical manipulation in litigation debate made British prejudices towards indigenous culture fair game. Commonly uttered in British criticism of Indian life and society was the opinion that devadasis were prostitutes and that women of a *zenana* (the women's quarters in an elite household) were ignorant intriguers of low character. Zamindar litigation had the effect of confirming these stereotypic notions.

The marriage of Raja Ramasami Setupati and Parvata Vardhani had resulted in two daughters. In 1830 Ramasami died without having specifically given Vardhani the authority to adopt a son, or so the Collector of Madurai later charged. By 1845 both girls had died and a year later Parvata Vardhani decided to adopt a boy, Muthu Ramalingam. In an attempt to thwart Vardhani, Muthu Virayi also decided to adopt a boy who could be an heir to the zamindari. After considerable negotiation, some of which is discussed above, the two women reached an agreement whereby Vardhani's right to adopt was recognised by the older woman. In 1847, however, the Collector of Madurai announced that Parvata Vardhani must convince *him* that she had a right to adopt under Hindu Law. Negotiations among Vardhani, zamindari kin and the Collector followed, to no avail. In 1860

[89] *Ibid.*, Supplemental Rejoinder in Record of Proceedings, p. 46.
[90] *Ibid.*, Record of the Proceedings. Case of the Respondents. Supplemental Answer, p. 4.

the Collector filed a statement saying that the Rani had failed to obtain the consent to the adoption of all of her husband's relatives.

Parvata Vardhani fared better in court. The High Court of Madras decided in 1864 that the majority of Ramasami's relatives gave their assent to the adoption, even if they had failed to do so at the time of the adoption. When the Collector took the case on appeal to the Judicial Committee of the Privy Council in London, he failed there as well. The Privy Council agreed that Parvata Vardhani had received the consent of enough of her dead husband's relatives to make the adoption legal in Hindu Law.[91]

During the years since Ramasami's death, a number of his relatives had challenged Parvata Vardhani's position as his heir (she was Guardian of his children and, then, of the minor Zamindar, whom she had adopted). The most serious of these challenges came from a former wife of Annasami, Kunjara, and her daughter.[92] Kunjara argued that she was the sixth wife of Annasami and that, since her daughter had a son, her daughter should be Rani of Ramnad and Guardian of a minor heir to the estate. She also challenged Paravata Vardhani's right to adopt. Kunjara's case was coupled with the Collector's and went thus to the High Court and the Privy Council.

Parvata Vardhani and her lawyers sought to discredit Kunjara and her daughter in their response to this challenge. Vardhani's lawyers argued that Kunjara was not the legally wedded wife of Annasami: She had been his concubine and, furthermore, her mother was the daughter of a devadasi and the concubine of another man.[93] Vardhani's suit asserted a tradition of concubinage in Kunjara's family by accusing Kunjara's daughter of following in 'the same course of life to this day'.[94]

Kunjara's defence was that, while she, an Ahambadiya woman, was not the same caste as her husband, her marriage had been legal according to Hindu Law because inter-caste marriages among Sudras were legitimate. Vardhani's side responded, however, that the 'fusion of castes' was not accepted among Maravars:[95] 'persons of different castes cannot marry.'[96]

The evidence presented for Kunjara showed clearly that she had been the sixth wife of Annasami. She was not a Maravar, but the judges at all levels decided that inter-caste marriage was permitted among Sudras in Hindu Law. Whether Kunjara was of illegitimate birth was not, the judges decided, relevant. However, because Parvata Vardhani's adoption of a boy, Muthu Ramalingam, was legal, Kunjara's daughter could not succeed to the title of Rani Guardian.

[91] See the decision of the Judicial Committee of the Privy Council in The Collector of Madura vs Muttu Ramalinga Sathupathi, 1868.
[92] Ibid., Case for the Respondent, pp. 3 and 9.
[93] *Ibid.*, Record of the Proceedings, second part, p. 4.
[94] *Ibid.*, Case for the Respondent, p. 4.
[95] *Ibid.*, Records of the Proceedings, second part, p. 5.
[96] *Ibid.*, Case for the Respondent, p. 9.

That Parvata Vardhani knew that Kunjara was the widow of the dead zamindar is indicated by the fact that she had been paying the maintenance due to Kunjara as a zamindar's widow. In this suit, however, the Rani and her lawyers were playing on the possibility that British judges, understanding little about caste, would assume that inter-caste marriages were not permitted according to Hindu Law (on occasion judges decided that inter-caste marriages were not permitted).[97] Living in the same palace as Kunjara, Parvata Vardhani would have known the marital status of the woman; furthermore, as the wife of a Ramnad raja, she would be aware that Ramnad rajas made political alliances among important groups in their domain and with other domain leaders through marriage, even if the women involved came of a different caste.[98] Before considering further the implications of the Rani's accusations, I present another lawsuit which took place among Ramnad royal kin at this time. This case developed out of the adoption conflict discussed above.

As a widowed Rani and Guardian of, first, her daughters and then Muthu Ramalinga Setupati, Parvata Vardhani was a woman of influence and high rank. The most powerful figure in zamindari politics at this time, however, was Ponnusami Tevar, Muthu Ramalinga's brother and the Manager of Ramnad, mentioned earlier in connection with Dorasinga Tevar. In the course of managing the litigation for the adoption suit, Ponnusami had become chief among royal kin.[99] However, as he attempted to line up consent to Muthu Ramalingam's adoption, Ponnusami met resistance from two male relatives. One of these men, Rama Raja, testified in court that he had not witnessed the adoption ceremony, suggesting that it had not taken place.[100] In so doing, Rama Raja challenged Ponnusami's authority and threated the existence of Ramnad as a zamindari. Ponnusami found a way to punish his rebel kinsman.

As mentioned earlier, Muthu Virayi had adopted a son, Sivasami, as part of her strategy to block Parvata Vardhani from keeping her important position as Guardian of the minor zamindar. In the agreement which the

---

[97] In the case discussed below (Privy Council. Ramamani and Kulanthai, 1871) the High Court decision asserted that 'mixture of castes' was said not to be allowed, nor could illegitimate children inherit from their father.

[98] Thomas R. Trautmann, *Dravidian Kingship*, pp. 387–94. Note the marriage of a raja of Ramnad and the sister of the Kallar caste head of Pudukkottai at the end of the seventeenth century, Dirks, 'Little Kingdoms of South India: Political Authority and Social Relations in the Southern Tamil countryside', PhD dissertation, University of Chicago, n.d., p. 174. See also Dumont, 'Hierarchy and Marriage Alliance', p. 12, and Privy Council. Collector of Madura vs. Muttu Ramalinga Sathupathi. Record of the Proceedings. The latter has a report from the Head of Police of the Zuft Zamindari of Ramnad, dated 2 April, 1820, giving evidence that Annasami was married to two Ahambadiya caste women, including Kunjara.

[99] Privy Council. Ramamani vs. Kulanthai, 1871. Record of the Proceedings, No. 62. Here a servant from the palace explains, 'Ponnusamy was the head of the family'.

[100] *Ibid.*, No. 64.

two women eventually reached, Sivasami was given a village, a comfortable monthly allowance, and Rs. 50,000 in a lump sum.[101] When Muthu Virayi died, Sivasami inherited her villages. When he died in 1862, his wife, Kulanthai, acted quickly to receive a government certificate as his heir.[102] One of her kinsman was the same Rama Raja who had challenged Ponnusami. He managed Kulanthai's affairs, and she appears to have decided to adopt his son as her heir, since she was childless.

However, two years later, another woman, Ramamani, instituted a suit for Sivasami's property, with the financial backing of Ponnusami. She argued that she was Sivasami's heir, having married him and having borne a boy and a girl by him.

Kulanthai's side responded with the allegation that Ramamani had not been legally married to Sivasami, that she was not a Maravar, and that she had been 'a notorious whore' – a devadasi.[103] Both sides lined up a long list of witnesses. Kulanthai's side produced fourteen people who claimed to have seen Ramamani dressed as a devadasi at various temples and to have seen her, thus dressed, dancing at Ramnad Palace.[104] Several witnesses claimed that Ramamani's mother had also been a temple dancer, suggesting that not only were Ramamani's children illegitimate, but that she had also been illegitimate. Ramamani had twenty-four witnesses for her side, including a Vellala headman of a zamindari village and his two sons.[105] These testified to be, respectively, Ramamani's father and her two half-brothers. Her mother was said to have been a Vellala woman who had died previously. Thirteen witnesses testified that they had been present at the marriage ceremony of Sivasami and Ramamani, while close relatives of Sivasami said that Ramamani had been Sivasami's second wife. They also said that a Maravar man could marry a Vellala woman.

In 1864 a district court found Ramamani – Ponnusami's client in this conflict – to have been legally married to Sivasami. A year later, however, the High Court found in favour of Kulanthai. These judges suggested that Ramamani's suit was dubious in that the Zamindar of Ramnad had backed it and that Ponnusami, Manager of Ramnad, had arranged for Ramamani's respectable royal witnesses to testify on her behalf. In their decision the High Court justices wrote that they believed the royal kinsmen to have lied in their defence of Ramamani: 'We have, however, daily and painful experience that the [high social] position of a witness by no means causes him to hesitate at perjury when there is for that perjury what appears to him an adequate object.'[106]

---

[101] Privy Council. The Collector of Madura vs. Muttu Ramalinga Sathupathi, 1868. Case for the Appellant, p. 5.
[102] Privy Council. Ramamani vs. Kulanthai, 1871. Record of the Proceedings, No. 64.
[103] *Ibid.*, No. 2.
[104] *Ibid.*, Case for the Respondent.
[105] *Ibid.*, Judgement of the High Court of Madras.
[106] *Ibid.*, Judgement of the High Court of Madras.

The Justices of the Privy Council, however, disagreed sharply with the lower court finding.[107] Writing in 1871, they decided that the evidence given by Ramamani's witnesses, though weak at some points, was generally persuasive. Nor were they suspicious of Ponnusami's financial support of the case: perhaps Ramamani was a widow in need!

Perjury such as that outlined above undermined the legitimacy of important symbols of royalty. In protecting worship, precolonial kings acted to generate power which could allow their kingdoms to prosper through (among other benefits) the 'good and timely' appearance of rains.[108] Devadasis, women who danced before the great god in a major temple, were 'married' to the ruling deity and were, as such, human embodiments of the god's consort. A king was homologous to the reigning deity and a king's first wife in particular was homologous to the divine consort. Thus devadasis were associated with kingship and were symbols of royal sovereignty. The power of the divine consort (sakti) was the energy source of the male god as well as the king. As human embodiments of the goddess, devadasis were associated with sakti. Like kings, they were regarded as auspicious and associated with fertility and, thus, with prosperity in general. Thus devadasis could be substitutes for the principal wife/ wives of a king both in public rituals and those which took place in seclusion. The dancers properly had sexual intercourse with temple Brahmins, but since they were married to the god, they were not supposed to bear children. They could not marry a human; however, it was not uncommon for kings to have intimate relations with these symbols of their sovereignty.[109]

By the eighteenth century, as part of the general devolution of royal cosmologies to lower levels of political organisation in south India, devadasis as symbols of auspiciousness had also become an important part of ritual celebrations in non-royal elite families; Kersenboom-story reports:

Another instance of their ... prestige was the code of politeness that prescribed that any dignified person of high social status should travel only with a retinue of devadasis. Important visitors ... [were] also received in the same manner.[110]

In describing Ramamani as a devadasi and associating Kunjara with a devadasi heritage, Parvata Vardhani and Kulanthai Nachiar created

---

[107] *Ibid.*, Decision of the Judicial Committee of the Privy Council.

[108] This discussion of the relationship between devadasis and kings is based on discussion in Frédérique Appfel Marglin, *Wives of the God-king: the Rituals of the Devadasis of Puri* (Delhi: Oxford University Press, 1985) and 'Kings and Wives: the Separation of Status and Royal Power', in T. N. Madan (ed.), *Way of Life – King, Householder, Renouncer: Essays in Honour of Louis Dumont* (Delhi: Motilal Banarsidas Publishers, 1982), pp. 155–68. The 'good and timely' appearance of rains is from 'Kings and Wives', p. 178.

[109] Marglin does not report this for her Orissan example; however, devadasis are commonly associated with rajas in southern Tamil country.

[110] Saskia C. Kersenboom-story, *Nityasumaṅgalī: Devadasi Tradition in South India* (New Delhi: Motilal Banarsidas, 1987), p. 66.

plausible scenarios in the eyes of the British judges. Ramamani and Kunjara's position under Hindu Law was vulnerable to begin with because they were not Maravar women. In practice a devadasi could not marry a zamindar and her offspring by a zamindar could not be legitimate. In the prudish eyes of colonial officialdom, the daughter of a devadasi was not considered a proper wife for a zamindar. In calling Ramamani a 'notorious whore', Kulanthai pointed to an interpretation of the relationship between zamindar rajas and devadasis which saw it not only as inappropriate, but immoral. This stance was a profound contradiction of royal ideology, which associated a devadasi with auspiciousness.[111] Such testimony contributed to the banishment of devadasis from Ramnad palace ritual at the end of the nineteenth century. As Parvata Vardhani and Kulanthai accused their competitors of being concubines of one sort or another, they degraded royal marriage practices and undermined sacred kingship in the public sphere.

Females as political actors in South India

As Julia Leslie recently noted, royal women in late precolonial polities had been active in the politics of royal households.[112] Strategic marriage and ties of kinship played an important role in political integration, at both local and regional levels, so it is only to be expected that females were politically engaged informally, if not formally.[113]

In both myth and actual practice in southern Tamil country, there were instances of women assuming formal responsibilities of governance. The most important mythic reference is the great goddess at Madurai, Minakshi, the only child of a king of Madurai, who was born with three breasts and was brought up learning the arts of warfare. Minakshi led her forces into battle against the armies of Siva; however, upon actual confrontation with the god, her third breast fell off as she recognised him as her future husband. Minakshi thus suddenly became shy; she married the god and proceeded to share the governance of Madurai with him. In Tamil the Minakshi story dates back at least to the fifth century AD, and appeared during the following centuries in Tamil and Sanskrit versions.[114] A well-

---

[111] The auspicious nature of devadasis and their function in warding off evil influences is a continuing theme in Kersenboom-story, *Nityasumangali*. She argues that their main responsibility in royal ritual was to protect the king from evil influences.

[112] I. Julia Leslie, *The Perfect Wife: The Orthodox Hindu Woman according to the Strīdharmapaddhati of Tryambakayajvan* (Delhi: Oxford University Press, 1989), p. 20.

[113] Pierre Bourdieu makes a useful distinction between public and official kin on one hand and private and practical kin on the other in discussing the political engagement of women in a north African locality in his *Outline of a Theory of Practice* (Cambridge: Cambridge University Press, 1977), pp. 34–43. The activities of females in the politics of kinship were, in his analysis, 'private' and 'practical'. See Dirks, *The Hollow Crown*, for a discussion of kinship and the organization of the Pudukkottai state, pp. 203–84.

[114] William P. Harman, *The Sacred Marriage of a Hindu Goddess* (Bloomington: Indiana University Press, 1989), p. 28.

known version in Pandyamandalam written by Parañcōti appeared in, probably, the middle of the seventeenth century.[115]

The presumed date of the Parancoti version is probably significant, indicating the possibilities for the formal rule of royal women in the late precolonial period. Rani Mangammal ruled the kingdom of Madurai as Regent from 1689 to 1704, when her grandson forced her to give up the throne. She was an active patron, supporting temples, road-building and the construction of (water) tanks, and her reign was popular, remaining a source for local tales into the first decade of the twentieth century.[116] Less well remembered was another queen regent of Madurai, Rani Minakshi, who ruled from about 1732 to about 1736. Her husband had no issue and chose Minakshi, his favourite wife, to succeed him (the other seven wives immolated themselves as satis). Minakshi adopted the son of a cousin of the dead king. The cousin, however, wanted the throne for himself and provoked a major war of succession.[117] In the course of the hostilities the kingdom became so weakened that enemy forces took control. The queen committed suicide and the Nayaka dynasty of Madurai came to an end.

Both the mythic history and the experience of the two ranis suggest an ambivalence about women as independent rulers in monarchical cosmology and political practice. The local goddess, Minakshi, had to marry and share her kingdom with Lord Siva, her superior. Both of the queen regents met with male resistance which eventually felled them, resulting in death.

As mentioned previously, during the period of the Vijayanagar Kingdom and the following centuries, sakti, the active female element in the cosmos, became an important theme in monarchical cosmology. During this period the Navaratri, the festival of the Goddess, was the most important ritual celebration of the integration of a royal domain. The prominence of a feminine-gendered concept of power (sakti) does not indicate unambivalent male acceptance of the assumption of formal ruling authority by women.

Analysis of the ritual of the Navaratri festival in the court of a sixteenth-century Vijayanagar king suggests conventional perceptions of the appropriate role of women in formal relations of rule.[118] The household domains of the king's chief wives received recognition in that the queens' many servants went in procession in groups during the ritual performances.[119] However, not only did the chief queens not appear, but their representatives did not take part in ritual exchanges in which specific persons honoured the king and received back marks of honour and rank. Women did not

---

[115] *Ibid.*, p. 27.

[116] Francis, *Madurai district Gazetteer*, p. 54.

[117] *Ibid.*, p. 56.

[118] Pamela Price, 'The State and Representations of Femaleness in Late Medieval South India', in *Historisk tidsskrift* (Oslo), no. 4, 1990, pp. 589–97, elaborates on the points below.

[119] Domingo Paes and Fernao Funiz, *The Vijayanagar Empire*, Vaundhara Felliozat (ed.), Robert Sewell (trans.) (New Delhi: National Book Trust, 1977) gives two descriptions.

participate in the ordered articulation of relations of power and authority in the kingdom.

Navaratri ritual separated the household domains of the queens from those under male control and suggested a qualitative difference between them. Here the domains of the queens were expressions of undifferentiated auspiciousness. This auspiciousness was not the function of individual political leadership and action, but existed, tensionless, to lend its rich and shining qualities to the wider realm dominated by male rulers, the king and his lords. The domains of the queens appeared thus encompassed as elements in the maintenance of the kingdom.

The role given to women in the Navaratri ritual expressed the common south Indian conviction that female power was auspicious when it was under male control and unpredictably dangerous if left to independent display. The absence of individual honouring of women indicated a mistrust in monarchical cosmology of formal, independent initiatives on the part of elite women. The orchestrated and undifferentiated appearance of palace women in the context of the honouring of men further suggested that this honour consisted, in part, of the appropriate (male) control of women.[120]

Vasudha Narayanan suggests a way to consider the nature of female subordination in medieval culture. She quotes a late thirteenth-century Sri Vaisnavite writer on the topic of the relationship of Sri, the embodiment of royal majesty, to her consort the Lord Vishnu:

Though you own will, you belong to the Lord. O Goddess, though both you and the Lord have such qualities as youthfulness, He has the masculine characteristics of not being controlled by others, controlling enemies, and valor ... [whereas] you have the feminine qualities of tenderness, being submissive to your husband, mercy, patience ... You two have thus split up the functions to enjoy [creation] ... [121]

Narayanan argues that at the same time as Sri and Vishnu were two parts of one, Sri was distinct and equal to Vishnu, subservient to him only because she herself willed it so. Elite men and women represented different and balanced qualities and requirements. One of the requirements of the beneficial possibilities in female power, however, was its orchestration by males.

The involvement of zamindari women in litigation took place outside political contexts which emphasised the complementarity of men and women. Anglo-Indian court procedure set litigants in adversarial relationships. Zamindari women stood forth as challengers to royal male authority

[120] See, in this connection, Pamela Price, 'Honor, Disgrace and the Depoliticization of Women in South India: Changing Structures of the State under Colonial Rule', in *Gender and History*, vol. 6, no. 2, 1994, pp. 246–64.

[121] Vasudha Narayanan, 'The Goddess Śrī: Blossoming Lotus and Breast Jewel of Vishnu', in John Stratton Hawley and Donna Marie Wulff (eds.), *The Divine Consort: Radha and the Goddesses of India* (Delhi: Motilal Banarsidass, 1984), p. 231, quoting Vedanta Desika, 'Srigunaratnakasa', verses 32 and 34.

in such a manner as to contribute to the loss of respect which zamindari houses suffered in the eyes of 'public opinion' in the course of the nineteenth century. At the same time, rigorous norms of female modesty and submission were taking hold in the constitution of nationalist identities.[122]

Zamindari litigation in the public sphere

From at least the 1840s,[123] English-language newspapers covered zamindari politics, sometimes including day-to-day reporting of testimony in court.[124] The district level proceedings of litigation, including documents and witnesses' testimony, as well as, sometimes, advocates' argumentation, were printed when suits went to the appeal level. How many copies were printed and who had access to them is not clear. The number of copies was probably quite limited. From the 1860s, decisions in the Judicial Committee of the Privy Council appeared in Moore's Privy Council Appeals[125] and important High Court decisions appeared in law reports and law reviews.

Litigation histories were hardly the stuff of cosmic confrontations with threats to the universe or the heroic poses in poetry and myth which royal patrons usually preferred. As they presented themselves in plaints and rejoinders filed in law courts, the only claim which zamindari kin had on kingship was a family membership upon whose legitimacy colonial judges decided. Succession politics thus individualised and domesticated Tamil kingship as it faced the wider audience of public life beyond the samastanam locality.

For ordinary and poor villagers and town-dwellers of nineteenth-century Maravar country, the kings of Sivagangai and Ramnad are likely to have retained important aspects of their royal dharmic and divine nature.[126] But for those men with access to information in the public sphere, for the people who defined themselves as 'public opinion', the heads of royal houses became less glamorous as members of a 'native aristocracy'. Through processes of litigation according to the 'personal' law of the Hindus, royal kin appear to have become associated in public opinion with categories which the law described. Zamindari litigants stood forth in print, each a

---

[122] Price, 'Honor, Disgrace and the Depoliticization of Women'; Dipesh Chakrabarthy, 'Postcoloniality and the Artifice of History: Who Speaks for "Indian" Pasts', in *Representations*, No. 37, 1992, pp. 14–15; and Rosalind O'Hanlon, 'Issues of Widowhood: Gender and Resistance in Colonial Western India', in Douglas Haynes and Gyan Prakash (eds.), *Contesting Power: Resistance and Everyday Social Relations in South Asia* (Delhi: Oxford University Press, 1991), pp. 62–108.

[123] A Madras newspaper called *The Hindu*, not to be confused with the later *Hindu* founded in 1878.

[124] The Madurai Mail covered litigation of local figures.

[125] Edmund F. Moore, *Reports of Cases Heard and Determined by the Judicial Committee and the Lords of her Majesty's Most Honorable Privy Council.*

[126] In Ramnad town in 1975 palace informants told me that villagers fell before Raja Ramanata Setupati (d. 1979) and worshipped him when he appeared at Rameswaram Temple.

potential raja or rani, as individual persons with a specific history as a member of a family wracked by particular conflicts. They shared much in this capacity with wealthy commoners who engaged in suits for partition.[127]

This litigation inadvertently provided a model in the area of changing norms about caste. The Setupati had been known as The Maravar or the Great Maravar in late precolonial Tamil country. In the locality of Maravar country, the Maravars as a group of clans sharing a 'caste' identity, acquired status from having the Setupati as the head of their community. In the course of succession litigation Maravar caste identity in the public sphere became universalised according to a scheme which gave the Setupati and the Raja of Sivagangai a lower status – or at least an ambiguous status – by virtue of belong to a 'caste' which had polluting habits. The discourse on caste in litigation proceedings replaced the special dharmic nature of rajas with a social identity which did not distinguish between the status of a title-holder of a zamindari and another member of the Maravar caste. As members of families who were subject to the definitions which Hindu Law gave their caste, zamindars entered the portals of ordinary humanity with the new, ambiguous status of 'aristocrats'.

The ideological damage of this type of representation was aggravated by the entrance of females as formal protagonists in competition for the title. The succession struggles of brothers and male cousins were common knowledge to the mass of people, familiar with the all-India epics, the *Mahabharata* and the *Ramayana*. Here mothers plotted for their sons, and the wives of the great heroes were models of submission. However, in the succession dramas which took place in colonial courts, royal women competed in public outside a mythic context which could frame them in complementary opposition to men. Those who were married did not conform to conventional images of royal wives as sources of kingly auspiciousness. Those who were widows confirmed the belief that, without husbands to control them, women were dangerous to men. Even though female litigants were allowed to protect their modesty by testifying in seclusion, in reports of litigation they were diminished as embodiments of sri and sakti, as sources of prosperity and power for communities.

In the late precolonial period one element of the high honour of men in public ranking was the representation of female submission. Zamindari litigation undermined royal honour by subjecting royal males to regular challenge in public by their kinswomen. Because of the conventions of legal

---

[127] In 1853 William Holloway published a list of families which had been published previously, in 1847, in a Madras city newspaper. These families, thirty-seven in number had, according to the newpaper, been ruined through litigation in the Supreme Court. The list told how much each family had spent on the litigation in question. The list included four 'Chittys', twenty-two 'Moodellys', five 'Pilleys', three 'Naicks', one 'Maistry', one 'Iyen', and an 'Ummal'. The families spent between one and forty lakhs apiece and Holloway said the total came to nearly two million pounds sterling. 'Notes on Madras Judicial Administration', Appendix, p. iii–iv.

to protect), a defender and a liberal man.[1] In monarchical cosmology, in appropriately allocating resources, the king, acting in accordance with dharma, protected the right order of things.

In precolonial inscriptions, the Setupati was sometimes identified as a 'Karna in giving', referring to a king in the *Mahabharata* who was noted for his great generosity.[2] In nineteenth-century Ramnad, largess became one of the most important methods through which zamindari kin developed networks of support and new domains of royal influence, in and beyond the samastanam. One constructed one's factional following and a great reputation with presents or bribes of lands, cash, clothes and jewels. In the absence of more direct tools of control, namely legitimate armies, largess gained in prominence. The zamindar as a vallal exerted the royal prerogative of social ordering, affecting the local status of his subjects through distribution of the resources of his domain.

Neither was the role of leader in conflict denied zamindari kin. The Anglo-Indian court system provided new weapons and arenas for local conflict and shows of influence and strength. A local leader demonstrated his capacity to mobilise and organise loans, lawyers, witnesses, legal and procedural expertise, government officials and a variety of faction followers and dependants, providing a variety of services. Litigation, often characterised as the main activity of zamindars and their managers, offered the opportunity for enemies to be vanquished with the marshalling of new kinds of forces. 'Chivalrous court fights' and the intrigue and events surrounding them provided the most talked about political spectacles of nineteenth-century Madras Presidency, affecting the lives and fortunes of, sometimes, hundreds of people for years at a time.[3] In his *Advice to the Aristocracy*, the Maharaja of Bobbili wrote concerning zamindari litigation:

Litigation nowadays is a very ruinous proceeding. Some Hindus assert that it is, though in another sense, as disastrous as wars. But in fact it is more disastrous. In battles, the conqueror, though his expenditure may be equal to that of his enemy, annexes the enemy's country, or secures certain commercial privileges. But in litigation, except in a very few instances, the winner gets nothing.[4]

The *cliché* of zamindari affairs, 'ruinous litigation', becomes comprehensible in local terms when viewed as an activity of political conflict, providing the occasion for shows of influence and support.

The sections which follow discuss the goals and forms of political authority in mid nineteenth-century Ramnad. These years were sprinkled with royal kin calling themselves Rani or Raja with varying degrees of

---

[1]   *Fabricius's Dictionary* p. 721. The dictionary was first published in 1779.
[2]   James Burgess and S. M. Natesa Sastri, *Tamil and Sanskrit Inscriptions. Archæological Survey of Southern India*, Vol 4, 1886, pp. 82 and 102.
[3]   V. V. Sayana, *The Agrarian Problems of Madras Presidency* (Madras: Business Week Press, 1949), p. 11.
[4]   Maharaja of Bobbili, *Advice to the Aristocracy*, p. 194.

'legitimate' claim to the title. The two most powerful figures of the period
were zamindari Managers, family members who were not, for one reason or
another, in a position to try for the throne directly through litigation. These
men were noted for having 'usurped' responsibilities, power and royal
status for themselves. Their stategies for status developed, it would seem, in
response to local expectations of appropriate behaviour for those claiming
royal authority.

The rise and fall of Muthu Chella Tevar

As noted in the previous chapter, the first Zamindar of Ramnad, receiving
the sanad in 1803, was a woman, Mangaleswari Nachiar. The Rani and her
husband, not having a natural heir, adopted Annasami. Raja Annasami
Setupati married several women, but had no living male offspring by any of
them. His chief wife was the strong-minded Muthu Virayi Nachiar, a near
kinswoman with two brothers (see *Figure 2*). Annasami eventually adopted
one of his wife's brothers, Ramasami, who became zamindar upon the
death of Annasami. Ramasami himself died shortly afterwards, leaving, as
we have seen, a wife, Parvata Vardhani, and two young daughters.
Vardhani was in her early twenties.

Muthu Virayi – 'a woman of great abilities, fully capable of directing the
affairs of the Zemindary' – had been the chief advisor of her husband.
When her adopted son/brother, Ramasami, died, he left a will making her
the Guardian of his wife and children and the executrix of the zamindari.[5]
He designated his and Muthu Virayi's brother, Muthu Chella, to be
zamindari Manager, subordinate to Muthu Virayi. According to the will,
when Mangaleswari, the young heiress, came of age, she would become the
Zamindarni. If she died, her sister, Doraraja, would become Rani. In either
case, the husbands of the young women might end up taking most of their
ruling responsibilities.

Rani Muthu Virayi was not able to control the actions of her brother
Manager, Muthu Chella, who succeeded in constructing strong networks of
support for himself within the zamindari and in Madurai town – signifi-
cantly, in the Madurai district Collectorate. He funded his activities with
zamindari resources, assuming the powers of the Executrix. She in turn
attempted in 1836 to expose his 'usurpation' to J. Blackburn, the Collector,
with the aim of having him removed. An investigation followed. However,
such was Muthu Chella's support in the Collector's own office, that the
Manager was cleared of the charges and, instead, Blackburn induced the
Government of Madras to remove Muthu Virayi from her position as
Guardian and Executrix. The Collector's staff convinced him that the Rani,
not her brother, was the person acting in opposition to the interests of her

---

[5]   Madura District Records, vol. 4678, 24 April 1830. To the President and Members of the
Board of Revenue from H. Viveash, Principal Collector to Madura, p. 126 (TNA).

grandchild's inheritance. Parvata Vardhani was asked to assume her mother-in-law's responsibilities.[6]

Vardhani turned to her own brother to help her carry on the struggle to depose Muthu Chella. However, Muthu Chella's allies in the Collectorate, including the Head Sheristadar, prevented reports of his activities from reaching Blackburn.[7]

With the two ranis stalled from effective action, Muthu Chella assumed the status of a royal personage. He allowed himself to be addressed as 'His Highness Maharaja Ragunada Muthu Chella Tevar' and moved into and expanded, at zamindari expense, a building in the palace compound called the Little Palace.[8] He took the king's role in the important arrow-shooting ceremony in the Navaratri festival and sat on the throne, receiving royal honours, during the Navaratri *durbar* assemblies.[9] Widespread acceptance of the Manager's power and status is indicated by his assuming, in the early 1840s, 'superintendence and authority' over the affairs of the great temple of Minakshi-Sundaresvarar in Madurai.[10]

Muthu Chella succeeded in marrying his son, Ramasami, to Mangaleswari, the Ramnad heiress. Her husband would be called Setupati, would take her place in public ritual, and would assume many responsibilities of rule. Concerning his own career, however, the Manager made a fatal mistake.[11]

In 1839 he formed a loose partnership with the British cotton merchant and landholder George F. Fischer, a major purchaser of Ramnad cotton. During an extended visit to the zamindari, Fischer learned that Muthu Chella had attempted for several years to convince the Government to reduce the Ramnad annual peshkash. The Government of Madras forbade the zamindar to collect the *moturpha* tax on tradesmen and artisans. Since the tax was included in the original peshkash demand, the Manager argued that the present demand should be reduced by the tax sum, 7,161 rupees, and that the zamindar should receive 250,644 rupees in back-payments. The Collector had prepared a report favorable to the request in 1832, but no action had yet been taken. Fischer prepared a memorandum on behalf of the Manager, with the understanding that Muthu Chella

---

[6] *The Hindu*, 15 December 1842. 'The Ramnad Zamindary and Mr. Blackburn', pp. 22–8.

[7] *Ibid.*, pp. 25–6.

[8] 'The Report of the Commissioners G.D. Drury and W. A. Moorehead', pp. 81–2 (TNA). Hereafter noted as Drury and Moorehead.

[9] 'Letters sent regarding Ramnad Zamindary while under attachment from the years 1842 to 1846'. Letters quoted were sent by the Collector J. Blackburn to the Secretary of the Board of Revenue. Hereafter noted as 'Letters'. 30 October 1842, p. 15 (TNA). The Persian word for royal assembly, durbar, was widely used in the nineteenth century.

[10] *Ibid.*, Letter number 98, 22 October 1842, p. 11, and 13 September 1843, p. 46.

[11] The following details are taken from 'Letters', 13 September 1843, pp. 41–4, and 12 August 1842, pp. 3–4. Breckenridge, 'Ramnad Zamindari: A Study in Early Nineteenth-Century Administrative History in Madras Presidency', unpublished Master's thesis, University of Wisconsin-Madison, 1971, pp. 36–45, gives a discussion of Fischer.

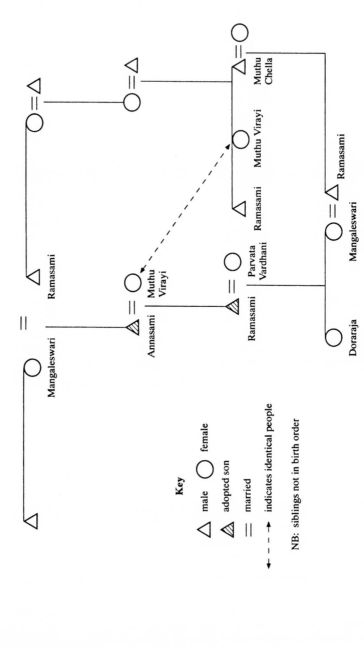

Fig. 2 The relationship of Rani Muthu Virayi to Raja Ramasami Setupati and Muthu Chella Tevar.

would give him one-fifth of whatever was recovered. The Government acted in favour of remission and payment of arrears in 1840. Fischer's memorandum had, however, little, if any, effect on their decision. Muthu Chella refused to pay the merchant his commission, claiming that his own contacts in Madras (where he knew Fischer to have no influence) affected the decision. When Fischer appealed to the courts, he was informed that it was the Executrix, Parvata Vardhani, not Muthu Chella who had the right to alienate zamindari resources in this situation. If Fischer wanted his money, he would have to appeal to her.

Reportedly held in 'thraldom' by her brother-in-law, Vardhani accepted Fischer's complaint. The Briton was one of the very few people with whom she could form an alliance who was capable of getting through the dense mesh of intrigue surrounding Blackburn. The Collector and Fischer had first met nine years earlier, in 1831, and, when Fischer later came to Madurai to purchase cotton, he stayed at Blackburn's house. The latter welcomed Fischer because, as he later wrote, he wanted 'to encourage the competition of a liberal European merchant'. Parvata Vardhani gave the merchant correspondence incriminating her manager as a forger and empowered him to act legally on her behalf. She intended to ruin Muthu Chella and obtain thereby 'the exercise of authority and power to which she was entitled ...'.[12] She and Fischer worked together to convince Blackburn that the zamindari should be taken under the management of the Court of Wards to enable investigation of Muthu Chella's activities. The merchant's own efforts were instrumental in documenting Muthu Chella's activities and, in 1842, when the Manager's end was in sight, Rani Parvata Vardhani granted Fischer a generous one lakh of rupees.

Victory over Muthu Chella and his web of supporters and dependants was not, however, easily obtained. George Fischer, outspoken and critical of Government officials, had many enemies in Madras; and Blackburn's reliance on the merchant and his private establishment for procuring evidence against Muthu Chella prejudiced the Government against the effort.[13] Furthermore, 'the principal men attached to [the Madurai] cutchery were merely so many puppets dancing on the wily wires of the Manager' and 'the manager [had] acquired friends in proportion to point [to him as] the fountain of truth, justice and equity'.[14] The Government, in fact, suspended Blackburn and appointed two commissioners to assume his functions and to compile a report on the bribes, forgeries and embezzlements which were alleged to have taken taken place in the Collectorate itself. After a seven-month inquiry, the Collector was reinstated and his enemies, the Head Sheristadar and Muthu Chella, were brought into criminal court to

[12] *Ibid.*
[13] *The Hindu*, 15 December 1842, p. 27.
[14] *Ibid.*

face charges of bribery.[15] Parvata Vardhani and her own network of brothers and brothers-in-law now gained control of the establishment of Ramnad Zamindari.

The uses of largess

In 1842, the Collector of Madurai described Muthu Chella Tevar as:

a man who could have no pretensions to exclusive or royal privileges except as a Manager of the Zemindary and he has been from time to time assuming higher honours till it ended in his sitting in state at the Dessurah festival [Navaratri] and presuming to shoot the arrow.[16]

The Manager did not earn his honours by becoming a crack zamindari administrator, famed for running an efficient and powerful revenue collecting establishment. Muthu Chella bore down hard neither on defaulting grain contractors nor on ryots. By 1842, he had allowed about three lakhs of uncollected tax balances to accumulate.[17] The main element in Muthu Chella's rise to high status and dominance was his wide liberality. Through bribes and presents the Manager developed the influence needed both to direct zamindari resources and to hide this embezzlement from the Collector. Blackburn ruefully admitted:

I have proof ... that hardly a servant of my office from highest [position] ever accompanied me through the Zamindary without finding provisions, etc., cost free. I have reason to believe all are in some degree implicated in the corruptions so widely and distantly spread by Mootoo Chella Tevar, and I have strong reason to fear one of my best accountants originally engaged in examination of the records was only using his ability with a view to falsify them and deceive me.[18]

Even the Government Vakil in Madurai was implicated. The Manager's 'malversation' of zamindari funds was calculated, by November 1842, to have exceeded twelve lakhs.[19] It is impossible to know how this sum was spent. A good portion would seem to have been used to pay for jewels which Muthu Chella accumulated and which were necessary for a splendid royal presence. Certainly these funds financed 'official secrets' and favoured arrangements from the Collectorate regarding zamindari affairs and the

---

[15] *Ibid.*, 1 January 1843, p. 43.

[16] *Ibid.*, 30 October 1842, pp. 15–16.

[17] 'Letters', 30 July 1844, p. 59. Blackburn writes that the balance under the main revenue categories came to 280,114 rupees for fusli 1252 (1842). During the following years, when the estate was under the Court of Wards, total collections came to between about 450,000 and 500,000 rupees per year. The government demand was 324,404 rupees, until the moturpha remission, when it became 317,243 rupees. Parvata Vardhani wrote that the balances under Muthu Chella were considerably more than three lakhs, saying that the number was six lakhs, *The Hindu*, 15 February 1843, p. 122, a translation of a letter to G. D. Drury, Commissioner in charge of Madura Zilla.

[18] 'Letters', 30 October 1842, p. 19.

[19] *Ibid.*, 18 November 1842, p. 21.

Manager's interests. The Head Sheristadar was convicted on charges of having taken, on one occasion alone, a bribe worth 35,000 rupees.

It would seem that not only substantial bribes, but also a wider 'generosity' earned for Muthu Chella great respect and a reputation for fine character. He contributed, for example, to festival expenses for Collectorate employees and their families and distributed widely cloths, shawls, grain, marriage presents and ready cash.[20] In Tamil society, to accept a present is to express one's subordinate position to the donor. Giving and receiving marks an order of relations. The Commissioners sent to investigate and report on malfeasance in the Collectorate noted this particular significance in Muthu Chella's vast charity:

> [A]mong the customs none is more cherished by the natives of this country than the deference toward men of wealth and rank and in the acceptance of provisions of ordinary consumption. The act is generally considered as a mark of respect towards the Donor, than as an act of bounty bestowed on the Receiver, and the high consideration in which the character of the late Manager of Ramnad Mootoo Chella Tevar was upheld throughout the District, and by the Principal Collector himself, may fairly be received in palliation of the conduct of the native servants – but that they ought not to have kept the Principal Collector in ignorance of the liberality of the Manager admits of question.[21]

An even more stark view of Muthu Chella's largess came from his sister-in-law, Parvata Vardhani: '[H]e has robbed the estate and embezzled its revenues and its riches ... [and] he has given and thrown away money upon numbers of people to aid and support him in his malpractices.'[22]

Usurpation in Ramnad and Sivagangai country

Muthu Chella used largess to establish his personal power and authority in and around Maravar country. One could argue, however, that when he took royal roles in ritual performances in public he was acting on behalf of the (formally secluded) females who had legal title to the zamindari. It appears, though, that the aim of his activites was to appropriate for himself the highest royal status in Ramnad.

As noted earlier, the concept of royalty was inclusive, not exclusive, in Tamil country. One could act like a king and receive royal honours and respect locally; however, one's hold on royal authority and pre-rogatives was vulnerable and had to be maintained with the continuous performance of a range of activities of protection. In the precolonial Tamil country a combination of continually manifested military prowess and persistent activities of largess and religious patronage over several generations was necessary for a line to secure its hold on royal status.

[20] Drury and Moorehead report, pp. 84–5.
[21] *Ibid.*
[22] *The Hindu*, 15 February 1843, p. 121.

In the process of accumulating the honours and titles of royalty a lineage was vulnerable to charges of inappropriateness and usurpation by its rivals. A famous precedent for the usurping actions of Muthu Chella Tevar took place just fifty years earlier in the contiguous kingdom of Sivagangai.

Chinna and Periya Marudu, brothers, came from an Ahambadiya clan in the Sivagangai Kingdom. The Ahambadiyas were warriors closely related to the Maravars in customs, though considered generally to be of a lower status. Like others of the Ahambadiya clans, Chinna and Periya worked as palace servants, in close association with members of the royal house. When the Raja of Sivagangai was killed in battle, and his chief minister died shortly afterwards, the brothers protected the widowed queen and her female heir. In 1780, with the help of a Mysore warlord, they succeeded in gathering and organising local forces.

In this period of great political strife and insecurity, the Marudu brothers became superb military leaders, supported both by their own Ahambadiya clansmen as well as by a number of Maravar chiefs and warriors in the kingdom.[23] Assuming military control, the Marudus became the *de facto* rulers of Sivangangai. To support their rule, they built *chattirams* (pilgrims' rest houses) and temples and they endowed older establishments.[24] They built a palace at Siruvayal and organised festivals. Their statues were placed in Kalaiyarkoil, a temple sacred to Sivagangai kingship, where special anointments took place.[25]

By 1785, Chinna and Periya Marudu had succeeded in acquiring wide popularity in Sivagangai. They could not, however, win the loyalty of all the important Maravar chiefs. The great Maravar chiefs called a durbar where they selected a new Maravar king and showed him royal honours. The chiefs also decided that their choice, the heir to the Padamattur Palaiyam in Sivagangai, a cousin of the king, should marry the royal heiress, Velu Nachiar. The Marudus themselves took part in the durbar and exchanged honours with the designated king, but they had no intention of surrendering their own lordship.[26] Fearful of the claim to kingship which marriage with Velu Nachiar could bring to the Padamattur heir, the brothers organised a marriage between the royal heiress and their own Maravar nominee. A Marudu daughter was also married to this warrior. Thinking that internal turmoil would not subside until a Maravar king was formally installed, the

---

[23] Kadhirvel, *A History of the Maravas*, pp. 177–8.
[24] Endowing such rest houses was a common form of religious protection in Maravar country because of the importance of Rameswaram Temple as a sacred place for pilgrims.
[25] These details are taken from Kadhirvel, *A History of the Maravas*, pp. 177–8; *Śivagaṅgaic Caritirak Kummiyum Ammāṉaiyum*, ed. by T. Chandrasekharan (Madras: Government Press,1954), p. 164; N. Cañcīvi, *Marutiruvar, 1780–1801* (Madras: Pāri Nilaiyam, 1968, third edition), plates between pp. 208 and 209 showing Periya and Chinna Marudu and their wives in sculpture at Kalaiyarkoil.
[26] T. V. Mahalingam, *Mackenzie Manuscripts*, vol. 1, Manuscript No. 56, 'Account of Neduvayal Palayapattu', p. 244.

Marudus had their puppet anointed at Kalaiyarkoil.[27] Their manoeuvres failed, however, when the British, in a strategem to win Maravar support, organised the installation of the Padamattur cousin, proclaiming him the new Raja of Sivangangai with all befitting honours and with splendour at the ancient capital of Cholapuram. Many heads of the villages and chiefs then shifted their support to Padamattur Oyya Tevar (also known as Gauri Vallabha) and the balance of support turned away from the Marudus.[28]

The Marudu brothers had acquired military power and leadership; however, ruling authority, *rāja-dharma,* demanded other activities. As they attempted to fulfil the requirements of the roles they assumed, the Marudus acquired wide support within the kingdom and beyond. Skilful military leaders, they played a major role in the palaiyakkarar wars, fighting against the East India Company, eventually being captured by Company forces and hanged. Approximately eighty years after their death, Chinna and Periya Marudu, still a focus for admiration and interest, were the subject of two long poems, written in folk meter, in Tamil.[29] In the twentieth century, at least one novel, one play, one movie and two histories have been produced concerning the Marudus.[30] Acts of heroism and liberality, forms of royal protection, earned long-lasting reputations for these two. In the short run, however, they lost: their enemies, who did not want to see non-Maravar groups become entrenched, turned to the newly emerging British overlord for aid in ousting the usurpers and their 'pretender'.

In a later and different political context – peacetime under an established imperial government – Muthu Chella's career holds analogies with that of the Marudus. During the existence of a minor ruler, the manager distributed resources of the zamindari domain such that he could reasonably claim, in the eyes of some observers, royal honours and status. He successfully influenced the choice of a mate for the female heir as part of a strategy to secure his authority. Vulnerable to objections to a rule not clearly sanctioned by formal installation, Muthu Chella had to control opposition with outstanding efforts. His lines of support had to be constructed widely, to prevent enemy factions from developing into serious threats. Muthu Chella's claim to high honours continued to be tolerated by the overlord until his enemies could show that his own base of support undermined imperial control. Then, seen as a criminal, he was ruined.

Elements of the Manager's strategy for honour and authority, like that of the Marudus, were shaped by ideas of raja-dharma. Muthu Chella endowed a chattiram and a temple and gained control over the superintendence of the famous Minakshi-Sundaresvarar temple complex in Madurai. His

---

[27] *Ibid.*, Local Tracts (Tamil), Section 9, 'Kaifiyat of Sivangangai Samasthanam', p. 163.
[28] Kadhirvel, *A History of the Maravas*, p. 200. Padamattur Oyya Tevar, as noted in Chapter 2, was also known as Gauri Vallabha.
[29] *Sivagangaic Carittirak Kummiyum Ammanaiyum.*
[30] *Civakankaic Cīmai* is the title of a play (by Kannadhasan), a movie, and a history (by Durgadoss S. K. Sami). Another history, as noted above, is Cancivi's *Marutiruvar.*

activities focused around the wide and generous spread of presents and cash. A 'Karna in giving', Muthu Chella turned to the vallal constituent of dharmic action left to Ramnad kings and would-be kings.

Muthu Virayi secures honours and a domain: Pederanendal

Muthu Virayi's attempt to oust her manager, as we saw above, resulted in the loss of her position as Guardian and Executrix to Parvata Vardhani. The older Rani had been powerful in zamindari affairs during the titleships of her husband and her adopted son/brother. A desire to establish independent ruling authority, as Executrix, is indicated by her founding a chattiram in 1833. To this she assigned the income from two villages. Throughout the period of Muthu Chella's ascendancy, she continued to supervise the affairs of the chattiram.[31] Muthu Chella's ambition, while conflicting with her own, had by no means destroyed it; and his fall provided Muthu Virayi with new competitors in the form of Parvata Vardhani and her kin-linked faction. A suit filed in 1843 for the title to the zamindari marked the beginning of a twenty-year struggle for legal control. The struggle was carried on first by Muthu Virayi and, then, by her legal heir, Sivasami Tevar. Chapter 2 discussed aspects of this conflict. Other points illustrate further the nature of goals in zamindari politics.

The defendants in Muthu Virayi's suit were listed as Parvata Vardhani, her daughter Doraraja, Doraraja's husband, and the Collector of Madurai. As Ramnad was still under the Court of Wards for the investigation of Muttu Chella's managership, the Collector had legal responsibility for the conduct of the case. Parvata Vardhani and her son-in-law, Muthu Vijia, however, wanted control of the litigation, arguing that the Collector, as Agent of the Court of Wards, would not pursue victory with the necessary skill, interest or zeal.[32] The Court of Wards would not, however, grant permission for her proceeding in the defence, saying that she ceased being the minor's guardian during the sequestration. Nevertheless, the Rani borrowed funds and went ahead to file a defence. The conflict was not left in the hands of her lawyers, however. Muthu Vijia assisted his mother-in-law in the conduct of the suit, agitating for funds from the Court of Wards and studying the relevant law.[33] At one point, the Collector sent fifteen copies of a Tamil translation of the Madras Regulations to the palace, along with translations of the Circular Orders of the Sadr and Faujdari Adalut.[34] Political leadership in the zamindari involved a capacity to control the activities surrounding the continuous litigation involving zamindari kin.

[31] 'Letters', Letter number 49, 4 March 1845, p. 82.
[32] *The Hindu*, 15 February 1843, p. 121.
[33] 'Letters', 4 March 1845, p. 81.
[34] *Ibid.*, Letter number 106, 3 May 1845, p. 88.

The first phase of the struggle between the two widows and their dependants ended with an agreement out of court in 1847. Muthu Virayi did not become Zamindarni of Ramnad; however, a domain within Ramnad was created for her. She was given the division of Pederanendal, comprising twenty-three villages. For the expenses of her palace establishment, Muthu Virayi received six of Parvata's privately held shares in a particular village. She was also given villages and land to help in 'continuing the charity of distributing food, &c, conducted by her in the choultry [chattiram] in Ramnad'.[35]

Within Pederanendal Muthu Virayi and her heir received the responsibilities of the zamindar. They maintained a revenue-collecting establishment, gave orders to village officers, granted *paṭṭās* (titles) to ryots, sold grain collected by their officers and, theoretically, paid tribute to the Setupati. The responsibility for irrigation repairs was theirs and they had authority to mediate disputes in the division.[36] The Pederanendal tribute was called peshkash. As a district Judge of Madurai later noted:

The use of the word peshkist implies that she is herself a Zemindar, independent in every way except that the older Zemindar chooses still to be the channel by which her payments pass to Government. Her position is far superior to that of a mere farmer or lessee.[37]

The compromise reached by Muthu Virayi gave her both a political domain and ruling honours. It stipulated her durbar order vis-à-vis her rival, Parvata Vardhani. The agreement between the two Ranis read:

The honours done by the Temple authorities and all other people on the days when Dasra and other festivals [are] celebrated in the palace of the zemindari aforesaid, should be done to plaintiff also equally.[38]

Muthu Virayi received payments of about 337,500 rupees. Her concern for cash was embedded in political aims, focusing around the recognition and maintenance of ruling authority. Protection of that authority became one of the continuing issues of conflict between the new Zemindarni of Pederanendal and her immediate overlord.

The 1847 agreement did not stipulate that the new zamindar would pay the *makamai* fees. These fees were little in monetary value, but had powerful symbolic value to the ruler of Ramnad. They were meant to pay for: (l) the maintenance of the palace temple of the Setupati family's tutelary goddess, Rajarajeswari; (2) the support of Brahmins who recited sacred verses for the continuation of the prosperity of the Setupati and of Ramnad samastanam; and (3) the maintenance of temples not directly under zamindari temple

[35] High Court of Madras. Documents and depositions in Appeal No. 22 of 1879, Exhibit A. pp. 1-3.
[36] *Ibid.*, pp. 33 and 71–72.
[37] *Ibid.*, p. 17.
[38] *Ibid.*, p. 2.

administration.[39] In 1850 and 1854 Parvata Vardhani attempted to have the charges declared legally part of the Pederanendal assessment. The Court refused her, saying that the charges formed 'no part of the recognized land revenue'.[40] In 1858 Vardhani included makamai fees in a suit for payment of arrears of revenue from Pederanendal and, two years later, non-payment of the fees was still a legal issue. The size of the sum was not the point of conflict. Parvata Vardhani spent, in pursuing this issue, more than she could hope or expect to receive. Payment of the fees symbolised the inclusion of the division zamindari in the Ramnad royal domain. Non-payment showed contempt for Parvata Vardhani's authority, a form of insult and dishonour.

On palace factions: introducing Ponnusami Tevar

Parvata Vardhani's victory over Muthu Chella Tevar and her success in stopping Muthu Virayi's claim was accompanied by the rise of new factions to importance in palace politics. These were organised around the Rani, her brothers and her brothers-in-law. Vardhani depended entirely upon close relatives in her choice of managers. Kottasami, her first Manager, held an unremarkable tenure. About him the Collector of Madurai intoned the common litany of complaint regarding zamindari administration: he 'lets villages on low leases, sells appointments, and neglects tank repairs'; many zamindari resources were 'expended in Law Charges & in remuneration and presents to Native Agents'.[41] Kottasami did not try to become independent of Parvata Vardhani and, perhaps with the memory of Muthu Chella's maneouvring, the Rani did not marry her daughter Doraraja to one of Kottasami's sons. The heiress married instead the brother of Kadambava, Vardhani's sister's husband.

When Doraraja contracted a fatal illness in 1845, Kadambava and his brother hastily organised an adoption by Doraraja of one of Kadambava's four sons, Annasami. The adoption, a scheme to gain control of the estate administration, was carried out without Parvata Vardhani's assent. The Government of Madras declared the will invalid, for technical reasons, and Vardhani turned to another sister's son for her own adoption of a male heir, Muthu Ramalingam (see *Figure 3*).[42]

Eventually, Kottasami either died or was dismissed and the father of Vardhani's heir, Sivagnana, became Manager in 1856. The following year

---

[39] T. Raja Ram Row, *Ramnad Manual* (title page missing), pp. 120–22. The makamai funds were established in the 1780s by Pradani Muthirulappa Pillai, *diwan* (chief revenue official) of Ramnad Kingdom.

[40] Documents and depositions in Appeal No. 22 of 1879, p. 63.

[41] Miscellaneous Correspondence for Madura District, 1851, to the Secretary of the Board of Revenue from R. D. Parker, Collector of Madura, 11 March 1851, pp. 377–8 (TNA).

[42] High Court of Madras. Documents, evidence and District Judge's notes in Regular Appeal No. 35 of 1873. The adoption of Annasami is the main point of the questioning of witnesses on pages 23–40. Details of kin relations for *Figures 2* and *3* come from this evidence.

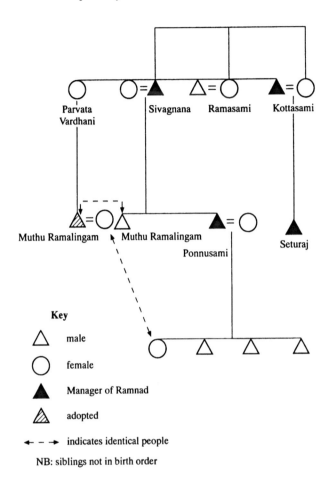

Key

△ male

○ female

▲ Manager of Ramnad

▨ adopted

◄ - - ► indicates identical people

NB: siblings not in birth order

Fig. 3 The relationship of Raja Muthu Ramalingam Setupati and Ponnusami
Tevar to Rani Parvata Vardhani.

Vardhani selected Sivagnana's other son, Ponnusami, to become Manager.
For several years she had favoured Ponnusami, who was ambitious and
talented compared to his less serious and passive brother, her adopted son,
Muthu Ramalingam. She would have adopted Ponnusami, had not the law
of adoption prevented adoption of an eldest son.[43] During the ensuing
decade, Parvata Vardhani exhibited contempt for Muthu Ramalingam,
who had 'an almost childish dread of anything to do with accounts' and
was 'more inclined to spend his time in hunting and music than office

[43] High Court of Madras. Regular Appeal No. 42 of 1874, p. 11.

work'.[44] When Muthu Ramalingam came of age in 1860, he was forced to bring a suit against his adoptive mother for the title of the zamindari. Even after she agreed to give it up, Parvata Vardhani continued until 1867 to call herself Zamindarni and to refer to Muthu Ramalingam in documents as her 'adopted son'.[45] As Ponnusami developed into a manager of power and authority on the scale of Muthu Chella, she did not try to stop him and was even known to side with him against the zamindar. Vardhani, in fact, had inaugurated Ponnusami's career as Manager by simultaneously making him a division zamindar, granting him Palayampatti, with eleven villages of the best land in Ramnad. She made this grant in response to a petition from Ponnusami, which, paraphrased below, shows the man's early ambition:

[Court Document letter I] recites a petition by Ponnusami for this sub-division of Palayampatti to enable him to keep up a respectable position, and then goes on to make the grant on the grounds of his close relationship, that he and his ancestors [his father was manager before him] had rendered faithful services to the zamindary, and that it was therefore incumbent on the Zemindar to maintain him in respectability.[46]

Dominance in Ramnad: Ponnusami Tevar, 1858–1868

Indications of Ponnusami's preoccupation with royal status are found in his successful acquisition of two divisional zamindaries and his interest in a third for his son. He built a grand palace in Ramnad town. He assumed the managership of temple administration in the zamindari. However, there are no accounts of the Manager taking the king's role in durbars or festivals in Ramnad. Perhaps because Parvata Vardhani became a jealous guardian of her own royal prerogatives and perhaps because Muthu Ramalingam was no longer a minor, but capable of taking part in ritual occasions, Ponnusami was forced to go outside the arena of ritual to show his grandeur: he became one of the most important patrons of music, poetry and Tamil scholarship in nineteenth-century Madras Presidency. Ponnusami played an important role in financing the editing and publishing of Tamil literary works, which carried reference to his support on the title page. Among the recipients of his largess were the well-known scholars Minakshisundaram Pillai and Arumuga Navalar;[47] (the latter received the royal honour of a

---

[44] Proceedings of the Board of Revenue (BP). June 1874, No. 1565, letter from W. McQuhae, Collector of Madura, to J. Grose, Secretary to the Court of Wards, dated 23 May 1874, enclosure no. 3, 10 February 1874, from J. Lee-Warner, p. 4408 (TNA); and Regular Appeal No. 42 of 1874, p. 17.

[45] Regular Appeal No. 42 of 1874, p. 11.

[46] *Ibid.*, p. 12.

[47] Subramania Aiyar, *Tamil Studies: Second Series* (Tirunelveli: Copies available from S. R. Subramania Pillai, 1970), p. 117. I am indebted to K. Kailasapathy for information on Ponnusami's wide sponsorship of scholarship.

Plate 3   Ponnusami Tevar's palace in Ramnad town

golden shawl from a math on the estate). Print thus carried the message of his vallanmai – the implications of this novel form of patronage will be discussed in a later chapter. Here the content of some of the poetry is an issue.

Patronage of music and verse was long an important element in Tamil kingship, going back to the Sangam period. Reports of seventeenth- and eighteenth-century kings and palaiyakkarars have many references to such patronage. In his lavish patronage of music, scholarship and poetry, the Manager seemed to focus on himself as Ponnusami vallal.

In a poem written contemporaneously about Ponnusami Tevar, a Tamil scholar and poet describes the Manager continuously as King, with a number of different Tamil synonyms, *mannar, nirupan, pūpālan,* and so on. The poet describes Ponnusami as the protector of Ramnad, a hero, as one who has the capacity to fight his enemies, as Setupati mannar (king), and, in particular, as a vallal.[48] This poem, one of many which the poet wrote about Ponnusami, reflected the Manager's prodigious patronage.[49] A. V. Subramania Aiyar has commented:

[48] *Tanippātal tirattu uraik kurippukkalutan* (Tirunelvēli: Tirunelvēli Tennintiya Saivasittānta Nūrpatippak Kalakam, 1964), vol. 2, pp. 137–45, by Cantiracekara Kaviraca Pantitar. I am grateful for the assistance of Kausalya Hart in translating this poem.

[49] *Kalaikkalañcayam,* vol. 4, p. 426. (This is a Tamil encyclopedia.)

Ponnusami Thevar was not only a great scholar and musician himself but enjoyed helping other Tamil poets, writers and musicians. During his ministership Ramnad was the centre of Tamil learning and culture in the Poligar world.[50]

Ponnusami paid to be praised in precolonial terms as vallal and as King, but his dominance (while it lasted), was like that of Muthu Chella, deeply anchored in colonial institutions and new tools of dominance.

Like his predecessors, Ponnusami did not develop a zamindari establishment capable of the efficient extraction of revenue. On the contrary, by the end of his tenure, zamindari ryots were about 973,500 rupees in arrears.[51] During his managership, royal control in areas of the zamindari was weakened by an acceleration in the process of the leasing of zamindari villages. This process had been in existence at least from the time of Muthu Chella. Under Ponnusami, however, more leases (called *cowles* or *kauls*), at more favourable rates to the *kauldar*, were given.[52] In 1870, two years after Ponnusami's dismissal, 322 villages (under 266 kauls) were under lease, compared to 899 unleased villages under direct zamindari revenue control.[53] The permanent kauls, land alienated permanently from zamindari control, numbered seventy-nine: twenty-nine were held by royal family members, seven were given for purposes of charity, one for irrigation repair service and forty-two for Chettiar bankers in connection with loans.[54] The gross profit for the kauldars from their leases ranged from 25 per cent to over 659 per cent.[55] Most of the high profit kauls had been given away by Estate Managers and, among the Managers, Ponnusami had given away the highest number.

Kauls were given mainly to relatives, to zamindari servants and officials and to Chettiar bankers. The person who received a kaul took over the functions of a zamindar with regard to his village.[56] Notice was sent from the samastanam office that village officers were now to obey his orders. The kauldar gave pattas and was responsible for the collection and sale of revenue grain and for the maintenance of irrigation works. A ceremony called *tōraṇam* expressed the authority and control assumed by the kauldar. A village caller would beat drums and announce that the village had a new master who had come for the toranam. Garlands of palm leaves, toranam – sometimes referred to as 'victory arches' – would be laid across village roads. These marked off, symbolically, the boundaries of the new master's

[50] A. V. Subramania Aiyar, *Tamil Studies* (Tirunelveli: Copies available from S.R. Subramania Pillai, 1969), p. 83.

[51] BP, no. 587, 17 November 1870, memo for orders on nos. 1230 and 1716 (TNA).

[52] BP, no. 389, 21 February 1874, enclosure no. 1, from J. A. Boyle, Acting Special Assistant Collector, Ramnad, to H. W. Bliss, Acting Collector of Madura, 26 October 1873, p. 868 (TNA).

[53] *Ibid.*, p. 870.

[54] *Ibid.*, p. 873.

[55] *Ibid.*, pp. 870–1.

[56] Details of the transfer of authority are taken from Documents, Evidence and District Judge's notes in Regular Appeal No. 35 of 1873, pp. 78–89.

authority with reference to a time when a village was taken by the victor in battle. The kauldar would then go to the main temple in the village where he would be shown honour through transactions of betel with prominent village ryots. Worship would be performed at the temple. The kauldar offered *pongal* (rice cooked with green-gram dhal) both to the main village god and to minor deities. The continuing authority of the zamindar, the inclusion of the kaul villages in the zamindari domain, was symbolised by the *uluppai* (offerings of food) which the kauldar, according to terms of the lease, was to send to the palace for special festival durbars.[57] On the village level, however, the kaul compromised the control of the zamindar and his official representatives.

By 1865 Parvata Vardhani and Muthu Ramalingam had lost all power to challenge Ponnusami's alienation of villages.[58] Ponnusami had taken away from them complete control of the process of creating new domains; such control lent validation for his own claims to royal status. Another aspect of his dominance in Ramnad was an outgrowth of this power of alienation – namely, control of major litigation.

In 1863 Muthu Ramalingam gave Ponnusami the division zamindari of Pandulkudy; and in 1865 he and Parvata Vardhani signed over all the powers of zamindari administration, retaining for themselves only the prerogative of signing bonds for the payment of zamindari debts with estate resources. Both documents gave as the reasons for such action the desire to recognise both Ponnusami's management of the zamindari and his conduct of zamindari litigation.[59] Ponnusami's leadership in the enormously expensive and complicated process of protecting Vardhani and Muthu Ramalingam's claims to the title of the zamindari had resulted in the acquisition of another small zamindari domain and in enhanced powers over the vastly larger one in which he was employed.

One of the suits of litigation at this time was the Ramnad Adoption Suit, discussed in the previous chapter. If the courts accepted that Parvata Vardhani lacked a legal heir, Ramnad Zamindari would have to be escheated to the Government of Madras upon the Rani's death. The domain would be dismantled and the territory would come directly under the Collectorate administration under a ryotwari settlement. The other important suit at this time was that of Kunjara and her daughter. Plaints for both suits were filed in 1860 and Parvata Vardhani's right to adopt was finally confirmed in the Judicial Committee of the Privy Council in 1868.[60] The announcement that the samastanam had been saved was met with great celebration in Ramnad. Muthu Ramalingam,

[57] See High Court of Madras. Appeal No. 57 of 1894, Documents and depositions, pp. 5–6 and 10.

[58] High Court of Madras. Documents in Regular Appeal No. 80 of 1876, no. 37, p. 59.

[59] Regular Appeal No. 42 of 1874, p. 12, and Documents in Regular Appeal No. 80 of 1876, p. 59.

[60] Moore, *Reports and Cases*, vol. XII, 1867–1869, pp. 397–447.

now secure in his title, organised entertainments, including music and dancing girls, and the distribution of sugar and betel to all who attended.[61]

The conduct of a major court case thus assumed considerable local significance. It involved organising and funding a variety of activities, including acquiring legal knowledge and the knowledge of Anglo-Indian court procedures, calling for legal assistance, hiring and consulting with great figures of the Madras and District Bar, and securing the support of witnesses, both truthful and dishonest. Associated activities included travelling back and forth between Ramnad, Madurai and Madras, talking with lawyers and government officials and picking up court gossip. One had not only the usual palace and zamindari dependants and supporters to please and to keep away from enemy influence, but the obligation to develop a wider group of dependants who, presumably, performed services more directly connected with the process of getting the litigation through the courts to a successful conclusion. This process, with attendant large expenditures, attracted dependants, minor lawyers or other people claiming influence in the law courts, access to special information or the capacity to perform some legal service. The services were often of dubious usefulness, certainly not worth the remuneration which these barflies received.[62] The development of a group of litigation dependants, appearing busy in the pursuit of one's cause in court, in the district capital, in Madras, or, even, in England, was an integral aspect of the conflict, a part of the political spectacle of litigation.

All of the activities of zamindari litigation demanded cash, in large, accumulating amounts. There were costs for stamp paper fees, for documents, translation fees, copying charges, support of witnesses during court attendance, processing charges, petitions, other fees of petitioning, not to mention the requirements of the dependants mentioned above.[63] Even for district level pleadings, major lawyers from Madras were hired and travelled to the district town for consultation before the court appearances and

[61] Documents, Evidence and District Judge's Notes in Regular Appeal No. 35 of 1873, p. 55.
[62] There are occasional references in court judgements to the existence of zamindari hangers-on who, in the opinion of the judges, took advantage of zamindars' gullibility, claiming influence in the courts and with government officials and receiving money for bribes never given; for example, the High Court of Madras. Select documents in Appeal No. 215 of 1895, from the judgement of Justice C. Sury in Original Suit No. 38 of 1888 in the Sub-Court of Cocanada, p. 87. The comment of W. McQuhae speaks directly to this: a 'Court Vakeel' had filed a plaint against the Agent for the Court of Wards for 1,000 rupees as a fee for professional assistance in a Ramnad suit. McQuhae wrote, 'It is usual in such suits for Zamindars to give Vakalats [making the receiver one's legal agent] to Pleaders for real or imaginary services rendered out of Court, and I do not know what this particular Pleader did ... We cannot pay the regulation fee to any one who obtained a Vakalat in consequence of the hopes or fears of the late Zamindar, and whose services, if any, were rendered out of Court.' BP, no. 65, 16 January 1874, W. McQuhae, Collector of Madura, to J. Grose, Secretary to the Court of Wards, 27 December 1873, no. 144, p. 124 (TNA).
[63] Selected documents of Appeal No. 215 of 1895, p. 145.

during court proceedings.[64] In a report discussing debts accumulated during Ponnusami's managership, both the Advocate General of Madras and the Government Solicitor agreed that 10,000 rupees was the usual fee which a major figure of the Madras bar received for taking part in an important case.[65] The enormous wealth of the great lawyers of nineteenth-century Madras, gained in good part from participation in zamindari cases, suggests that large sums indeed resulted from their association with this litigation.[66] One of Ponnusami's district lawyers received 10,000 rupees in the year 1866 alone and a Madras lawyer who also acted as a banker for Ponnusami received 150,000 rupees over the course of the Adoption litigation.[67] Ponnusami himself received 10,000 rupees for a trip to Madras in connection with the suit.[68] An agent was sent to England, at a cost of 42,000 rupees.[69]

The need for such large sums of cash created a dependence on the powerful Nattukkottai Chettiar banking families who lived in the Sivagangai and Ramnad estates and who had served as creditors to the royal families since the Permanent Settlement. A major responsibility for Ponnusami, then, was to negotiate loans for litigation expenses. The complexities of negotiation are suggested in his borrowing 10,000 rupees to pay a third party for help in securing one loan.[70] The Chettiars were aware that, usually, zamindars could not be depended upon to pay back the principal; however, a powerful incentive for loaning was the possibility of receiving a kaul, even if only at some time after the initial loans were made.

It is difficult to determine the cost of zamindari litigation during Ponnusami's managership. Part of the difficulty stems from deciding what can be defined as a cost. If one thinks of major litigation as having meaning and significance beyond the legally phrased concerns of the several parties named in the plaints, then 'litigation expense' covers a broad spectrum of related activities. By 1868, Ponnusami Tevar had involved Ramnad in debt for at least 14.5 lakhs. A sum of 4 lakhs, attributed to litigation expenses,

---

[64] BP, no. 587, 17 November 1870, 'Opinion', by John Bruce Norton, Advocate General, and I. W. Handley, Government Pleader, 16 November 1870 (TNA). Hereafter, 'Opinion'.

[65] *Ibid.*

[66] K. Chandrasekharan, son of the leader of the Madras bar, V. Krishnaswami Aiyer (1863–1911), and a lawyer and a scholar, said in an interview that zamindari cases provided a major source of income for the great lawyers. His father's older associate, V. Bhashyam Iyengar (1844–1908), was the first Indian lawyer in Madras to get a significant portion of zamindari litigation. For many years the cases were argued by British barristers such as John Bruce Norton and John D. Hayne. Interview in Madras, 28 May 1974.

[67] High Court of Madras. Regular Appeal No. 43 of 1874 and Regular Appeal No. 46 of 1874, pp. 15–16. The Madras lawyer was V. Sadagopacharlu, who with his brother, V. Rajagapalacharlu, was one of the first Indians to become prominent and wealthy at the Madras bar. See V. C. Gopalratnam, *A Century Completed (A History of the Madras High Court): 1862–1962* (Madras: Madras Law Journal Office, n.d.), pp. 263–5. Both were associated with Ramnad litigation.

[68] Regular Appeal No. 43 of 1874 and Regular Appeal No. 46 of 1874, pp. 15–16.

[69] 'Opinion' (TNA).

[70] *Ibid.*

was paid off to one Chettiar with interest and with presents in appreciation of the aid.[71] Of the remaining 10.5 lakhs, the Advocate General and Government Solicitor decided that about 290,000 rupees out of 575,000 rupees claimed for litigation expenses could be considered legally chargeable against the the inheritance of the zamindari[72] (the heir of a zamindar could not be forced to pay out on debts run up by his or her predecessors against the interests of the family or zamindari estate, as defined by the courts). Another government official, commenting on this decision, found the definition of the costs of litigation to be too narrow. He argued that almost all of the remaining debt of 10.5 lakhs, including that marked as having gone for payment of peshkash, should be attributable as litigation expenses. The insecurity of the position of Parvata Vardhani and Muthu Ramalingam during the period, the continual need for cash to meet 'extraordinary expenses', and the concentration of attention on the suits – drawing away from matters of revenue management – were all functions, he believed, of an extended and difficult litigation.[73] The President of the Board of Revenue seemed to share something of this view when he wrote that 'the greater part of the resources of the zamindary' had been devoted to legal conflicts.[74]

When Parvata Vardhani and Muthu Ramalingam cited Ponnusami's managership and his responsibilities with regard to their suits as reasons for giving him new lands and for making over to him their powers, they were recognising the two main sources of his dominance. From these two positions, the Manager had directed the movement of land and fortunes of cash. He had used his control (or the promise of control) over villages as a base for the lavish organisation of people in Ramnad, Madurai, Madras and England for extended conflict. The activities of the legal struggles against Kunjara and her supporters and, most threateningly, against the Government of Madras had provided a structure for leadership, recognition and patronage both within and far beyond the territory of Ramnad.

Ponnusami did not establish his dominance without arousing the development of opposing factions. One local Judge articulated a common, negative assessment of the man in saying: '[T]his mere name in this District at once suggests daring intrigue and unscrupulous litigation.'[75] That he was not unique in his active use of the courts is suggested by a local authority on the history of litigation in the Madurai area, who noted that the majority of the local contestants 'had a penchant for mutual ruination

---

[71] *The Law Reports: Madras Series* (London, 1879), vol. VI, 1878–1879. p. 172.
[72] 'Opinion' (TNA).
[73] BP, no. 587, 17 November 1870, memo for orders on no. 3580 (TNA).
[74] Revenue Department, no. 1762, 1871, A minute by His Excellency the President of the Board of Revenue, 4 May 1871, to the Secretary to the Government of India, Home Department (TNA).
[75] High Court of Madras. Plaintiff's and defendant's documents and depositions of defendant's witnesses in Appeal No. 22 of 1879, p. 61.

by revengeful attacks on [the] persons of their opponents or their properties before the advent of the British, [and] now began to do the same by subtler means in civil and criminal forums.'[76]

In 1866 serious resistance to Ponnusami's dominance emerged.[77] Muthu Ramalingam gained the strategic support of a near kinsman, Seturaj, when he gave him two villages. Seturaj became closely tied to the interests of the Zamindar and persons who had been important allies of Ponnusami began, discreetly, to draw away from him. The Manager attempted to stop the threat by the distribution of heavy largess to dependants and by cutting off supplies to the palace. He threatened to stop his conduct of the Adoption Suit and he settled accounts with the Chettiar bankers. This he did to prevent them from making separate arrangements for payment from Muthu Ramalingam, becoming supporters of the cause of the Zamindar. Cut off from access to cash or grain, the Zamindar began to borrow from Parvata Vardhani. Ponnusami then took further precautions and ordered all the local revenue collections to be remitted directly to Madurai. He screened all applications for audience with Muthu Ramalingam and let it be known that any samastanam officials found speaking against him in the palace would be severely punished. Over the next eighteen months, Ponnusami forced his brother into a series of humiliating agreements, making him sign away rights to revenues in villages and giving kauls to Chettiars with low rates unfavourable to zamindari interests. During the struggle, Parvata Vardhani wavered back and forth in her loyalties, finally siding with the Manager. In the end, however, Muthu Ramalingam had the upper hand: as soon as he received word of the success of his suit in the Privy Council, he wrote the orders for the dismissal of Ponnusami. Seturaj became the new manager.

Thus Ponnusami Tevar's greatest achievement contained the instrument of his destruction. As the Privy Council confirmed Muthu Ramalingam's title and as the extended litigation came to an end, the Zamindar's dependence on his ambitious manager ceased. An agent for the Court of Wards in Ramnad wrote concerning Ponnusami's career:

This short sketch is broken off at the point when Ponnusamy had reached his highest ascendancy in Ramnad. The process had occupied him rather less than ten years; but the results were gigantic. While his younger brother was reduced to beggary, his own star had been proceeding from the misty horizon, at first slow and measured advances; but when it had fairly mounted, by borrowing light and lustre freely all around, it rapidly culminated in splendour in 1868. But accomplishment of so great a plan had cost him all his strength. To such a climax as this necessarily there succeeds the anticlimax, and let the lawyers shift the scenes for us, the curtain may

---

[76] R. Ganapathyraman, 'The Birth and Growth of Rule of Law in Madurai', in *Madura Bar Association: Souvenir, Centenary Celebrations: 1872–1972* (Madurai: no publisher, n.d.), no pagination.

[77] BP for the month of December, 1874, vol. 42, Madras. Proceedings of 2 December 1874, no. 3,490, enclosure no. l, J. Lee Warner, Provisional Assistant Collector, Ramnad, to W. McQuhae, Collector of Madura, 14 November 1874, no. 228, pp. 9266–8 (TNA).

yet arise upon justice limping, with sure steps, after the usurper, overtaking him in his borrowed plumes, and hurling him down from his false position.[78]

Cash in the construction of new domains

According to the former tutor of Raja Dorasingam Tevar of Sivagangai, J. Rengasamy Iyer, a zamindar was best known as 'a man who gives things to others'.[79] To illustrate his point, he told of a twentieth-century Sivagangai zamindar who decided to enter an election. His men told voters in the zamindari, 'He and his family have always given to you. Now you can give him your vote.' Examining the careers of two men who attempted to acquire royal authority in Ramnad, we find Rengasamy Iyer's simple formulation to be apt. Control over movement of land-holding and of cash, not the acquisition or hoarding of these, appears to have been their significant aim. Raja-dharma was still protection; however, elements of this protection received new emphasis and meaning in the nineteenth century.

Vallanmai had been a strong element in the definition of royal protection since Sangam times. Now it gained in significance as other strategies for royal status were cut off. In the process of their redistribution, aspirants to royal status created new domains of royal control and influence. Ponnusami constructed one of legal resources, human and material, and Muthu Chella put together a network of control within the Madurai Collectorate. Predominance over the heterogeneous groupings of major and minor domains within Ramnad zamindari required, in the new context of nineteenth-century empire, bureaucratic forays and leadership over a litigation army.

Nicholas Dirks has argued that zamindari redistribution of land under the Permanent Settlement was not the same phenomenon as the gifting or affirmation of landed domains in precolonial realms in Tamil country. He finds that precolonial royal gifting imparted sovereignty because it sustained 'relations of service, loyalty and honour' and that nineteenth-century gifting departed from this ethic because it involved 'pay[ing] off political debts'.[80] The language of the law, because it did not contain the precolonial allusions to 'honor, protection, loyalty, kinship, service, property, and privilege ... [with] specific relational and operational meanings' deprived nineteenth century redistributions of establishing sovereignty.[81] Legal agreements in the nineteenth century which were available to us here did, however, refer to honorific privileges and to services which had been rendered. Ramnad royal kin draped their redistributional activities in the new legal context with the ideological trappings of Tamil monarchical cosmology. In order to

[78] *Ibid.*, p. 9268.
[79] Interview in Sivagangai, ll May 1975.
[80] Dirks, 'From Little King to Landlord', p. 331.
[81] *Ibid.*, p. 332.

comment on the nature of the change which took place, however, we need to examine not just land, but movable gifts such as cash, cloth, jewels, and so on.

The gifting of precolonial kings had been strategic, with a wide range of possible motives.[82] The gifting which took place in ritual performances in public lent the relationship between transactors formal qualities, outlining the political structures of lordly domains. A good part of the zamindari redistribution which we have examined here had a very different nature. Zamindari lords gave movable gifts which maintained, for the most part, *informal* networks of influence. Transactions between Muthu Chella and the employees of the Madurai Collectorate outlined relationships which could not survive public disclosure. The lordship which was represented by Muthu Chella's becoming Manager of the great Minakshi-Sundareswarar Temple in Madurai was over a domain network which was mostly hidden from the view of the overlord. The redistribution in which Ponnusami engaged as he set in motion the many actions surrounding the Ramnad Adoption Case created a similarly ephemeral realm, one which he attempted to substantiate through the patronage of poetry and scholarship.

In considering the altered meaning of royal largess in mid nineteenth-century Ramnad we look to the nature of the relationship between a zamindari samastanam and the colonial regime. The work of Wink and Kolff on inter-domainal relations suggests that locality lords in the late precolonial period used gifts to gain influence outside the immediate areas of their control.[83] The direction of the flow of such gifts was, like the borders of the domains themselves, continually shifting, but givers could, to a certain extent, decide in which direction they wanted to move politically. In the institutional context of the Permanent Settlement, the relationship between the establishment of a zamindari lord (with or without legal title) and the organs of the empire was stable and the outline of formal duties and responsibilities clearer. Possibilities for interference from the overlord were vastly enhanced. To protect his developing authority and growing control in Ramnad, Muthu Chella had little choice in the direction of the flow of his largess. The Madura Collectorate was the source of imperial interference in the locality, an interference which, from the perspective of indigenous monarchical culture, would be best dealt with through the construction of a domain of influence hidden inside the imperial bureaucracy. The official nature of gifts of land threatened exposure of the political engagement; security

---

[82] André Wink, in *Land and Sovereignty in India*, p. 249, takes the position that the language of dharma and service was just a screen for the rivalrous activities of fitna. I do not think one needs to divest raja-dharma of moral integrity in order to appreciate the tensions in monarchical polities, but Wink's argumentation and evidence provide a provocative view of the order in the seeming disorder of Maratha political relations.

[83] Wink, *Land and Sovereignty*, and Dirk Kolff, 'The End of an *Ancien Régime*'.

required movable, secret gifts. Cash acquired special importance as a political tool in the politics of liberality.[84]

Ponnusami Tevar directed a good part of his political focus towards imperial involvement in the management of disputes, including the Collector's dispute with the Ramnad royal house. Much of his redistributional activity was concerned with getting control of disputing processes; here, again, cash was of paramount importance. The Manager leased out rich villages on terms disadvantageous to the financial position of the zamindari in order to gain access to cash in creating a shadow realm – 'pockets of influence' – inside and around litigation processes.

Because of the nature of overlord rule in the nineteenth century and because of the desire of zamindari lords to resist and/or influence aspects of this rule, largess in the form of movable gifts assumed increasing importance. The political focus turned increasingly outwards, towards the institutions of the overlord. The descendants of battlefield warriors became more interested in manipulating the terms of land-holding as a source of cash than in acquiring new holdings. Physical defence of land or the seizing of new land could no longer mobilise men for political action under the constraints of imperial rule. A would-be little king now set defensive and offensive actions in motion mainly through the strategic use of movable gifts. In so doing he created openings for new types of land-holders to enter into zamindari politics. The Nattukkottai Chettis eventually acquired so much land and influence in Ramnad district that, at the end of the century, one of their families established a new kind of rulership in the area, that of an austere merchant line.

Nattukkottai Chettiar bankers in Ramnad and Sivagangai

From the beginning of the nineteenth century to the mid-point, Nagarathar interest in Ramnad and Sivagangai affairs centred mainly on moneylending and grain marketing. Several merchant families consistently made loans to help the zamindars meet their financial obligations. Nagarathar willingness to forward loans for peshkash payments stood between the continued existence of zamindar local domination and imperial sequestration. Merchant money financed a raja's or rani's attempts to retain the title to the zamindari or, conversely, permitted a contender from another faction of kin to claim it. Important for the attempted reproduction of royal status were loans which permitted largess. As the writers of an early twentieth-century encyclopaedia noted:

[84] That 'fluid', 'liquid' resources entered royal polity importantly in the Nayaka period is shown in Narayana Rao, Shulman and Subramanyam, *Symbols of Substance*, pp. 80 and 118. Cash becomes signficant in new ways in political development under the Permanent Settlement.

Arunachellam Chettiar ... played a most conspicuous part in contributing to the prosperity and fame of the [Ramnad royal] family, and furnished the groundwork for the princely benefactions, characteristic of this reputed house.[85]

Before 1800, the maintenance of Maravar warrior clan organisation was a major element in the protection of royal claims. After the Permanent Settlement, the capacity to take part in the local spectacle of litigation politics depended on cultivating Nagarathar support. The relationship of certain merchant families to zamindari administration and the affairs of royal kin was close, complex and, sometimes, intimate. Nattukkottai Chettiars were occasional witnesses to major transitions of power among the royal Maravars.[86]

Nattukkottai Chettiar interests appear to have been both several and changing over the course of the century. Motivation in the first half of the century may have been related to the orthodox code of merchant service to kings. In Nagarathar folk histories, great service to kings was rewarded with high honours. Service to a king was participation in the sacred endeavour of maintaining prosperity and dharmic order as the king redistributed the loan to others who served the realm.

Chettiar willingness to enter a seemingly bottomless pit – financing *samastanam* politics – also had economic motivation, in the desire to take advantage of opportunities for trade in zamindari grains. When Government officials were not making one of their periodic attempts to restructure or abolish grain contracting in the two zamindaris, major Nagarathar merchants held responsibility for selling the grains. A sub-collector observed in 1828:

It was formerly the custom to deliver over the ... grain to a few rich merchants who of course made a considerable profit by the assistance they afforded the Zemindars in relieving them from the burden of disposing it on the market.[87]

Even with changes in the contracting system, which followed periods of government sequestration, the main merchants retained significant control over grain marketing. The major dealers in Sivagangai grain contracting from mid century appear to have been the same figures who dealt in zamindari moneylending.[88]

[85] 'Zamindar of Devakottai', in V. L. Sastri *et al.* (eds.), *Encyclopedia of the Madras Presidency and the Adjacent States* (Madras: Oriental Publishing Company, 1921), p. 478.

[86] Madras High Court. Documents in Appeal No. 21 of 1887, Exhibit V, p. 145 and Exhibit VII, p. 179.

[87] Boards' Consultation, 14 April 1828, back no. 47, Extract from the Proceedings of the Board of Revenue under date the 14 April 1828, on the settlement of the Ramnad Zemindary for FS. 1235 and 1236, p. 4. (TNA)

[88] Throughout the Miscellaneous Correspondence volumes for Madura District for the years 1850, 1851 and 1853 drafts drawn by Nattukkottai Chettiars for Ramnad and Sivagangai Nattukkottai Chetti grain contractors are listed. Some of these names correspond to zamindari creditors. All are directed to the Sub Treasurer, Fort Saint George, from R. D. Parker, Collector of Madura (TNA).

In the first decades of the nineteenth century, Nattukkottai Chettiar creditors appear to have been fairly lenient with the royal houses. Villages may have been mortgaged for security, but there is no evidence of crippling foreclosures. By the middle of the century, however, a change in relations between the merchants and the houses had begun to occur. In negotiating and renegotiating loans, greater emphasis began to be placed on repayment according to schedule, with mortgaged villages or divisions as the forfeit.[89] In this mid-century period, Chettiar creditors began aggressively to force the terms of mortgage bonds and to press for land sales.[90]

Because of dynastic absorption in succession conflicts, zamindari revenue establishments, never geared to efficient collection in the first place, suffered. Peshkash payments became increasingly dependent on loans. The merchants gave *hundis*, as needed by the zamindars and then, at a later point, might negotiate a mortgage bond in which whole taluks or sub-divisions of each zamindari would be mortgaged. In Ramnad, during the 1860s and early 1870s, two taluks were mortgaged to two Nattukkottai Chettiar brothers, Chidambaram and Subramanian; three divisions to two cousins, Narayan and Vairavan; two divisions and one fourth of the rent of another division to Ramanadhan Chetti, who came to play a major role in Ramnad affairs in the 1880s and 1890s; other portions to the heirs of Arunachalam, one of whom, Ramasami, became Ramanadhan's major rival for influence in the zamindari.[91]

In the 1870s, as Raja Muthu Ramalingam Tevar failed to make his payments, these merchants refused renegotiation and took him to court. Ramnad Zamindari was saved from extinction by the premature death of Muthu Ramalingam Setupati and the decision of the Court of Wards to make agreements with the Chettis for payment with Government funds.

Conclusion

The fragmentation of monarchical cosmologies in Tamil country occurred unevenly in the nineteenth century. Maravar royal kin figuratively battered symbols of their rule in the discourse of litigation, but in face-to-face exchanges of their localities they were more successful in reproducing systems of ideas and symbols which defined Tamil kingship. Largess

---

[89] See, for example, *Ind.Dec. N.S. (M.H.C.R.)*, vol. I, pp. 810–11.
[90] See, for example, *Ibid.*, Pitchakutti Chetti v. Ponnamma Natchiyar, 17 January 1863 decision, pp. 99–100.
[91] See: Documents in Regular Appeal No. 80 of 1876 containing the Judgements for Original Suit No. 1 of 1872 (Chithambaram Chetty v. Raja Vijia Regunada Muthuramalinga Saithupathy, Zemindar of Ramnad), p. 12; Original Suit No. 3 of 1872, Narainen Chetty and Vyravan Chetty v. Vijia Regunada Moottooramalinga Saithoopathy, Zemindar of Ramnad, p. 17; in the Judgements relating directly to R.A. No. 80 of 1876, see in the High Court printed collection, Original Suit No. 5 of 1874, The Collector of Madura and Agent to the Court of Wards on behalf of Baskarasami Setupati, Zemindar of Ramnad v. Ramasami Chetti son of Arunachellam Chetty, p. 3.

emerged as a powerful tool for protecting and enhancing royal authority in the attempt to fulfil common expectations of appropriate behaviour for a royal personage. However, the nature of this largess changed as the redistribution and use of cash achieved increasing importance in political strategies.

The colonial overlord penetrated the institutions of local rule more thoroughly than previous overlord regimes. This overlord could not be appeased with the granting of rights over village produce, the precolonial method of negotiation. Therefore, new techniques for protecting local authority and control needed to be devised. The effective ruler of the zamindari samastanam had to develop new constituencies, in the bureaucracy and in the activities surrounding dispute processing. Cash and other movable gifts became essential for the development of secret domains of influence among local servants of the state. In extravagant attempts to influence the outcome of litigation, zamindari politicians supported the development of a wide range of legal practitioners and semi-professionals specialising in the manipulation of the colonial system of dispute management. Ponnusami's patronage of the new literary and religious scholarship and its publication indicates a preoccupation with the fate of kingship in the emerging public sphere. However, the full implications of this kind of political involvement would not emerge until the end of the nineteenth century. Royal authority thus had to be maintained and honour acquired through a new range of transactions, within both the little kingdom and the larger structures of the colonial state within which it was embedded.

4

Human and divine palaces in the fragmentation of monarchical cosmology

The protection of royal honour and authority in Tamil country traditionally depended on the transactional processes besides those emanating from royal courts. The redistributional systems of temples and shrines played an important part in articulating major elements in monarchical cosmology. Precolonial royal kin gave high priority to the establishment and maintenance of ritual and administrative links to the temples of high-status worship. Under colonial rule the ritual and myths of worship continued to inform and influence notions of honour and legitimate authority in villages and towns. In nineteenth-century Maravar country the royal houses continuously attempted to recruit priests and temple administrations to the support of their reproductive agenda. However, what appears to have been a low-lying tension in the relationship between royal courts and establishments of divine worship developed into an antagonism which had an impact on the development of political ideology in public spheres. The relationship between zamindari houses and temples and shrines in the zamindaris became aggravated because of the new context of political competition under colonial rule. Zamindars and their estate managers had to compete for ruling honour and authority not only within the little kingdom, but also within colonial legal and civic arenas.

In precolonial Tamil country the ideologies outlining monarchical cosmologies had encompassed competitive tensions within and among elite groups. Rivalries over honour and rank took place in a political field defined by ritual schemes of royal integration. Smaller domains might break out of larger ones, as Ramnad did from Madurai and Sivagangai and Pudukkottai did from Ramnad. But the sustaining aim of smaller domain lords was ritual association with lords more magnificent than themselves. Such association took place through participation in durbar assemblies and in the endowing of acts of worship in temples. It also took place in the arranging of marriages.

With the onset of the Permanent Settlement and the consolidation of British colonial rule, high-status ideological totalities, containing conflicting principles of political action, fragmented into heterogeneous landscapes of occasionally adversary domains. These domains emerged in the course of the nineteenth century with relatively distinct identities. Politically they were connected in the common requirement of coming to terms with the administration of the colonial state.

Examining the accommodation of the ruling houses of Maravar country has shown the intensity with which their members struggled to maintain their political and social salience. Great was their frustration to find that institutions which had previously played important roles in sustaining monarchical ideologies were no longer committed to this end. In the course of the nineteenth century, temples and maths in Maravar country charted out their own strategies for political survival under colonial rule. Whether they completely altered their identity (as in the case of the family math of the ruling house of Sivagangai) or sustained major elements of their former responsibilities of worship, the heads of these institutions sought more autonomy in relationships with the former political authorities of their localities. While the new proximity of the imperial overlord had resulted in the scaling down of the political scope of the rajas, colonial rule gave administrators of temples and shrines opportunities to extend their authority in local society.

Scholarship interpreting the meaning and structure of transactions within temples and between temples and kings gives the impression that no opposition of interests could exist between the two types of institution.[1] However, there were possibilities for tension between human and divine courts: a devout servant of Lord Shiva, for example, could decide that his duties to the divine lord were more important than those to his human lord.[2] At the same time as precolonial maths and temples participated in ritual schemes of monarchical integration, they constituted domains of control which had their own complex and distinctive religious and political identities.[3] As related below, the desire to protect these identities could result in resistance to the directives of a royal house.

The western, colonial style of conflict processing played a significant role in the evolution of innovative relationships between royal houses and the religious institutions of their patronage. In the proceedings of courtroom

---

[1]   Carol A. Breckenridge, 'The Sri Minaksi Sundaresvarar Temple', Appadurai, *Worship and Conflict under Colonial Rule* 1981; Appadurai and Breckenridge, 'The South Indian Temple'; Dirks, *The Hollow Crown.*

[2]   Poems in Hank Heifetz and V. Narayana Rao, trans., *For the Lord of the Animals – Poems from the Telugu: The Kālahastīśvara Śatakamu of Dhūrjaṭi* (Berkeley: University of California Press, 1987), pp. 20, 36, 41, 50, 51, 84, 103 and 118 illustrate this tension for a former minister of a Telugu king. In his 'Afterword', Narayana Rao notes that 'The temple poet did not recognize the sovereignty of the human king.' p. 144. See also, Glenn Yocum, 'Brahman, King, Sannyasi and the Goddess in a Cage: Reflections on the "Conceptual Order of Hinduism" at a Tamil Saiva Temple', in *Contributions to Indian Sociology (N.S.)*, vol. 20, no. 1, 1986, p. 36.

[3]   See, for example, Yocum, 'Brahman, King, Sannyasi', and Marie-Louise Reiniche, 'Le Temple dans la Localité: Quatre Exemples au Tamilnad', Jean-Claude Galey, ed., *L'Espace du Temple: Espaces, Itinéraires, Méditations, Puruṣārtha* no. 8 (Paris: Éditions de l'École des Hautes Études en Sciences Sociales, 1985), pp. 75–119.

litigation protagonists became politically integrated in new ways as they took part in novel public encounters. They confronted each other formally as adversaries participating in processes which emphasised antagonistic interests. In the litigation process participants were encouraged to formulate distinct boundaries of authoritative control. It was significant for political development in the nineteenth century that conflicts between religious institutions and zamindars were not managed within an ideological framework which assumed essential complementarity in these relationships. The ideological totalities of monarchical cosmology shattered into splinter domains which publically defended their sovereignty against all but an invincible colonial state. An example from Sivagangai zamindari illustrates the way in which zamindari samastanams became ideological minefields under the Permanent Settlement.

One of the most cherished bits of the mythic history of the royal house of Sivagangai told of the early meeting of Sasivarna Tevar, the founding hero, with a forest ascetic, Sathappier, who predicted his future greatness. Annasawmy Ayer related the story in 1899, complete with identifications for a European readership:

Sasivarna Peria Oodaya Thevar, while passing through the jungles of Kaliarkovil ... met a Gnani (sage) by name Sathappier who was performing Thapas (meditation) under a jembool tree near a spring called Sivagangai. Sasivarna, being much struck with the austere devotion of the Gnani, prostrated himself before him and narrated all the previous incidents of his life. The Gnani sympathised deeply with his unfortunate condition in life, asked him to bathe in the spring, gave him sacred ashes, whispered a certain Mantra in his ears (Mantra Opadesam) and advised him to go to Tanjore and kill (by virtue of the Mantra Opadesam) a ferocious tiger which was kept by the Rajah especially to test the bravery of men and so obtain his friendship.[4]

The sojourn in Tanjore was successful, as noted earlier, and a war resulted in the establishment of the kingdom of Sivagangai. As he consolidated his rule, Sasivarna established the Sathappier math for a practice of worship and learning which would commemorate the sage and his initial protection of the royal house. The terms of the original endowment of 1734 stipulated that the *paradesi*, the religious and administrative head of the math, should be an ascetic.[5]

After the Permanent Settlement, however, the paradesis were married men or widowers.[6] By 1864 the original math building was a ruin. Not even a promise to an imperial commission, investigating land grants with privileged status, could induce the paradesi to rebuild it with funds

---

[4] Annasawmy Ayer, p. II.

[5] *The Indian Law Reports: Madras Series*, vol. XIV, 1891, January-December, pp. 1-17, gives the following details.

[6] *Ibid.*, p. 10. The fifth paradesi was a widower; it is not clear that he had joined an order of ascetics.

from the math endowment. Rani Kathama Nachiar attempted to remove this paradesi, saying that he had not been appointed by a zamindar; however, the High Court decided in 1867 that paradesis legally appointed their successors. By the 1880s the same paradesi had ceased all performances of the *Sivayogi nishtai* and *gurupujas* for which the math had been founded. He had mortgaged portions of the endowment for his family needs and attempted to turn the entire trust into his own family property, so that his son, who was not a disciple, should inherit it after his death.

Founded as 'an act of religious charity which would ensure the prosperity of [Sasivarna's] family', the math theoretically played a role in maintaining the prosperity of the kingdom.[7] However, what began early in the nineteenth century as a challenge to the authority of the ruling house gradually evolved into a denial of its cosmological significance. The Sivagangai samastanam gradually lost its identity as a community whose well-being was intimately related to the fate of the royal house. The criteria of judgement in the Anglo-Indian legal system were geared to the protection of the math endowment as property with specific rules attached to its management, not to paradoxical and subtle issues of the intertwining of human and divine authority.

Royal protection of worship in Maravar country before the permanent settlement

The number of temples and donated villages in Maravar country attests to the significance attributed to temple worship by Maravar chiefs and kings and other lords, distant and near, in their attempts to establish ruling authority in the area. Of the sixty-three major temples listed in the *Ramnad Manual*, thirty-three were founded by Pandyan, Chola, or Setupati kings and four by ministers of the Setupatis. Seven were founded by Setupatis, two in the seventeenth century and five in the eighteenth.[8] Approximately 366 villages of the kingdom's 2,167 villages had been given as endowments to temples by the end of the eighteenth century.

Perhaps as important as temple-building in the eighteenth century was the construction and endowing of chattirams, houses of rest and nourishment for the thousands of pilgrims who came from all parts of India to Rameswaram. Of forty-four chattirams built in the Ramnad kingdom, one was built by a Setupati towards the end of the seventeenth century, and twenty-seven were built or received a starting endowment in the eighteenth century. Sixty-seven of the kingdom's villages were given as endowments to

---

[7] *Ibid.*, p. 6.
[8] Raja Ram Rao, *Ramnad Manual*, pp. 81–5. The other temples were founded by the following: Brahmins and gurus – six; Vellalas – one; gods – five; Chettis – one; rishis – seven; Tevars – one, unknown – five.

chattirams.[9] Most of the 431 *dharmasanam*[10] villages given by the end of the eighteenth century were grants to Brahmins.[11] Thus, by the end of the eighteenth century, a considerable portion, approximately 865 villages out of the total of 2,167, had been given to the service of various religious institutions which were expected to support the honour and authority of ruling houses.

Ritual redistribution in larger temples, made possible through royal, dharmic gifting, articulated aspects of the political order. The endowment of chattirams fulfilled the Setupati's responsibility as protector of Rameswaram Temple and its pilgrims. Grants to Brahmins justified the title, *Āriyamānaṅkāttān*, or protector of the honour/dignity of the Brahmins.[12]

In granting and endowing almost half the kingdom, Ramnad Rajas did not relinquish royal authority over these lands and people. The king fulfilled another important definition of royalty in superintending the activities surrounding the gods of the temples, including worship, festivals, distribution of temple income and so on. One of the important Setupati titles reflects this function: one who bears the charge of the activities of the god Ramanada, chief of the gods at Rameswaram.[13] The raja also superintended affairs of the chattirams and of Muslim and Christian religious establishments in the kingdom, in particular, mosques and shrines.

The issue of what 'superintendence' or 'management' involved in the late eighteenth century and in the nineteenth century will be discussed further in this chapter. Here it is sufficient to point out a few elements of late precolonial supervision. The raja or his appointed jury was the final appeal in major factional conflicts in temples.[14] He might order the sequence of worship or aspects of ritual and designate ritual performers, as well as settle disputes about access to crops and tank water.[15] He maintained a revenue establishment for the collection of the light rent owed to him by holders of temple and dharmasanam lands. The raja's responsibility of protection included checking abuses in temple management. He also confirmed the selection of religious heads and in cases of disputed succession might choose the heads himself.

9   Raja Ram Rao, *Ramnad Manual*, pp. 91–119.
10 Gifted in religious charity.
11 Raja Ram Rao, *Ramnad Manual*, p. 285.
12 Burgess and Natesa Sastri, p. 79.
13 In Tamil the phrase is: *Srīrāmanātacuvāmi kāriyaturantaran*, Burgess and Natesa Sastri, pp. 65–6.
14 See Rameswaram Copper Plate, Plate 30, in possession of the Raja Sahib of Ramnad. A copy of this was made available to me by R. Nagasamy and Burton Stein.
15 Burgess and Natesa Sastri, Setupati Copper Plate Grants numbers 5, 6, 8, and 16, ranging in years from 1658 to 1763. High Court of Madras: Documents in Appeal no. 21 of 1887, Exhibit PP, p. 96, translations of cajan orders from Raja Muttu Vijaya Tagunatha Oyya Tevar of Sivagangai to the managers of a mosque.

Changing Raja-dharma and Devastanam 'mismanagement'

During her brief reign as Istimirar Zamindarni, Rani Mangaleswari Nachiar (1803–1807) carried on royal activities of state formation through dharmic gifting to temples, chattirams and Brahmins. Mangaleswari founded or rebuilt four chattirams during her reign. During the following years, only two more would be built.[16] Mangaleswari also endowed four temples and a math. Her greatest charity was to return eighty-six villages, which had been taken from mainly Brahmin grantees in the late eighteenth century. The other zamindar noted for religious endowments was Rani Parvata Vardhani, who endowed two temples and several chattirams upon assuming her title after her long conflict with Muthu Chella.[17]

From 1803 to 1889, the years for which there are records, Ramnad zamindars gave the produce of the lands of thirteen villages to temples, sixty-two to chattirams, and two to maths. Apart from the eighty-six villages of Mangaleswari, no more lands were granted as dharmasanams.[18] Most of the granting appears to have taken place in the first forty years of the century, with the greatest incidence occurring in Mangaleswari Nachiar's reign.

Not only did the rate of alienation of land for religious purposes considerably decline and major temple-building cease, but throughout the nineteenth century the zamindari establishments struggled to retrieve some of what had been given away. Court cases were initiated to recover lands, a common argument being that the families in question had alienated holdings which had been granted for the performance of a religious service. If the lands no longer supported the service, they had to be returned to the raja.[19] By the end of the nineteenth century, however, ryots on temples and chattiram lands had won the right to alienate or mortgage their holdings.[20]

Under the Permanent Settlement zamindars maintained *devastanam* revenue establishments (collecting revenue from places of worship) and were designated managers of the temples and chattirams. They were no longer, however, the final appeal on significant issues facing these institutions. The zamindars became, in effect, mediators between the Collector and families or religious heads who held lands with privileged tax rates and who had grievances or problems. Several examples will give an idea of the character of this mediation. The zamindar or his manager might report on a shrine which had lost its tax base during the Permanent Settlement.[21] They would call on the Collector to settle conflicts along district borders over the

---

[16] Raja Ram Rao, *Ramnad Manual*, pp. 118–9.
[17] *Ibid.*, p. 264.
[18] *Ibid.*, p. 477.
[19] Madura District Records, Volume 4778, dated 6 March 1830, p. 8205 (TNA).
[20] Raja Ram Rao, *Ramnad Manual*, p. 286.
[21] Board's Consultations, the Board of Revenue, dated 7 November 1833, back number 24–25, latter dated 13 March 1833 (TNA). Hereafter referred to as BC.

collection of revenue from devastanam villages.[22] When temples which held claim to pearls from the Gulf of Mannar believed that pearl-fishers were not paying their due portion of the catch, the zamindar informed the Collector of their grievance.[23] On occasion the raja would bring action against a devastanam village accountant who misappropriated temple funds.[24]

No longer sovereign in respect of religious establishments in their domain, the royal houses needed ways to describe themselves officially which would still suggest special qualities in their relationship with these institutions. A series of incidents in 1870–71 indicates the evolution of a new formulation.

In 1870 Shaik Mira, a Muslim, was digging near his field, close to an elevated part of a tank, when he discovered a ruined temple and some 5,000 rupees worth of idols and copper vessels. Upon being informed of the discovery by the local police, the Sub-Magistrate of Tiruvadani took the objects into his custody and sent them on to the Civil Court. Although Muhammad Mira, the brother of Shaik Mira, claimed the area of discovery to be in his field, a commission which investigated the matter found the land in question, the tank, to belong to the Zamindar of Sivagangai. Two parties stepped forward to claim the vessels and idols: Muhammad Mira (his brother having died) and the Zamindarni of Sivagangai, Kathama Nachiar. The Rani pursued the suit to appeal to the High Court. There her lawyers argued that the idols belonged to the 'Hindus' of the zamindari, the worshippers of the gods, and that Kathama Nachiar had claim to the items because of her special position vis-à-vis this community. She was the:

head and representative of the Hindus residing in the zamindari, and ... the recognised manager of all the Hindu religious institutions in the estate, [and therefore] entitled to have charge of the idols, to be by her deposited in one of the temples of the village [where they were found] for the use of the said community ...[25]

Neither the Justices of the Civil Court nor those of the High Court, however, found this argument convincing. They chose to question the definition of the 'whole Hindu community'[26] and to ask whether or not the zamindarni's ancestors could be proved to have been the trustees of this ruined temple.[27]

In claiming political significance in this case, the Rani tried to associate herself with a social (as opposed to political) category which officials of the empire might understand: the 'Hindu community'. The colonial proclivity

[22] Madura District Records, vol. 4678, 6 March 1830, p. 825 (TNA).
[23] *Ibid.*, 8 April 1830, p. 117 (TNA).
[24] Madura District Records, vol. 4682, 30 September 1834, pp. 425–6 (TNA).
[25] J. M. C. Mills, *Reports of the Cases Decided in the High Court of Madras in 1871–1874* (Madras, 1875), Civil Miscellaneous Special Appeal no. 363 of 1871, p. 153. Hereafter referred to as MHCR.
[26] *Ibid.*, p. 155.
[27] *Ibid.*, p. 158.

for distinguishing Indian subjects, socially, in terms of their worship had made its mark. In Anglo-Indian legal discourse, zamindars were stripped of the moral and sacred qualities which they sought through participation in palace and temple ritual. In court the Zamindarni depended on definitions implied by the regulations of the Board of Revenue. Her responsibilities for the maintenance of worship and as mediator between religious establishments and the Board of Revenue were translated to be 'representative' and 'managerial' in nature.

In the course of the nineteenth century 'management' of institutions of worship became, in fact, one of the most important strategies among royal houses for the reproduction of high honour and status. In the meantime the notion that indigenous rulers properly transcended sectarian boundaries became mitigated.

One reason for the continuing significance of royal superintendence of temples and shrines was the role of royal models and symbols in worship in Maravar country and beyond.[28] Tamils conceived of gods and goddesses as ruling the cosmos as divine kings and queens, and royal symbols denoted the protective functions of gods and goddesses in the lives of their worshippers. Temples, in a sense, served as repositories of monarchical values, symbols and models. In temples and shrines important aspects of monarchical cosmology were enacted regularly in ritual performances. Social and political ordering through processes of redistribution in temples, large and small, continued to play important roles in the organisation of political relations in villages and towns.[29] Temples remained important for rich and poor people as they dealt in their lives with both practical and existential issues.

The superintendence of temples, or 'management' as it came to be called, had the added advantage for cash-pressed zamindars in that, far from involving the alienation of resources, it brought control over funds. Despite their occasional letters to the Collectors of Madurai drawing attention to devastanam conflicts, distress and abuses, the zamindars of Sivagangai and Ramnad did not notably pay close attention to the regular and accurate performance of temple rituals, the maintenance of devastanam irrigation tanks or the upkeep of religious buildings. They were, however, active in the politics of establishment control. Access to interest-free loans from temple funds was only one motive for this involvement, however. Disputes over the distribution of temple funds were also conflicts over the distribution of

---

[28]   See Breckenridge, 'The Sri Minaksi Sundaresvarar Temple', and C. D. F. Mosse's study of worship among Christians and Hindus in a village in contemporary Ramnad district, 'Caste, Christianity and Hinduism: A Study of Social Organization and Religion in Rural Ramnad', PhD dissertation, University of Oxford, 1986. I am grateful to Dr Mosse for making his study available to me.

[29]   Breckenridge, 'The Sri Minaksi Sundaresvarar Temple'; Appadurai, *Worship and Conflict*; Dirks, *The Hollow Crown*; Mosse, 'Caste, Christianity and Hinduism'; Bayly, *Saints, Goddesses and Kings*.

authority in the temple domain. They were conflicts over status in the ritual hierarchy.[30]

In 1815, the Collector of Madurai, Rous Peter, brought the lands of all the devastanams in Ramnad under his supervision, remarking:

The lands granted for the use of [almost all the religious establishments in Ramnad] ... have become much involved, the ceremonies have been overlooked, and a proper regard to their decorum & respect been much neglected ... I have in consequence assumed the lands of all, and have appointed Circar Servants to manage them, as well as to see that the accustomed ceremonies of each Pagoda are performed.[31]

The Collector also assumed charge of temple villages in Sivagangai for four years, as accusations of the misappropriation of funds abounded.[32] In 1834, amid other charges of misappropriation, Acting Principal Collector, J. C. Wraughton, explained to his superiors that he had been unable to send on a statement of religious endowments in the two zamindaries because:

... the accounts are kept in a most imperfect and irregular way ... I find that there are no accounts in this cutcherry regarding the Shevagunga Devastanoms and I am unable to ascertain the number of villages granted for that purpose.[33]

The nature of zamindari devastanam management is found in a report made by the Collector of Madura concerning royal supervision of chattiram buildings, lands and accounts in Ramnad between 1859 and 1868. The report indicates that what the Collector's establishment saw as poor or inadequate record-keeping was not necessarily the result of insufficiently developed management techniques. Zamindari management also served as a method to facilitate control over chattiram funds. The funds of the thirty-three chattirams under the zamindar's management were consolidated, and the endowment of one chattiram appropriated casually to the use of other chattirams. When the stock of supplies at a chattiram was diminished, the local manager would prefer to obtain an advance from local Chettis, rather than to appeal directly to the raja's supervising establishment. In this system of loose supervision and accounting, it was simple for the zamindar or his manager, when available cash ran short, to supplement the samastanam treasury with chattiram funds. Over nearly ten years, 42,549 rupees had been loaned interest-free to the zamindar. The average yearly assessment on chattiram lands was 22,507 rupees. During this same period chattiram buildings deteriorated and the tanks went unattended. Only 2,617 rupees were spent on the upkeep of the thirty-three chattirams; 3,452 rupees were spent on the seventy-two tanks which fed chattiram lands. As the Collector

---

[30] Appadurai, *Worship and Conflict*, pp. 111–14, 212–15, and Breckenridge, 'The Sri Minaksi Sundaresvarar Temple', *passim*.

[31] BC, back numbers 64–5, dated 8 October 1832, extract of Mr Peter's letter to the Board dated 5 February 1816, no. 3 (TNA).

[32] Madura District Records, vol. 4682, 3 March 1834, pp. 115–16 (TNA).

[33] *Ibid.*, pp. 50–2.

noted, the balance which should have gone for repairs had gone in loans to the zamindar.[34]

When Ramnad went under the Court of Wards in 1872, it was found that the systems of accounting had not changed. Not only the chattirams, but the entire devastanam establishment was characterised by a lack of clarity as to income and expenditure, with no statements of yearly transactions. Some temple accounts were missing.[35] To imperial officials this loose accounting and appropriation had only material advantage as its aim.[36] It must also be seen in the context of the struggle to protect or expand royal authority. The sums mentioned in connection with zamindari management were relatively insignificant in the context of the financing of major litigation. Control over temple and chattiram accounts served as an important expression of continuing royal authority in the context of the Permanent Settlement – a time when supervision over the movements of cash, as opposed to land, was acquiring new political significance in the redistributive schemes of south Indian monarchy. Sivagangai and Ramnad zamindars argued continually that maintenance of their status required such 'management' responsibilities and they struggled to remain managers of the devastanam managements when their zamindaries went under the Court of Wards or were leased.[37]

Temple officers were not passive witnesses to either zamindari or imperial attempts to exert control over their resources. Religious establishments resisted samastanam attempts to gain control over their affairs with long bouts of litigation. For over seventy years the rajas of Sivagangai fought with the heads of the Trivanamalai Math – which in turn managed five temples – for the privilege of closer supervision.[38] The conflict which best illustrates the complex issues of devastanam–zamindar struggles was that between the royal house of Ramnad and the head officer of the famous and wealthy pilgrimage temple of Rameswaram, the Setu Pandaram. As happened typically, however, important ideological issues became clouded in the process of conflict management in the colonial legal system.

Factions in both the temple establishment and among royal kin struggled to acquire imperial support for their cause and appealed consistently for imperial intervention. There appears to have been hope on each side that it could incorporate imperial initiatives as part of its strategy

---

[34] The Proceedings of the Board of Revenue, 21 March 1871, Proceedings dated 6 February 1871, no. 298. Under the arrangements worked out under the Court of Wards, the loan was repaid with interest (TNA).

[35] Raja Ram Rao, *Ramnad Manual*, p. 348.

[36] BP of 12 May 1874, vol. 5, no. 1,105, dated 24 March 1874, p. 3196 (TNA).

[37] In 1871, for example, the Raja requested that he be allowed to retain mangement of the devastanams and chattirams 'in order to keep up his rank'. BP, 21 March 1871, no. 198, dated February 6, 1871 (TNA).

[38] High Court of Madras. Appeal No. 21 of 1887, p. 44.

of contest. This appeal may be interpreted as a continuation of the traditional proclivity for using imperial overlords to seek advantages in major local conflicts. With the cessation of warfare in southern Tamil country, however, there was also the lifting of pressures for political accommodation and compromise between the major domains of Maravar country. The security and political integrity of both small and large communities in the area were no longer threatened by open and prolonged antagonism between the major institutions of community integration. Temple administrators grew bolder as royal sovereignty diminished and colonial officials took all or part of the zamindari under attachment in cases of financial distress or unclear succession.

In the litigation between Rameswaram administrators and the Zamindars of Ramnad, officers of the government clearly stated the interest of the colonial state in managing the relationship between a subcontinentally famous temple and its royal patrons. The king-temple relationship became refashioned in a process of dispute management that had as its first priority the articulation of the sovereignty of British imperial government.

Superintendence and management, 1793–1837

The century-long conflict between Ramnad Zamindars and the Pandarams of Rameswaram centred legally around the question of who was to have the authority to appoint or dismiss the Pandaram, the official with the greatest supervisory responsibilities. This issue was embedded in conflicts among the participants over the nature of royal honour and status under the Permanent Settlement, over the extent and nature of royal authority, and over control of temple resources.

The beginnings of the conflict are found in disruption in the governance of Ramnad Kingdom in 1772 after the capture of Raja Muthu Ramalingam Setupati by the Nawab of Arcot. Preceding this disruption, it appears that Ramnad rajas had played a significant role in the managing of disputes among temple factions. We do not know how often or at what stage in a conflict a raja was called upon, but he selected the supervisors of endowments and had designated ritual responsibilities and honours among priestly groups.[39] The Setu Pandaram, while supervising one of the most prestigious kattalais (endowments), had not previously possessed administrative authority over the other endowments of the temple.[40] The Nawab, however, in the absence of the Raja, appointed the Pandaram chief over all of the

---

[39] Burgess and Natesa Sastri, Setupati Copper Plate Grants numbers 5, 6, 8 and 16, ranging in years from 1658 to 1763; Plate 30, Rameswaram Copper Plate in Possession of the Raja Sahib of Ramnad, from the reign of Muthu Vijaya Ragunath Setupati (1734–1747). See Carol Appadurai Breckenridge, 'From Protector to Litigant – Changing Relations between Hindu Temples and the Raja of Ramnad', in Stein, ed., *South Indian Temples*, pp. 88–94, for an interpretation of the copper plate grants.

[40] BC 8 October 1832, back nos. 64–5, enclosure no. 6.

twelve kattalais. The Pandaram, for his part, signed a statement promising to relinquish his authority when the Raja was returned.[41]

The kattalais were returned to their various superintendents when Muthu Ramalingam resumed his rule. In the course of building a new hall, however, when it was necessary to destroy the supply cells of the various kattalais and consolidate the stores, the Pandaram was again put in general supervisory capacity.[42] He was accused in this connection of misappropriating ('embezzling') 20,000 pagodas and of failing to attend to the proper performance of temple worship.

Raja Muthu Ramalingam dismissed the official and appointed, first, Ragunatha Gurukul and then Subaray Iyar to the management of the endowments. Before the disgraced Pandaram died, however, according to practice, he appointed his successor from among his relations, a child of four years named Chinna Ramanadan. If practice had been followed entirely, Chinna Ramanadan would have received an ochre robe (a *caushauyum*) from his dying predecessor or other kin, and he then would have been confirmed in his office by the Raja. The Raja would then have issued an order to the *kurukuls, stanikars* and other officers of the temple to show the new Pandaram respect and to give him one of the highest temple honours by tying the *parivattam* cloth around his head.[43] In this succession, however, Raja Muttu Ramalingam refused to allow the caushauyum to be given. Thellaynoyagum, Chinna Ramanadan's father, conducted temple affairs for the next six months and, after his death, was followed for a year by his nephew, Arunachellam Pillai.

At this point, in 1793, Muthu Ramalingam consented to have the child made the Pandaram and entered into an agreement with Chinna Ramanadan and his agents. In the agreement the responsibilities of the office were outlined. These concerned the regular performance of worship, the administration of temple villages and the maintenance of loyalty to the interests of the samastanam.[44] This novel agreement was to become a source of much discussion in later years, as it stressed the authority of the Raja over the Pandaram: the Raja was stated to have nominated the new Pandaram and is referred to as the Sovereign Lord of the Pandaram; the Pandaram was referred to as the 'servant of the palace' and agreed to abide by the order of his sovereign in the case of disagreements.

Raja Muthu Ramalingam did not have an opportunity to consolidate the gains he made in the agreement of 1793. Company forces succeeded in surprising him in Ramnad in 1795 and deposing him. The next six years were unstable ones in Ramnad with uncertainty as to the Raja's successor and military uproar. The favourite of the rebellious Maravar chiefs was

---

[41] *Ibid.*
[42] *Ibid.*
[43] BC 8 October 1832, back nos. 64–5, enclosure no. 6, dated 3 February 1816 (TNA).
[44] BC 8 October 1832, back nos. 64–5, enclosure no. 9 (TNA).

beheaded in 1801 and Mangaleswari did not receive the sanad until 1803. Possibly during this period the Setu Pandaram succeeded in strengthening his position. In any event, the powers of supervision and control which the office had acquired were not relinquished upon the death of Chinna Ramanadan's predecessor. The Pandaram and his kin had built a dense network of support in the temple and had acquired information about the temple lands and treasures which could be denied to the king's appointee. Without this information supervision was severely hampered.

Like his predecessor, Chinna Ramanadan was also accused of misappropriation and inattention to ritual performances. By 1815, his contemporaries credited him with having:

... appropriated many of the covil [temple] property & built Bungalows, purchased horses and Bandies, sent for 4 or 6 Dancing Girls from Madura and Tinnevelly & gave each 4 & 5 Pagodas from the Covil fund & made away with the Pearl weighing 18 5/8 Rauthel which was sent from the Fishery for the head-dress of the swamy [god] and which was sealed and kept in the covil room and also made away with the utensils &ca of the 12 different [kattalai] cells, & made jewels to the said Dancing Girls from the Ornaments that were in the byrooms, and mortgaged and Hypothecated some of the abovesaid & borrowed 64,000 and odd Pagodas by the above specified means & expended the said amount for the Dancing Girls & their relatives, and thereby caused ruin to the said covil.[45]

The Collector found that temple rituals and festivals had been neglected and that temple village lands had been mortgaged or alienated. Concerning the latter he wrote,

The many claimants to the produce of these villages clearly [show] how much the Revenue has been anticipated. If the Lands be continued under attachment, I shall be enabled to discover how far they [the claims] are just, as I have at present reason to believe that many Bonds have been granted without the knowledge of all parties concerned.[46]

Chinna Ramanadan had involved the temple in debt to 140,000 rupees.[47]

Despite the 1793 agreement, royal supervisory powers had proved inadequate and had not prevented the expansive activities of an ambitious pandaram. In 1809 and 1811, both the zamindar and claimants to the royal title had made complaints to the Madurai Collector; action by the Collector was not, however, taken until 1816. Meanwhile, Chinna Ramanadan had died and a succession struggle had ensued in the Temple. Vizea Gopal – the husband of Sivagami Nachiar, a claimant to the Ramnad throne – claimed that Ramanadan had not appointed a successor, but that two other officials, in collusion, had selected Venkatachellam to be Pandaram, giving him the symbols of office. Vizea Gopal further wrote that these officials intended to

[45] BC 12 November 1832, back nos. 17–18, dated 29 September 1832 (TNA).
[46] BC 8 October 1832, back nos. 64–5, enclosure no. 2 (TNA).
[47] *Ibid.*, enclosure no. 8.

tie the parivattam and to take Venkatachellam in procession as a Pandaram. He asked the Collector to prevent the final ceremonies and to put his (the Collector's) men in charge of the temple treasure.[48]

Rous Peter, the Collector, found that he could not dismiss the new Pandaram nor remove him from his position of supervision over temple jewels and funds. Peter followed the advice of his assistant, Narrain Row, who wrote:

... as it would be difficult to find out what property there are and what of them [are] lost should either of them be ... [missing] and as Travellers & pilgrims, from distinct counties would not have proper attentions shewn to them, or the customs of receiving Emoluments from them be known should Circar [government] servants only be appointed to superintend the affairs, it appears expedient that the Pundarom should be continued to superintend the affairs of the covil.[49]

Nevertheless, the temple lands were put under Collectorate supervision; the temple came under attachment with its affairs conducted jointly by the new Pandaram, Venkatachellam, and Collectorate servants, subject to the orders of the Sub-Collector.[50] Ramnad Zamindari, which was experiencing confusion of rule during the dislocation of its long succession dispute, was also taken under attachment at this time.

In 1816, Peter instructed Narrain Row to conduct an inquiry into the practice of Pandaram appointment. Narrain Row found temple factions arguing opposing views on the issue of the Zamindar's role, some holding that a dying Pandaram could select his successor and give the caushauyum, others arguing, with support from zamindari people, that the Raja customarily appointed a new Setu Pandaram.[51] On the issue of Venkatachellam's assumption of office, more than twenty-five priests, officials and accountants claimed that he had been picked 'jointly and clandestinely' by two people with no authority to do so.[52] Peter could not settle either issue, but was obliged to allow Venkatachellam to stay in office for lack of any other person who could assume the responsibilities of supervision. The controversy over who had the authority, according to established practice, to pick a new Pandaram had only just begun. Factions led by the Vellalar families of the Pandaram line were ranged on one side, and those led by royal family members, on the other. The zamindari party focused on Muthu Ramalingam's selection of Chinna Ramanadan as representing custom. In the years to come, this succession was their only proof of a claim to nomination.

With the assumption of kattalai superintendence by the Setu Pandaram, two generations of officials had shown the financial possibilities of the

---

[48] *Ibid.*
[49] *Ibid.*
[50] *The Law Reports, Indian Appeals*, vol. I, 1873–4, p. 212. Hereafter referred to as IA, 1873–4. Rameswaram Temple held seventy villages in Ramnad Zamindari.
[51] BC 8 October 1832, back nos. 64–5, enclosure no. 6 (TNA).
[52] BC 12 November 1832, back nos. 17–18, dated 29 September 1832 (TNA).

position: it gave access to cash through the supplies and treasures of the various kattalais and through the prerogative of mortgaging temple lands. Peter's descriptions of Chinna Ramandan's activities suggest that he used this access to temple funds and properties, including jewels, to enhance his rank. The acquisition of horses and his association with devadasis were symbolic of enhanced, royal status.[53] It is not surprising in this context that Ramnad zamindars did not want to return to the custom of merely ratifying the nomination of a new pandaram, a practice which had been established during the period when the pandaram was only one of many administrators, with an only slightly augmented status.

In 1828, the Judicial Committee of the Privy Council decided the Ramnad succession in favour of Ramasami Setupati and in the following year the zamindari attachment was removed. Both zamindari and devastanam management were given to the new zamindar. The management of Rameswaram villages was also given to Raja Ramasami. When Venkata-chellam protested, asking for the entire Rameswaram responsibility, the Zamindar responded by claiming that he, not the Pandaram was the Dharmakarta of Rameswaram and, therefore, entitled to the management of the temple.[54] The term *dharmakarta* (master of the charity) had two meanings. It could signify any person who had supervisory rights over a temple by virtue of being its major patron or it could refer to a temple official who held these responsibilities.[55] The term was often used by kings in South Asia.[56] The new Collector did not attempt to settle the issue at this time, but simply allowed the devastanam villages to stay under Raja Ramasami's management as a temporary measure.

The Government of Madras decided four years later that the Pandaram should be placed in full management of the temple, including the seventy devastanam villages and their lands.[57] They were guided in this decision by a report of the Collector (Vivash) who stated that the zamindar had not held exclusive management since the Permanent Settlement and that it was generally agreed that in the recent past these responsibilities had gone to the Pandaram. Vivash did, however, suggest a general supervisory role for the zamindar, not on the basis of past practice involving ideas of the Setupatis' dharmic responsibility, but because, 'the country of Ramnad is under the management of the zamindar's family'.[58] The Government of Madras

---

[53] C. J. Fuller found the authority of the chief priest of the Minakshi temple in Madurai to have expanded after the fall of the Nayakas and, further, in the nineteenth century: *Servants of the Goddess: the Priests of a South Indian Temple* (Cambridge: Cambridge University Press), 1984, pp. 76–7 and 109.

[54] IA, 1873–4, p. 213.

[55] The two definitions are illustrated in Ponduranga vs. Nagappa (*Indian Law Review: Madras Series*, vol. 12, 1889, January-December) and in Krishnasami Tatacharyar vs. Krishnama-charya (*Indian Law Review: Madras Series*, vol. 5, 1882, July-December).

[56] Eivind Kahrs (personal communication).

[57] IA, 1873–4, p. 215.

[58] *Ibid.*

would examine past relationships in order to decide on specific management responsibilities in Rameswaram, but it was not willing to examine more abstract notions of the relationship between the raja and the temple on any terms except those defined by Anglo-Indian law. Throughout this controversy, the Government attempted not only to draw the outlines of authority between the Pandaram and the raja, but it also sought to articulate the principles by which zamindar authority was substantiated.

Ramasami Setupati died in 1830. The new Zamindarni, Muthu Virayi Nachiar and her brother and Manager, Muthu Chella Tevar, refused to turn Rameswaram village management over to Venkatachellam. They suggested as a compromise that both zamindari men and those of the Pandaram should manage the lands jointly and they continued the campaign to have the Government recognise the zamindar as head manager of Rameswaram. In 1832, Rani Muthu Virayi and Muthu Chella sent a letter to the Governor in Council explaining their position. Rameswaram, they pointed out, had been built almost entirely by the royal family of Ramnad. The Setupatis had established the major endowments and had given jewels and vehicles of precious metals for the gods. They had appointed the superintendents over endowed villages. Furthermore,

... our ancestors had from time immemorial superintended the affairs of the Temple as Durma Kurters, owing to which the zamindary acquired fame and honour and the title of Saidobathee.[59]

A Setupati had appointed the original Setu Pandaram to the supervision of the Tirumalnayak kattalai and he 'was subject under the control of the Saidobathees'.[60] The letter told again the story of Muthu Ramalingam and Chinna Ramanadan, leaving out the passing of the Pandaram to his position of authority during the time of the Nawab. Venkatachellam, who, they maintained, had never been properly appointed in the first place, was acting contrary to custom in assuming the title of Setu Pandaram and in claiming authority over the management of Rameswaram Devastanam. Here, the Rani and Manager combined the two issues of the nature of Pandaram succession and the limits of Pandaram dominance in temple affairs. It would be easier to win on the issue of right to nomination, than to allow the enemy to receive office and then attempt to take his powers from him.

Two weapons were then brought out. If the Setu Pandaram were meant to hold authority over the temple villages, he would have received at the time of the Permanent Settlement a sanad to that effect. He would have been made a zamindar. Furthermore, proof that the Pandarams' party did not have the authority which they now claimed was the absence of their

---

[59] BC 12 November 1832, back nos. 17–18, dated 26 September 1832 (TNA). The original letter was written in English.

[60] *Ibid.*

own charities toward the temple. If they were authoritative, where was their dharmic gifting? Statues of Setupati donors existed in the temple, to which rituals were regularly performed: 'Such charities were never founded by the Pundaroms, and they have never been entitled to such marks of respect.'[61]

Having swung back and forth between Anglo-Indian procedures and precolonial conceptions of ruling legitimacy, the writers of the letter again appealed to Anglo-Indian regulations:

[A]s Regulation VII of 1817 does not intend that the donors of charitable institutions should be excluded from right of controul over Servants who they may employ for the due administrations of the affairs over which they are placed, and as the right of nomination may be visited with us & that we superintend its affairs under such restrictions as the Government may be pleased to direct, & not that Pundaroms themselves assume dignities to which they are not entitled to with contempt towards our authority, because it cannot be possible to suppose that they originated of themselves & that the title of Saidobathee is of non-effect.[62]

Muthu Virayi and Muthu Chella elaborated on the requirements of the ancient lineage title:

Accounts may be rendered by us to the Collector, and our immediate check and superintendence of the affairs of the Temple is necessary to establish us to the title of Saidobathee. If that privilege is taken away from us, the title is also lost.[63]

Sister and brother moved on several fronts in their letter, intertwining the issues of honour and authority with control over accounts. The Setupati function of protection, which in the past had included in its definition the endowing of lands and the construction of buildings, was now spoken of only in terms of management of endowed lands and their accounts. This new definition of protection as mainly comprising management of accounts was the offspring of imperial rule. Not only was this definitional change one that could be encompassed by political understandings of the Government of Madras, but it might appeal to the Government's ideas of the proper authority for a zamindar. The Government defined the Raja of Ramnad as one who held the management of Ramnad estate. Similarly, here the complex temple-royal donor relationship would be simplified into a single concept which turned on the question of who controlled the accounts. The Rani and zamindars after her, far from resisting this change, promoted it. Aspects of legitimisation in the former temple-king relationship became diminished as new ideas of the establishment of authority developed. 'Temple management', a notion that colonial rulers could understand, would serve to simplify the more ambiguous arrangements of royal temple supervision and would place tools of control – financial control – directly into the hands of the zamindar and his or her establishment.

[61] *Ibid.*
[62] *Ibid.*
[63] *Ibid.*

The Setu Pandaram had a powerful weapon at his disposal, ample witness to the custom of appointment by the dying predecessor. The Rani and her Manager brother, though, had touched a tender spot in pointing out that the Setupatis could make authoritative claims based on their earlier privilege and capacity as the major Temple donors, substantiated with statues in the temple. Venkatachellam fought back by destroying a number of copperplate inscriptions in the temple and by forging new ones, which depicted a great sage, Ramanada, as having repaired the temple and built mandapams:

In the year Kālayukti, which is in the midst of the Kali years, the ruined prākāram of the god that was consecrated on the Sētu by the lord of the Raghu family [Rama], for the pacification of all his sins, was first repaired with the additions of many rows of beautiful mandapams by Rāmanātha, the prince of sages, who is well versed in all the rites and Agamas of the Saiva system.[64]

In an attempt to authenticate his inscriptions and substantiate his authoritative claim, Venkatachellam also mutilated several statues of associates of Vijaya Ragunatha Setupati (dating from the early eighteenth century), by having them chiselled into ascetics, attaching beards of lime.[65]

This aspect of the conflict, focusing on legitimate authority as derived from the protection of worship through donations, was carried to a greater extent thirty years later. In 1863 and 1864, the contending Pandaram, Periya Nayakam Pillai, endowed acts of worship in Rameswaram and had copperplates made and attached to the temple walls. He did not identify himself in these plates as Pandaram, only as 'Manager and Dharmakarta', with the English word transliterated into Tamil script.[66]

The letter from Muthu Virayi and Muthu Chella received a short but direct response from Acting Collector, R. J. Sullivan. He noted that, according to the stanikars, the Pandaram had superintended temple affairs since the Nawab's time. The zamindar might supervise the Pandaram's management, but:

it would by no means be beneficial to the devastanam estate to allow him to have control over the funds. The revenues of the devastanam should be paid into the Circar treasury, from which also the monthly disbursements should be issued; in this case, the surplus which remains could be expended as occasion requires for the benefit of the Rameswaram Devastanam.[67]

The Collector's office would be the most appropriate source of village supervision, he suggested. With the implacable logic of a bureaucrat, he

---

[64] Burgess and Natesa Sastri, 'From Rameswaram', wall and sculpture inscription no. 7. Burgess points out the forgeries. See also inscriptions number 8, 9 and 10. Original diacritics.

[65] James Burgess, 'The Ritual of Rameswaram', in *The Indian Antiquary, A Journal of Oriental Research*, vol. 12, 1883, December, p. 316.

[66] Burges and Natesa Sastri, 'From Rameswaram', inscription nos. 21 and 22.

[67] IA, 1873–4, p. 216.

went on to deny the Setupatis their own traditional and special authority in relation to Rameswaram:

The Manager of Ramnad seems to be of opinion that he has a right to superintend in consequence of endowments made by his ancestors. This ground of claim, however, cannot be justly urged, because two-thirds of the revenues are derived from Maneyam [*inam*] villages in the Tinnevelly, Tanjore and Shevaganga districts, and all the Ramnad devastanam villages are excluded from the permanent settlement.[68]

In 1835 the Board of Revenue, after examining evidence from both sides and the reports of Madurai Collectors, decided that Pandaram succession belonged with a dying Pandaram. The zamindar was given the function of appeal, from Pandaram appointments and dismissals in the devastanam establishment, and was allowed an accountant to keep records of temple receipts and disbursements to be sent to the zamindar. Special mention was made of the desired behaviour of the accountant, who was to show the Pandaram 'as much deference and submission as he would towards his own master'.[69] The accountant's presence in the temple was not to be construed as symbolic of superior authority and status on the part of the Raja.

Two years later, after continued disputation, the zamindar and Venkata-chellam came to an agreement which served to settle the terms of the relationship for the next fifteen years. Part of the agreement was that neither party would claim the title of dharmakarta. The zamindar would not manage temple funds; however, the Pandaram compromised by granting willingness to 'abide by the directions of the said zamindar' in regard to village management and expenditures of the temple.[70] The accountant was to continue his work in the temple.

The struggle for management, 1854–1874

In 1852, the calm was broken and, in 1854, the conflict took on new virulence, as Venkatachellam died and the issue of Pandaram appointment arose again. Venkatachellam appointed a successor who, in turn, died in 1857. The Pandaram appointed in 1857 also died, shortly after appointing Ambalavana Pillai. The Rani of Ramnad, Parvata Vardhani, refused to recognise any of these appointments, having, in 1856, made her own selection.[71] Protracted litigation followed in the Zillah Court and the case came before the High Court of Madras in 1865. During this time, Ambalavana Pillai had died and a minor, Ramanada Pandaram, had succeeded him. Ramanada's guardian, Periya Nayaka Pillai, prosecuted the case. The Raja of Ramnad, Muthu Ramalingam, lost his case in the High

[68] *Ibid.*, pp. 216–17.
[69] *Ibid.*, p. 219.
[70] *Ibid.*, p. 220.
[71] *Ibid.*, p. 221.

Court and took it to the Privy Council. There, nine years later, in 1874, the Law Members gave their decision for the Pandaram. In the appeal before the Privy Council, the lawyers of the (now minor) Raja, Baskara, argued for inclusion of Rameswaram Temple in his domain using the arguments discussed above. The arguments of the Pandaram and the representatives of empire stretched the authority of the temple administration still further: the domain of the temple was seen as free of the Raja. The Privy Council, on the other hand, protected the sovereignty of the Government of Madras against local claims of the Raja.

J. B. Norton and his associate, for the Pandaram, noted that temple endowments had not come entirely from Ramnad kings.[72] If the king had not granted all of the lands, managership stemming from residual proprietorship could not be said to remain with him. Referring to early inscriptions, the lawyers found that Setupatis had not founded the temple. Setupati construction of Rameswaram was overlooked. To show precedence of recent autonomy, it was argued that Rameswaram villages had not been included in the Permanent Settlement and that, in 1816, temple lands had been attached separately from those of zamindari.

Along with arguing the case for a separate domain, the lawyers returned to a tactic used by the Pandaram since 1834,[73] that is, denying the Setupati superior status by stating that he was ritually inferior to the Pandaram. Since the Maravars ate flesh and the Pandarams were of 'pure Shiva caste', it was inconceivable that any Setupati could have invested the new appointee with the symbols of sacred office.

The argument for the Pandaram did not, however, deny the Raja of Ramnad continued local rule or any role at all in temple affairs:

It is asserted on the part of the pandaram that the pagoda of Rameswaram was an independent endowment, in which the Rajahs Setupati had no rights of patronage, or control, other than the general authority they assumed as the rightful or de facto rulers of the district, to prevent abuses in the management of its affairs, and to see that its laws and usages were properly observed.[74]

The Pandaram was willing to grant that from continuing, de facto Ramnad rule came the obligation to maintain laws and customs of the area. A zamindar's dharma, however, did not include the role of Dharmakarta of Rameswaram Temple.

The Judicial Committee of the Privy Council decided on a number of different fronts that the Setupatis did not have authority over Rameswaram management. The endowment had not come solely from Setupatis; the Temple had not been founded by Setupatis; the 1793 nomination did not establish proof of custom; and the 1816 attachment had been separate. The

---

[72] *Ibid.*, p. 224.
[73] Madura District Records, vol. 4682, 7 January 1843, p. 14.
[74] IA, 1873–4, p. 227.

Law Members' greatest interest was in the Setupati argument of continuing sovereignty in Ramnad:

It appears ... to be highly probable that the Setupatis in the days of their power exercised control over the pagoda, not, however, in virtue of any proprietary right of patronage, but as the rightful or de facto rulers of the district. The powers they enjoyed as sovereigns, whatever they may have been, have now passed to the British Government, and the present zemindars can have no rights with respect to the pagoda other than those of a private and proprietary nature, which they can establish by evidence to belong to them.[75]

The history of the relationship between the Government of Madras and devastanam management in the Madurai-Ramnad area was reviewed, showing the new government to have taken over the responsibilities of the former sovereigns. The lawyers of the Raja of Ramnad had argued that, previous to Regulation VII of 1817, the actions of the Collectors during the Rameswaram attachment, 'could only have proceeded from ... the rights of the zemindar vested in them under the attachment'.[76] Further, the lawyers of the zamindar suggested, since 1817, that it could still be argued that the Collectors had acted under the supervisory rights of the Zamindar. Their Lordships responded by stating that proof of the Collector's superior authority lay in his order to Rani Muthu Virayi that she must relinquish her responsibility for management of the temple villages to the Pandaram: 'so far from relying on the right of the zemindar, he [the Collector] acted in direct opposition to the claims of his guardian [the Zamindar].'[77] The ruling legitimacy of the zamindar existed solely in terms of rights deriving from the rule of the Government of Madras. The traditional relationship between the former king and the temple was not to serve as grounds to evade British legal and political understanding. Their Lordships summed up:

Taken by itself, [the 1837 agreement between the Raja and the Pandaram] would certainly appear to recognise the manager as superintendent in right of the zemindar; but ... their Lordships think that the acknowledgement must be referred to the power entrusted to the zamindar as the nominee of the Government. Even if it had been shown that some power of superintendence resided in the owners of the zemindary, it would not at all follow that the right to interfere in the appointment belonged to them.[78]

In the view of the Pandaram, the Raja of Ramnad still retained sources of legitimacy which were independent of the Government of Madras, but such legitimacy gave the Raja only a weak caretaker role over temple accounts. The view of the speakers for the empire denied any right to rule which was not grounded in Anglo-Indian law with its new conceptions of

[75] *Ibid.*, pp. 233–4.
[76] *Ibid.*, pp. 235.
[77] *Ibid.*, p. 238.
[78] *Ibid.*, p. 240.

imperial sovereignty and responsibility. The judgement was given: the Raja of Ramnad could neither nominate nor dismiss the Setu Pandaram of Rameswaram.

The Raja becomes manager: Baskara Setupati

The last major temple-zamindar crisis of nineteenth-century Ramnad saw a variation in the previous tripartite struggle. The Government of Madras, having differentiated its instruments of rule and moved closer to affairs of rural governance,[79] no longer felt the necessity to protect its local prerogatives against threats which a great zamindar like Ramnad could pose. At the end of the nineteenth century the Raja of Ramnad could become the Manager of Rameswaram, for it was undeniable that the Zamindar was Manager by the choice of the state. Temple officials went into battle with the courts to establish control over the appointment, frustrated by the success of their old enemy in using the tools of Anglo-Indian legitimacy to achieve his goal.

One way to fight back was to point to the Zamindar's performance as a temple administrator on the same terms which colonial officials used to evaluate titleholders to estates, as incompetent. The other strategy was to draw attention to the Maravar king's low caste status, according, again, to criteria which colonial officials had shown themselves to prefer. On this basis the young Raja's enemies at the great temple attempted to deny his family temple-based honours which designated high ruling status. Accused of being an ordinary human of low status, the Raja of Ramnad was left with the less spectacular consolation of aristocratic class rank. At the same time, however, Rameswaram, like other great temples, acquired an identity which emphasised its 'religious' nature, narrowly defined, and diminished its own capacity to play a role in the representation of earthly rule.

In 1882, eight years after the Privy Council decision, the subordinate court of Madura East removed Pandaram Saminatha Pillai from office.[80] The departing Pandaram was not allowed to select his successor. The District Court assumed direct responsibility of appointment and selected Mahadeva Aiyar as a Receiver.[81] The Court next settled on Tirugnana Sambandha Pandaram Sannadhi of Madura to be the Pandaram. Within several years of Tirugnana Sambandha's assumption of office, however, he was dismissed, under unclear circumstances, and Baskara Setupati, the young, ambitious and flamboyant new Raja of Ramnad, was appointed by the District Court to become the Manager of Rameswaram. There were

---

[79] See D. A. Washbrook, *Emergence of Provincial Politics: Madras Presidency, 1870–1920* (Cambridge: Cambridge University Press, 1976) for an extended discussion of this process.

[80] *Madurai Mail*, 16 March 1895.

[81] *Ibid.*, 20 April 1895.

indications that the Pandaram Sannadhi had abused his position.[82] Charges followed that Baskara himself had bribed Tirugnana Sambandha, to assist his appointment.[83] The Zamindar's version of his appointment was that the District Judge had recognised his 'hereditary claim' as the Dharmakarta.[84]

This selection mobilised factions in the Temple community against the Raja. The Arya Maharashtrian Mahajanan (a priestly group in the temple), including stanikars, *nainars* and *mirasidars*, and the high-ranking Karkartha Vellalas, claimed that the right of appointment under circumstances of dismissal belonged to them.[85] As they lined up their attack, including petitions to the Court and a lawsuit, these temple officials focused their argument on Baskara's poor capacities as a manager:

[T]he chief of [their complaints is] that his administration has not been altogether a success and that his incapacity for the management of any large estate, his extravagance and embarrassed circumstances, his wholesale alienations and lease of many parts of his estate including Devastanams, Chuttrums, &c., charitable institutions are all within the knowledge of the Court, having been brought before it both at the time of his appointment as Manager and at the recent trials in the two sessions cases of ... this year.[86]

For the temple factions, the struggle was now defined in terms of the extention of a zamindar's estate management to management of the temple and his poor capabilities as a manager.

Baskara Setupati's interest in Rameswaram, on the other hand, was part of his extravagant attempt to assume local pre-eminence in a style of rule which drew both on precolonial precedents and the themes and values of the new public opinion of the nineteenth century. Baskara Setupati's enhancement of his royal status, involving as it did his assuming the Managership of Rameswaram, did not meet with universal sympathy by powerful factions of temple officials at the temple, though he retained support from some sections. Not only did his enemies, as seen above, attack him in the court for being a poor Manager, they also played on the theme of Maravar caste identity and status. They insulted the special status of royal family members, declaring, again, that they were simply 'Sudras', of inferior ritual purity. The outline of this strategy is found in the following newspaper report of the funerary celebration of Baskara's deceased mother.

When the party taking the remains [of the deceased senior dowager Rani of Ramnad] reached Kaddo Pillayer Kovil, they were received by the officials of the temple with becoming honours. One Somanatha Iyer, an intelligent and old Stanikal of the Devastanam, was made to mount the temple elephant with the remains. Then a grand procession was formed and it moved with great pomp through the town

---

[82]   *Ibid.*, 24 August 1895.
[83]   *Ibid.*, 18 May 1895.
[84]   *Ibid.*, 20 April 1895.
[85]   *Ibid.*, 12 May 1894.
[86]   *Ibid.*

towards the temple in front of which a parivattam was tied round the vessel containing the remains as a mark of respect. Then the remains were taken to the ditch near Thanushkoti [on Rameswaram Island] and left to sink into it. We learn that the Arya Mahajanems met on the evening of that day and passed a vote of censure on the said Somanatha Iyer for his having taken part in the ceremonies and excommunicated him from society for his having handled the polluted remains of a Sudra before the performance of karmam and insisted on the temple elephant undergoing a Pryaschittam before being used for temple purposes.[87]

The following week the correspondent noted that such behaviour on the part of the temple officials was a departure from practice; Baskara's father and Rani Parvata Vardhani had received these honours without incident.

This conflict between an important ruling house and the administrators and ritual practitioners of a great temple was indicative of a major shift in the relationship between priestly groups – generally Brahmins – and dynastic heads in south India. The final two chapters show that Baskara did not let attacks on the status of his ruling house and the honour of its members pass without aggressive reaction. He appears to have followed the lead established by his uncle, Ponnusami Tevar, in supporting a movement of religious 'reform' which challenged the primacy of the learning of temple priests. Unable to win control of temple establishments in their local domain, both men sought influence in the public sphere. In this manner they presaged zamindari leadership and financial support of the Justice Party in the early twentieth century, challenging the new political dominance of south Indian Brahmins under colonial rule.[88]

Conclusion

The long conflict between the zamindars of Ramnad and administrators of Rameswaram Temple describes the partial disintegration of the ideological and institutional structure of an Indian royal domain under colonial rule.[89] In the course of the conflict, priests from Rameswaram still took part in ritual performances organised by the Ramnad court. However, even if radical discontinuity in ritual exchanges did not occur, the political nature of the little kingdom changed as relationships altered among its major institutions of rule. The radical discontinuity which this conflict illustrates is the change in modes of imperial political integration which attended the consolidation of colonial rule in India.[90]

In late precolonial regimes, ritual ranking and the management of major

[87] *Ibid.*, 13 April 1895.
[88] For one aspect of this shift see Price, 'Ideology and Ethnicity under British Imperial Rule'.
[89] Somalay (ed.), *The Saga of Rameswaram Temple: Kumbabishekam Souvenir* (Rameswaram: Arulmigu Ramanathaswami Thirukkoil, 1975), contains a photographic portrait of the late Ramanatha Sethupathi (d. 1979), identifying him as Hereditary Trustee and Chairman of the Board of Trustees from 1967.
[90] The following argumentation was provoked by correspondence with David Gilmartin.

disputes did not necessarily occur in separate political processes. This is because much disputing in major assemblies appears to have involved competition over honours, ritual usage and succession to domains of various types. The distribution of honours in temple and court settings involved deciding whom among claimants to an office or title the ruling authorities would favour. The rhetoric of ritual in dispute processing-cum-ranking allowed winners of major disputes to enter the charmed circle of those who shared in the ruling authority of divine and human rulers.

Participation in the Anglo-Indian legal system allowed for – it required – the formal representation of the heads of remaining elements of precolonial systems of rule, such as the rajas and temple administrators discussed here. This representation and (from the indigenous point of view) ranking took place in litigation processes in district and metropolitan courts of law.[91] However, the colonial legal system controlled the terms of that representation in such a way as to prevent these entities from sharing in the formal authority and sovereignty of the imperial state. The colonial regime denied indigenous institutions of rule the representation in dispute processing which would have allowed them to incorporate into their own local political identity colonial symbols of rule. In the main arenas of the colonial state where local elites could regularly appear and be ranked vis-à-vis each other, they were denied the right to appropriate, formally, the symbols and substance of colonial sovereignty. The conflict discussed shows justices carefully protecting the prerogatives of the imperial regime.

In the Anglo-Indian legal system, on the contrary, the appearance of zamindari rajas and temple administrators served to define negatively their formal political significance under colonial rule: they were not representatives of the public domain of the state, but were distinguished sharply from colonial institutions of governance. Through the legal system the colonial state attempted to differentiate between legitimate and illegitimate attempts to exert authority and control on behalf of the state. Here powerful Indians experienced the meaning, for example, of a distinction between an institution or issue of a private or 'personal' nature and those of a public (official) nature. The conceptual language of Anglo-Indian law served to separate little kings and temples from the ideological and administrative structures of the colonial state and denied them a share in formal ruling authority under colonial rule.

Participants in litigation experienced the distinction between political administrative responsibility and that which was apolitical. The rhetoric of litigation mangled the complex issue of the sharing of authority between a king and the god who ruled from the temple. Legal terminology translated indigenous concepts of ruling authority into issues of control over procedures of accounting. The world of 'management' was concerned with

---

[91] For discussion of an important case involving caste ranking and ritual usage in Madras Presidency see my 'Acting in Public versus Forming a Public'.

efficiency, effectiveness and accuracy. This world was incongruous with the cosmologies of personal, dharmic authority, honour and status which supported the visions of high-status temple officers and little kings. The procedures and rhetoric of colonial litigation also, thus, contributed to those processes which separated ideologies of worship from formal ideologies of governance in India. Baskara Setupati would paradoxically build on this distinction in his support of Hinduism as a world 'religion' and his campaign against priestly 'ignorance' and degenerate practices.

5
Ritual performances, the ruling person and the public

At the end of the nineteenth century the arena of conflict between royal kin and temple establishments moved from the law-courts to the palace in Ramnad Zamindari. Here, through newsprint, Baskara Setupati acquired some control over the representation of the relationship between kingship and divinity in both the samastanam and the public sphere. Baskara's words and actions were aimed at undermining priestly status and authority. These actions also worked, however, to change the sacred nature of Ramnad kingship, since they involved acceptance of a distinctly 'religious' conception of the practice and doctrine of worship. However, the royal house laboured simultaneously to protect a special status for the person of the ruler. This special status would eventually subsume other issues in the emergence of a new style of leadership in Tamil political practice, not only in Ramnad, but beyond. A discussion of ritual developments at the court both illustrates Baskara's attempts at religious reform and reveals aspects of the continuing focus on the person of the leader in monarchical politics in the nineteenth century. It points to Baskara Setupati's innovative strategy of royal reproduction as he attempted to bridge the gap between the universal requirements of recognition in the public sphere and the particularities of political authority in his locality.

The privilege of taking part in kingly rituals and organising elaborate ritual performances celebrating royalty had distinguished high-status rulers in precolonial Maravar country. Some of these rituals took place in seclusion, while others were performed in public. Participation in both added to the 'name and fame' – the honour – of men who must also continually demonstrate their prowess in a range of activities, both violent and peaceful. Precolonial Maravar rajas addressed varied audiences in their ritual performances, including the heads of important domains – military, religious, kin and commercial – within and beyond Maravar country. This visual, representational aspect of monarchy was one which was still available to zamindars after the Permanent Settlement. The significance of these ritual performances, however, changed under colonial rule.

Precolonial audiences for royal ritual performances did not constitute a 'civil society', separate from the state. Monarchical symbols informed the meaning of the myriad ritual exchanges which bound niches of local authority into a continuous web of religio-political ties, the loosely organised domains of the monarchical state. In this manner did 'state' and 'society' interpenetrate each other, precluding the development of a public.[1] Even village gods ruled and wore the clothing of *pōrvīraṅkaḷ* or war heroes,[2] and metaphors of governance and battle articulated the protection which villagers sought in local shrines and temples.[3] Local concepts of authority were inextricably bound to notions of dharmic rule resonating with political visions emanating from palaces and forts.

Under the colonial regime, printed rules and regulations, not the exchange of gifts in public, outlined the organisation of the state. Domain heads still received honours in village and town temples and shrines, but these honours no longer had formal significance vis-à-vis the state. The concern of the new regime was with allegations of the misuse of the funds endowing ritual exchanges.[4] Otherwise the principle of the colonial government was non-interference with the 'ceremonial' concerns of its subjects.[5] The conceptual distinction of authoritative boundaries between the colonial state and indigenous institutions of rule provided, thus, an ideological basis for the emergence of civil society.

A public sphere characteristically includes people who share interests which bind them together across local hierarchies and separate them from the institutions of the state.[6] Throughout much of the nineteenth century the politics of indigenous institutions tended to be focused on particularistic issues of local ranking and thus did not constitute the activities of a public sphere. At the end of the nineteenth century, however, Raja Baskara Setupati wove trans-local themes of 'religious' reform and progress into palace performances in Ramnad and there occurred a blending of the particularistic politics of the little kingdom with the universalistic concerns of metropolitan civic arenas.

It was rare that nineteenth-century zamindars joined in the activities of public opinion. In his defence of British rule in Madras Presidency,

[1] The concept of the 'public sphere' here borrows from Habermas with an attempt to respond to the south Indian context. See Sandria Freitag 'Introduction', in *South Asia. New Series*, vol. XIV, no. 1, 1991, pp. 1–13 and Pamela Price, 'Acting in Public versus Forming a Public'.
[2] Stephen Robert Inglis, 'Village Arts of Madurai District: Some Notes on Technique and Style', unpublished paper, Madurai University Tamil Department, 1975, p. 18.
[3] Mosse's thesis, 'Caste, Christianity and Hinduism', describes the historical and political consciousness of villagers he studied in Ramnad district. Alf Hiltebeitel's studies of myth and ritual in contemporary Tamil Nadu, *The Cult of Draupadi*, vols. I and II (Chicago: University of Chicago Press, 1988 and 1991) describe village cultures formed by monarchical cosmologies. For the late nineteenth and early twentieth century see Henry Whitehead, *The Village Gods of South India* (New York: Garland Publishing Company, 1980, first published, 1921) and H. Krishna Sastri, *South-Indian Images of Gods and Goddesses* (Benaras, 1974, first published in 1916).
[4] Breckenridge, 'The Sri Minaksi Sundaresvarar Temple', *passim*.
[5] *Ibid.*, p. 363.
[6] See Price, 'Acting in Public versus Forming a Public'.

published in 1893, Srinivasa Raghavaiyangar wrote sympathetically concerning the political consciousness of zamindars:

It is true that the Zemindars as a body have as yet done nothing to assume their proper position as leaders of social and industrial movements; but in fairness to them, it must also be remembered that to a great extent circumstances have been against them ... Brought up in the old traditions, with no sphere of public [i.e. governing] usefulness open to them to develop their better qualities or enlarge their minds, they have hitherto, with some notable exceptions, formed an idle and dissipated class. Recently, however, a change has become perceptible. Several of them are being educated, and the proceedings of the Landholders Association recently organized distinctly show that they are beginning to realize their duties and responsibilities and to feel that if they do not rise to the requirements of the present *regime*, they will lose all social influence and importance and be doomed finally to disappear.[7]

Zamindari kin were acquainted with actors in public life in Madras and the district capitals. Their local politics had, in fact, created a financial base for leading participants in the new politics. The most prominent men were Brahmin lawyers who had made sizeable fortunes in zamindari litigation.[8] Appearing in the public sphere, however, implied that one shared with other participants a common political status in relation to the state. Sharing status on those terms did not, generally, interest zamindari kin. Their primary concern was to establish and maintain ruling status vis-à-vis an unco-operative imperial regime, sharing – if possible – in its authority. Zamindari interest was with constructing hierarchies which penetrated the state, not sharing platforms with those who confronted it.

With his heavy patronage of Tamil writers in the mid nineteenth century Ponnusami Tevar had played a role in the production of literary and scholarly material which later became important to actors in civil society in Madras Presidency, in particular to founders and supporters of the non-Brahmin movement.[9] Regular action in public informed by issues of civic arenas emerged first in Maravar country, however, in the person of Baskara Setupati. With heavy doses of royal largess and well-advertised commitment to goals of progress and social well-being, Baskara created a new political style in Tamil country. A discussion of nineteenth-century palace ritual provides a background for examination of this style.

In the midst of cosmological fragmentation and the emergence of public

[7] S. Srinivasa Raghavaiyangar, *Memorandum on the Progress of the Madras Presidency During the Last Forty Years of British Administration* (Madras: Government Press, 1893), p. 248.

[8] Price, 'Ideology and Ethnicity Under British Imperial Rule'. Note the Madurai lawyer elected to serve on the Temple Committee of Minakshi Temple in 1878, in Breckenridge, 'Sri Minaksi Sundaresvarar Temple', p. 351.

[9] For the development of the non-Brahmin movement see Eugene Irschick, *Politics and Social Conflict in South India: The Non-Brahman Movement and Tamil Separatism, 1916–29* (Berkeley: University of California Press, 1969).

opinion, zamindari political cultural kept a powerful focus on the person who was the ruler of a domain. The theme of the special nature and status of the ruling person pervaded attempts on the part of zamindari kin to protect local sovereignty. A dominant message of the hierarchy in palace ritual was that the existence of the political community depended on the capacity of the leading person to affect the well-being of others.

In the late precolonial period the status of the ruler was conventionally articulated in terms of honour, mariyatai. This was a person's value relative to others in a fluid political system where actors, hierarchically ranked, shared ruling authority. In the context of a new type of imperial integration under colonial rule the concept of mariyatai as relative status was joined by the concept of an absolute status, held by virtue of the influence which wealth brings. In southern Tamil Nadu today this status is widely known as *antastu*.[10] Tied to quantitative wealth, antastu is not a relative quality.

Mariyatai carried connotations of the recognition of social boundaries.[11] The distinctions of mariyatai were vulnerable, taking place in a shifting political universe. The model for antastu expressed a fixed hierarchy, describing the storeys of a building, 'being one above the other'.[12] Abstract dictionary meanings for antastu were 'degree of dignity, rank, position';[13] 'rank, condition, position, state';[14] or 'dignity, prestige'.[15] The word came into use during the Vijayanagara period[16] and may reflect the increasingly important role of liquid resources in monarchical politics. Possession of cash proved to be a more reliable tool of influence and control than the promises of service implied in ritual exchanges in the assemblies of great lords. The emphasis in the colonial regime on bureaucratically defined statuses and absolute rights supported the increasing importance of antastu.

Conceptualising status as antastu did not preclude preoccupation with the more fluid and vulnerable mariyatai. For evidence of this we have the wide documentation of conflict over showing and receiving honour from the Vijayanagara period to the present in Tamil Nadu.[17] Zamindari kin

---

[10] Interviews in villages and towns in Madurai district that I carried out with my field assistant, Velraj P., in 1991 are reported on in Pamela Price, 'Revolution and Rank in Tamil Nationalism', (forthcoming). Antastu is derived from the Sanskrit *antaḥstha-*, meaning being in the midst or between, M. B. Emeneau and T. Burrow, *Dravidian Borrowings from Indo-Aryan* (Berkeley: University of California Press, 1962), p. 11. Emeneau and Burrow's source for meanings of antastu is L. V. Ramaswami Aiyar, 'Semantic Divergences in Indo-Aryan Loanwords in South Dravidian', in *Journal of Oriental Research, Madras*, vol. 8, 1943, pp. 252–66, and vol. 9, 1935, pp. 64–77. I am grateful to Klas Hagren for his help in tracing meanings for antastu and mariyatai.

[11] *Fabricius's Dictionary* p. 778, and Emeneau and Burrow, *Dravidian Borrowings*, p. 53.

[12] *Kittel's Kannada-English Dictionary*, M. Mariappa Bhat (ed.) (Madras: University of Madras, 1969), first edition, 1894, vol. I, p. 68, and Emeneau and Burrow, *Dravidian Borrowings*, p. 11.

[13] *Kittel's Kannada-English Dictionary*, vol. I, p. 68.

[14] *Fabricius's Dictionary*, p. 21.

[15] Emeneau and Burrow, *Dravidian Borrowings*, p. 11.

[16] Vijaya Venugopal (personal communication).

[17] For southern Tamil country see, for example, Bayly, *Saints, Goddesses and Kings*;

continually sought to protect and reproduce the status of mariyatai honour. In winning the legal title to an estate, they also acquired the desirable antastu. The absolute sum, the peshkash or revenue, the zamindar annually owed the Government of Madras was a representation of this status.

The official peshkash demand indirectly designated zamindars as particularly privileged financially, even if they often defaulted in their payments. It was the rare commoner who could have borne such a responsibility. Under the new regime, the peshkash-owing zamindar occupied a position fixed in a universalistic, absolutist legal framework. Assiduously protected by the state through a variety of administrative mechanisms, this fixed status placed the large zamindars among the wealthiest subjects of the Government of Madras in the nineteenth century.

The absolute status of antastu, which reflected the personal influence of the holder, combined with the glamour of royal mariyatai to create the major elements of political charisma in the career of Baskara Setupati.

Navaratri and the celebration of monarchy

As dharmakarthas or as managers of temples, rajas or their representatives received high-status temple honours.[18] Other important settings for the distribution of honours were festivals in the palace, in particular, those festivals highlighting the zamindar/ni as a special person, holding the highest rank in the locality. The festival of the Goddess, 'nine nights' or Navaratri, was the most important festival to this end.

Ostensibly the Navaratri festival celebrated and invoked *Devi*, the archetypical Goddess who was sakti, the power which infused the cosmos and the force and energy which were life or which protected life in all forms. Devi – in English, the Goddess – was the initial form, the creatrix, from whom the other female goddesses emanated, in forms appropriate to a situation. While the Navaratri celebrated and invoked the power of Devi generally, the story of Durga was the most important festival story. A basic outline of the story follows.

The heavens were seriously threatened by the most powerful and terrible demon of them all, Mahishasura. Because of a vow made to the demon, Siva, Vishnu and Brahma and the other *devas* were powerless to act to save themselves. No male deity could destroy the demon, according to the vow,

Hardgrave, *The Nadars of Tinnevelly*; and Mosse, 'Caste, Christianity and Hinduism'. An all-Tamil country discussion is included in Arjun Appadurai, 'Right and Left Hand Castes in South India', in *The Indian Economic and Social History Review*, vol. 11, nos. 2–3, 1974, pp. 216–59.

[18] Breckenridge notes that in 1874, of 191 large temples in Madurai district, the zamindars of Ramnad and Sivagangai continued to supervise, respectively, 59 and 81. 'The Sri Minaksi Sundaresvarar Temple', pp. 350–1.

and so the devas created a female goddess who contained all of the divine powers within her. Vishnu gave her his weapons, the conch and the disc, to aid her in her struggle. The Goddess rode to battle on a lion and, with her sword, cut off the buffalo head of Mahishasura (it is also said that she felled him with arrows).

On the tenth and final day of festival, *vijaya dasami* (technically, a day not part of the 'nine nights'), the battle between Durga and Mahishasura was re-enacted with the king ordinarily taking the role of goddess, carrying a sword to the battleground outside the capital city and shooting arrows at a tree symbolising the fearful threat to dharma. The previous nine days of the festival were devoted, in three-day periods, to worship of Devi as Durga, Mahalakshmi and Mahasarasvati.

Stein has discussed the festival during the Vijayanara period, seeing it as an 'encompassing form of public ritual' with 'incorporative meaning'.[19] He focused on the king in his interpretation of the festival's function of incorporation:

Kingly ritual power is expressed in numerous ways: in the manifestation of wealth displayed and elaborately redistributed at many points of the nine day festival; in the various consecratory actions involving the king's weapons as the means of his royal fame and protection; and also in the king's frequent and often solitary worship (and ultimately his identity with) the deity who presides with him over the festival and in whose name and for whose propitiation the festival occurs.[20]

The incorporative elements Stein saw in the festival centred around displays of the king's authority; following Hocart, he speaks of 'the subordination of all gods and all chiefs to the King'.[21]

In the course of several centuries the ruling lineages of Ramnad and Sivagangai invested a fair portion of their resources in the building and management of temples to Siva and Vishnu and associated their rule in iconography and insignia with Saivite and Vaishnavite traditions. Their tutelary deity was, however, Rajarajeswari or Goddess of the King of Kings, a form of Durga. Durga was associated with the protection of ruling lineages throughout India. Celebration of her annual festival was especially appropriate for the royal houses of Maravar country in their attempt to sustain a royal regime, for she was an anomaly as a goddess of the orthodox pantheon. Durga (and her counterpart Kali) alone demanded animal sacrifices and possessed terrifying and warlike countenances. In the Madurai-Ramnad area, when villagers picked the name of a goddess from the Sanskritic tradition for their female guardian deity, they called her

---

[19] Stein, 'Mahanavami: Medieval and Modern Kingly Ritual in South India', in Stein, *All the King's Mana: Papers on Medieval South Indian History* (Madras: New Era Publications, 1984), pp. 311 and 318.

[20] *Ibid.*, p. 318.

[21] *Ibid.*, p. 319.

Badhrakali. The identity of the Goddess was associated with the Badhra-kalis of the villagers.[22]

The festival of the divine warrior, because of her nature, expressed values, images and concerns which fitted with those of the vast majority of zamindari subjects in Maravar country, preoccupied as they were with stories and symbols of violence in the struggle for existence. The blood which was shed in village sacrifices represented the violence, broadly conceived, which protection could involve. The abundance which needed to be protected and which was won with blood included the abundance of fertility, female fertility. The concept of protection, particularly as it referred to the activities of goddesses, evoked themes of sexuality as an element in the reproduction of village communities.[23]

Within the encompassing framework of the Navaratri festival the raja could recognise and support the protecting deities of his villagers and their divine rule, a rule without exclusive Brahmin mediation.[24] Durga, as a deity of the orthodox pantheon, however, received Brahminical attention and was identified as the active agent of Siva and Vishnu. Receiving both vegetarian and non-vegetarian *puja*, the worship of Durga incorporated both ritually pure priests from Rameswaram Temple and the non-Brahmin officiants who performed animal sacrifices in village shrines. Documents from the early twentieth century show that the Raja of Ramnad organised and attended celebrations at Kali and Aiyanar temples in the capital city immediately before the Navaratri festival.[25] In this, he sought their protection for the city during the ten-day period of the festival.[26] In the course of the festival, the pots and terracotta horses of polluted ritual practice were integrated, with the mediation of the king/zamindar, into a single religio-political system of ideas which left the lords of Rameswaram and Kaliarkoil inviolate and still at the top.[27] In this fashion the kingdom could be conceived of more vividly as one divinely protected area.

The zamindars of Ramnad and Sivagangai maintained the performance of Navaratri throughout the nineteenth century. The Sivagangai house conducted Navaratri even when the estate was under lease.[28] In the early

[22] Kasinath Dorai, brother of the last Zamindar of Ramnad, interview in Ramnad, 26 April 1979.
[23] Alf Hiltebeitel, 'Sexuality and Sacrifice: Convergent Subcurrents in the Firewalking Cult of Draupadi', in Fred W. Clothey (ed.), *Images of Man: Religions and Historical Process in South Asia* (Madras: New Era Publications, 1982), pp. 72–111, and Brenda E. F. Beck, 'The Goddess and the Demon: A Local South Indian Festival and Its Wider Context', in *Autour de La Déesse Hindoue: Études Réunies par Madeleine Biardeau. Puruṣārtha*, no. 5. (Paris: Éditions de l'École des Hautes Études en Science Sociales, 1981), pp. 83–136.
[24] Whitehead, *Village Gods*, pp. 18–19.
[25] *Srī Sētu Samstānam virōtikirutu Mahā Navarāttiri Mahōtsavattil Vittuvānkaḷ Pātiyapatalkaḷ* (Madurai, 1912), p. 2. I am grateful to M. Anjali Anna Bai for her assistance in translation.
[26] Kausalya Hart (personal communication).
[27] Kaliarkoil was the main temple of Sivagangai Zamindari.
[28] High Court of Madras. Documents in Appeal No. 57 of 1894, p. 2, and Documents in Appeal No. 14 of 1898.

part of the century the Court of Wards financed its performance in Ramnad when the estate was under its charge.[29] Following the financial fiasco of Ponnusami's managership and the death of his brother, the Zamindar, it seemed that the festival might be 'hopelessly discontinued'.[30] Baskara, however, revived the festival lavishly.

Earlier chapters have shown that zamindari politicians developed new types of domains of influence in the course of the nineteenth century at the same time as older domain relationships were experiencing fragmenting tensions. The ritual exchanges in palace durbars, involving both temple priests and local big men, became increasingly anachronistic as outlines of political relationships vital to the functioning and existence of a zamindari samastanam. New definition of relationships and rights appeared in the Regulations of the Government and the procedures and rhetoric of the legal system. The rajas became diminished in significance as figures who sustained and protected dharmic order. Decreasingly representing cosmic energy and redistributional control, the status of the zamindar was becoming increasingly a function of his personal wealth and his capacity to affect the fortunes of others through its disposal. The zamindar or zamindarni were shown mariyatai in settings which reflected dharmic concerns, but his or her status increasingly contained qualities of antastu, reflecting the practical influence commanded as a function of wealth. What remained salient was the focus on the special status of the zamindar as the embodiment of political authority. This status slowly evolved from an emphasis on the dharmic character of the ruler's honour (mariyatai) to an emphasis on his personal influence (antastu). The raja became someone who, by virtue of his wealth and access to important official and unofficial persons and institutions, could affect the fortunes of those he favoured. It was advantageous for zamindari title-holders that the monarchical system of values and symbols supported the king as being, appropriately, wealthy. A less sacred symbol of domain abundance, the zamindar became a model of the personal prosperity for which individual subjects longed.

Navaratri in 1863 : the coronation of Rani Kathama Nachiar

Two extended eye-witness reports of Navaratri performances in Sivagangai and Ramnad exist, one from 1863, in Sivagangai, and the other from 1892, in Ramnad. The 1863 report, a British journal article, describes vijaya

[29] BC 10 October 1831, back nos. 60–61. Statement showing the gross charges and surpluses of zamindaries under the management of the Principal Collector of Madura for July 1827 to July 1828. Ramnad Detailed Account Particulars, July 1828 to May 1829. See item, 'dusserah feast charges'.

[30] BP for September, Proceedings of 24 September 1874, no. 2,760 from W. McQuhae, Collector of Madurai to J. Grose, Secretary to the Court of Wards, 17 August 1874, enclosure no. 1, memorandum from J. Lee-Warner, Manager of the Ramnad Zamindari, to W. McQuhae, Collector of Madurai, 30 July 1874, no. 126, p. 7538.

Plate 4   Temple to the tutelary goddess of the royal family of Sivagangai.
The coronation mandapam is to the right of the temple

dasami, while the 1892 report, originally from a Madras newspaper, concentrates mainly on the first day of the festival. Festival puja (worship) aimed ostensibly to prepare the ruler to carry out his or her responsibilities, as well as to honour the Goddess. For most of these purification and propitiatory rituals, performed by Brahmin priests with the raja or rani occasionally participating, ordinary samastanam subjects were not present. The durbar assemblies, the arrow-shooting ceremony and the royal processions to and from these occasions required the presence of people of the samastanam, either as participants or observers.

John D. Shortt, who took the eye-witness account of Robert Fischer, was particularly interested in the events of vijaya dasami in 1863.[31] He may have focused on this day because Rani Kathama Nachiar, who had just won the title to Sivagangai Zamindari after thirty-five years of litigation, chose it as her coronation day. In this choice of ritual juxtapositions, the Rani associated the initiation of her titleship with the time of dharma which was to follow victory over *adharma*, when Durga vanquished Mahishasura – for Kathama herself had just won a long and arduous battle. The triumphal procession back to town after the arrow-shooting ceremony properly

---

[31]   John Shortt, 'Habits and Manners of Maravar Tribes of India', in the *Memoirs Read Before the Anthropological Society of London*, vol. III, 1870, pp. 209–15.

represented Durga's sovereignty over the capital (which, itself, represented the totality of the samastanam).[32]

On vijaya dasami morning, in 1863, the royal flags showing Hanuman (the monkey general of Rama) and Garuda (the vehicle of Vishnu) flew over the palace in Sivagangai Town.[33] People were beating tom-toms and firing cannons. After the Rani carried out her morning puja to Rajarajeswari, the *purohit* (the palace priest) presented her with *prasadam* (food from the ritual offering to a god or goddess) and asked her permission to begin the day's ceremonies. He departed then to the palace temple of Rajarajeswari, where several hundred Brahmins had gathered and, at an auspicious hour, began a ceremony to purify the palace. The Brahmins carried out several pujas, including the *chakra puja*, or worship with the metal plate, which organised and concentrated sakti. This puja was preliminary to the *pattabhishekam*, the installation of the rani. In the worship, prayers for the success of the new queen's reign were chanted simultaneously with the invocation of sakti, represented by the chakra and brass pots.

During the chakra puja, George Fischer, the Briton who managed Rani Kathama's successful recovery of the zamindari, brought forth and handed to the purohit a crown, which was shaped like a ducal coronet. The purohit placed the crown at the foot of a Vinayaka icon, a conical mass of ground turmeric representing the son of Siva, while water was prepared for the *abhishekam* (purification through pouring liquids).

At eleven o'clock in the morning, the Rani, having finished her own puja, came forth attended by her female relations. She was led to a small granite *mandapam* containing a marble platform, which served as the installation place in the palace. Surrounded by her close family and various relations, Kathama sat while the officiating priest and his assistants recited verses and poured water into a silver perforated strainer which they held over her head. Water from the chakra puja pots was included. Fischer, Kathama's agent, placed the crown upon her head while attending Brahmins invoked eternal blessings for the Rani and her lineage: 'The usual din and uproar from tom-toms and congratulations made the place resound again.'[34]

The Englishman, George Fischer, was not an imperial official and, as noted in an earlier chapter, was free to attempt a mediating role between the government and the participants in zamindari politics in Ramnad district. Kathama Nachiar was sufficiently impressed by his efforts on her behalf in Sivagangai to give him an important role in her installation ritual. As we saw earlier, she also gave Fischer most of her zamindari in lease to cover her debts. The crown which Kathama Nachiar used in her installation was that of a European-style aristocrat, not an independent monarch. With plans to give up her zamindari in lease to an Englishman, Kathama appears not to

---

[32] Rengasamy Iyer, interview in Madurai, 16 October 1978.
[33] The following details are taken from Shortt, 'Habits and Manners'.
[34] Shortt, 'Habits and Manners', p. 211.

have cherished illusions as to the autonomy of her own ruling status. However, the festival she organised and the rituals in which she participated clearly supported the idea that, even under European-style centralised administration, she was a person of (semi-) divine substance.

Dripping in water, Kathama returned to her quarters, changed into her white widow's sari, ornamented herself with jewels and smeared herself with sacred ashes. Then she returned to the palace temple, worshipped Rajarajeswari, and proceeded again to the installation place. There she performed the abishekam ritual of looking at her reflection, first, in ghee (clarified butter) and then in gingely oil, using a mirror. She distributed coins to her relatives, who departed, and gave to Brahmins ten gifts which the Sastras prescribed for the absolution of her sins. The abhishekam ceremony ended with the priests placing a few grains of rice upon Kathama's head and smearing ashes upon her forehead, invoking blessings.

After the Brahmins left, Kathama sent her son to represent her in the more public ceremonial acts of vijaya dasami. As a Maravar royal woman, she could not appear in public. The son prostrated himself before the deities in the palace Rajarajeswari temple and then received from the Rani the five arrows which he would shoot. He, in turn, gave these to the Brahmin who had, up to this point, conducted the Navaratri ritual. Kathama's heir went in procession through the palace grounds to the entrance gateway, where the palace elephant stood waiting. Leading the procession out to the *maidan* was an icon of Vinayaka placed in his vehicle, a bandicoot, on a cart dragged with ropes.[35] The Brahmin who had received the arrows followed next on an elephant. The white elephant holding Kathama's son and two of her brothers came next, accompanied by devadasis and a large crowd of people.

An enclosed shed had been erected on the maidan. Through an arched door one could see a *vanni* tree. The procession circled the shed twice. As it circled a third time, the Brahmin shot an arrow first east, and then towards the other three cardinal points. A sheep was sacrificed at each point where the four arrows landed. The fifth arrow he shot at the tree, which represented the demon Mahishasura, and the procession returned to the palace.

Kathama awaited her son's arrival at the installation place where, together, they underwent a ceremony to ward off the 'evil eye'. The Rani and her heir then moved to the marriage hall, where a durbar of relations was held. Here Kathama's children, her relations and her female servants prostrated themselves before her.

That evening the grand vijaya dasami durbar took place and the heir, once again, appeared for Kathama. At this durbar, representatives of major

---

[35] In Sivagangai and Mysore (as seen from a mural in the royal residence in Mysore City) a Vinayaka icon went to the maidan in the procession. Vinayaka did not take the place of the Goddess, but lent his auspiciousness to the proceedings.

domains on the estate honoured the Rani's representative and heir. The main officials of orthodox temples in the zamindari took precedence. The 'chief Stanigal' sat down before the son and offered him two bowls containing prasadam from his temple. The heir accepted the bowls by touching them, and an attendant emptied them and returned them to the stanikal. The latter rose, smeared holy ash upon the brow of the heir and left, to be followed by the heads of other temples and maths, each bearing prasadam from his temple. The next group of people to pay their respects were the heads of landed domains, *nāțu*, as these were called in Sivagangai. Bringing offerings of sheep, the *nāțțar* prostrated themselves before the heir and begged his protection for their customary rights and privileges in the samastanam. The third and final group mentioned were described as the 'chief' Brahmins of the zamindari. These may have been representatives from *agraharam* villages (villages granted to settlements of Brahmins). Five hundred in number, the Brahmins sat before Kathama's son, gave Sanskrit blessings and each one presented a coconut smeared with saffron. Simultaneously at the palace gateway approximately two thousand rupees were distributed to other Brahmins who had gathered. Following the durbar, twenty-four sets of devadasis performed. The installation vijaya dasami celebrations continued all night until daybreak, at which time sandalwood, betel nut, and garlands of flowers were distributed in profusion.

The Navaratri in 1892

Issues of *The Madras Times* carried descriptions of Baskara Setupati's Navaratri celebration in 1892.[36] The festival in Ramnad reflected many themes from Sivagangai. This report, however, brings out more clearly than the one from 1863 the ways in which ritual in Navaratri focused attention on the person of the ruler. The report describes the most distinctive rituals of the festival, those which attended the Raja's vow to protect the Navaratri and to conduct it properly, to make himself fit to shoot the arrows.

On the first day of the festival, beginning at about four o'clock in the morning, Baskara Setupati was first shaved and then anointed. In Ramalingam Vilasa, the Zamindar performed puja to the granite seat upon which, according to mythic memory, had sat the founder of the Setupati dynasty as Rama himself appointed him guardian of the Setu, the causeway to Lanka. Baskara then underwent an abishekam. He sat upon the granite seat as water which had been consecrated by Saiva ritual texts was poured over his head through a silver sieve. More waters were then poured – waters

[36] Ramanatha Sivasankara Pandiyaji and S. S. Venkataram Aiyanger, 'Celebration of the Navaratri Festival at Ramnad in 1892', *The Miniature Hindu Excelsior Series*, English Number IV, 1896. The authors explain that descriptions appeared in issues of the *The Madras Times* in 1892. Carol Breckenridge discusses this particular festival performance in 'From Protector to Litigant'.

consecrated by *vyasoktamantras* (sacred verses), waters from Rameswaram Temple, from sacred springs of surrounding districts and from the Ganges. The ceremony was attended with 'deafening cheers and various kinds of music and vedic hymns'.[37] The Raja's relatives prostrated themselves at his feet and pledged their loyalty, after which time he distributed gifts and went to worship Rajarajeswari.

This icon of the goddess was in the form of Mahishasura Mardani, the eight-handed Durga. According to the reporters of the event, a Nayaka king of Madurai had given the icon to the Setupati lineage, following a successful military venture. The green stone upon which she sat was another trophy of war, from Mysore, and was said to have originally been brought from the Himalayan home of Siva by the renowned philosopher, Sankaracharya. This stone, the Marakata pitam, concentrated sakti. After Baskara's puja, the goddess and the pitam were brought to a special mandapam, where the ceremony of the consecration of the pots took place. Sitting between the goddess and the pitam, the Setupati performed puja to nine clay pots filled with earth. Puja to nine metal pots, filled with water and with evergreen leaves at the mouth, followed. The pots were emblems of sakti.

The next set of rituals formed the *kāppukkattu* ceremony, when Baskara made his vows to refrain from meat, liquor and sexual intercourse and not to leave the palace grounds until the successful completion of the nine-day series of rituals.[38] Three officiating priests bound the *kāppu*, a thread rubbed with turmeric, three times around Baskara's wrist, intoning *slokas* (Sanskrit verses) for the successful conduct of the festival. The kappu, an emblem of prosperity, symbolised the Raja's protective vow. The Raja and the priests circled the green pitam several times and the chief officiating priest presented Baskara with the royal sword and sceptre. These had been placed at the feet of Rajarajeswari during the pot puja. He who contained sakti, represented by the pitam, deserved to rule. At the completion of the kappukkattu rituals, Baskara entered into several hours of meditation upon the Goddess, joined periodically by several of his male kin.

Two major durbars were held this day, each one following periods of worship of the Goddess. At three o'clock, Baskara Setupati returned in procession to the durbar hall. Whenever the Raja moved across the palace grounds, he was surrounded by a retinue both announcing and guarding him. The procession to Ramalinga Vilasam (the durbar hall) was a particularly grand one. Devadasis representing different temples of the samastanam came first, joined by their musicians. Groups of *nagaswaram* (wind instrument) players from various parts of the Presidency followed. Then came the palace band, playing both British and Carnatic music and leading the palace lancers, sepoys and liveried retinue, marching in military

---

[37] Pandiyaji and Aiyangar, 'Celebration', p. 3.
[38] Ramanata Setupati, Raja of Ramnad, interview in Ramnad, 1 March 1975.

order. Samastanam officials came next in the procession, followed by special guests of the Raja and then the royal relatives. Baskara appeared in royal dress, flanked by servants holding two silk umbrellas, royal insignia. On either side were torch-bearers and bearers of other ancient royal insignia. The official part of the procession ended with *pandits* (learned Brahmins) and groups of singers singing *bhajans* and songs from the Saiva canon. Thousands of people had entered the palace grounds to watch the procession; some greeted the Raja, who responded with salutations. Lines of elephants reared up to greet the Setupati as he passed by and the lancers and sepoys presented arms and saluted him as he entered the durbar hall.

Surrounded by portraits of past zamindars and their estate managers, of the Viceroy and of Queen Victoria, Baskara received the respects of the gathered assembly. The constituents of the durbar included new categories when compared to the 1863 description from Sivagangai. First came the stanikars and officiating priests of the devastanam temples, those controlled by the Raja's establishment. They were followed by the representatives of maths and Brahmin pandits, singers and, it seems, Brahmin estate officials. Special guests showed the Raja honour, as did non-Brahmin samastanam officials. Last came Maravar male kin, throwing before them a cloth as they prostrated. The same procession accompanied Baskara back to the zenana (women's quarters).

The evening worship of the Goddess took place in a magnificent set of temporary buildings and passages which Baskara had erected at great expense for the duration of the festival. Rajarajeswari sat in a silver vehicle with a painting of Durga slaying Mahishasura behind her and with the consecrated pots before her. Mahalakshmi and Mahasarasvati were also present in paintings, with Minakshi and Siva, the ruling deities of Madurai city, and Gajalakshmi (the goddess of wealth) and Vishnu nearby. Baskara arrived in another grand procession for evening worship of the Goddess. In the course of the puja, he sat upon a throne placed near the sacred pitam and held another durbar. Musicians performed for the durbar audience. The officiating priest took from the feet of Rajarajeswari consecrated arrows and gave them to the Raja, who returned them to the priest. The durbar closed and the Brahmins left the mandapam, before animal sacrifices were made to the Goddess. The next eight days included more durbars and similar pujas to Devi. With the kappukattu ceremony, Baskara had been recognised as the chief devotee of the Goddess; now he had to carry out his responsibilities.[39]

The activities surrounding the arrow-shooting ritual on vijaya dasami were, according to the festival description, 'the grandest of all the festivities'.[40] People came from all over the zamindari to observe. In the afternoon of the tenth day, Baskara mounted the state elephant and:

---

[39] Rengasamy Iyer, interview in Madurai, 16 October 1978.
[40] Pandiyaji and Aiyangar, 'Celebration', p. 14.

with two side elephants bearing his characteristic umbrella and flags, issued out of the palace amidst constant firing of guns, flourish of trumpets, and the deafening cheers of the multitude that greeted him, and forced his way through the dense crowd to the arrow-shooting plain.[41]

The other protective deities of the town had gone in procession earlier to the maidan. Upon reaching the field, Baskara circled it several times, passing the assembled gods and goddesses. Under the guidance of the chief priest of the festival, he shot the arrows. The icons were then taken from the maidan and the royal procession returned to the palace.

The most magnificent of the festival durbars was held that evening. Again, priests from devastanam temples gave honours and blessings, followed by other groups of Brahmins. The royal relations once again prostrated themselves and swore 'fealty to their paramount chieftain'.[42] In this durbar non-Brahmin officials and samastanam servants followed the Maravar kin. During the next two days the palace organised sports, firework displays and nautch parties – performances by devadasis. The Raja fed thousands of Brahmins and poor people and directed that scholars, musicians, artisans and 'other deserving persons' should receive money and presents.[43]

Observations on the accounts

During the Navaratri celebration, rituals which focused upon the king (or queen) were embedded among rituals which sought to honour and propitiate the Goddess. In Ramnad, there was an exchange between the king and the Goddess. She received the royal sword and sceptre, which were returned to the king. He was given the Goddess's arrows, which he returned until taking them for the arrow-shooting ceremony. While the king was honoured and, in a sense, worshipped in the evening durbar, priests simultaneously worshipped Rajarajeswari. Rituals which sought to create or renew royal substance, the abhishekam, were performed amid a series of rituals which sought to empower the tutelary deity of the lineage and to make her the great Goddess of all the samastanam. At the climax of the festival, king and Goddess shared a single identity as, together, they preserved dharma and created conditions for prosperity in the kingdom.[44] King and sword, joined by priest and arrows, slew Mahishasura.

Rajarajeswari ordinarily did not leave her palace temple, where only members of the royal family, joined on occasion by special guests, worshipped her. The chakra and the pitam, representing sakti, were used in daily palace puja. During Navaratri, however, the guardian deity of the

---

[41] *Ibid.*, pp. 14–15.
[42] *Ibid.*, p. 15.
[43] *Ibid.*, p. 16.
[44] Kasinath Dorai, interview in Ramnad, 26 April 1979.

royal house appeared strengthened as Mahakali, Mahalakshmi, Mahasarasvati and, finally, for all to see in the annual procession, Mahishashura
Mardini. Simultaneously Rajarajeswari became identified with all the *kāval
tēvam*, protecting deities, of the kingdom. The evening durbars celebrated
both expanded identities, containing puja of fruit as well as, after the
Brahmins departed, meat. Village religious practice also joined orthodox
practice in a single performance in 1863. As a Brahmin priest shot the
arrows, where each landed a sheep was sacrificed.

Durbars were an essential feature of Navaratri, as a festival of samastanam integration. Before the Permanent Settlement in Madras Presidency,
durbar assemblies – or *capai*, to give the Tamilised Sanskrit word – served
as occasions for heads of major domains of the kingdom to meet with the
raja and consult with him.[45] Kings announced their gifts of villages and
lands in durbars.[46] Warriors and land-controllers were affirmed in their
positions of local authority and ranked vis-à-vis each other.

After the Permanent Settlement, Navaratri and Pongal, both harvest
festivals, provided occasions for major zamindari durbars. During these
festival meetings, as we have seen, heads of temples and maths, kinsmen,
samastanam officials, Brahmins and 'special guests' offered prasadam, fruit,
cloths or sheep to the raja, according to their status. The Ramnad durbar,
with its 'special guests' and its estate officials illustrates new categories of
zamindari notables being incorporated into the recognised set of heads of
zamindari domains.

In available accounts telling of durbar gifts, all but royal kin brought
presents of food. The Maravar relatives threw down cloths called *tiṭṭi cēlai*,
'evil eye' cloths, meant to protect the raja from ill fortune.[47] All other gifts
mentioned were products of agriculture. In 1863 durbaris brought prasadam, sheep and coconuts. An 1894 account mentions limes, garlands and
coconuts.[48] These were the items of puja, and *kumpiṭu*, meaning to worship,
was a word used to describe the prostration before the raja.[49] In the durbar
the raja was worshipped as a god.[50] It would be an exaggeration, perhaps,
to suggest that in durbar prostrations and presentations the subjects of the
king were thinking of him as one of their deities. An analogy with puja is
viable here in that durbaris were empowering their ruler, feeding him and
honouring him as they would a god. In the fashion of a god and so
honoured, he would protect dharma and enable all to prosper.[51]

[45] The Raja of Sivagangai, interview in Sivagangai, 15 May 1975. Capai is commonly
translated as 'assembly'. The term was used before the adoption of durbar by the nineteenth
century.
[46] Rengasamy Iyer, interview in Sivagangai, 11 May 1975.
[47] Rengasamy Iyer, interview in Sivagangai, 10 May 1975.
[48] *The Madurai Mail*, 13 October 1894.
[49] Rengasamy Iyer, interview in Sivagangai, 10 May 1975.
[50] Velu Dorai, Sivagangai royal relation and estate Devastanam official in the 1930s, interview
in Sivagangai, 7 May 1975.
[51] These contemporary accounts of durbars in Maravar country do not mention either the

The king gave durbaris betel nut in return for their offerings, carrying the analogy with puja further. The prasadam which was given to worshippers in temple worship represented leavings from the divine meal. These leavings were not polluting. Generally, only family members willingly shared a substance touched by another's saliva. A deity's devotees, as his loyal subordinates, shared the divine leavings as an expression both of their acceptance of the deity's superior nature and their desire for an intimacy which claims divine protection. Betel nut, grown on a palm, is chewed for its taste and its narcotic effect. When the king's subjects accepted his betel nut, they ostensibly expressed a willingness to accept his superiority and to be faithful in his service.[52] South Indian brides took betel nut from their husbands during the wedding ceremony to indicate both a new intimacy and a subordinate status in that intimacy. According to this logic, so should the heads of zamindari domains enter into a metaphoric intimacy with the raja where treachery would occur at the cost of breaking a bond of 'kinship'.[53]

Zamindari durbars constituted persistent attempts at domain integration on the part of both title-holders and various other participants. Participation in the durbar constituted royal recognition of a subordinate's dominance in a local domain and thus a strengthening of his local claims. The pleas of nattar lords in Kathama Nachiar's vijaya dasami installation durbar can be examined in this light. The zamindar had the power to challenge claims to villages and lands, even if the instruments of the throne were more in the nature of lawyers and courts than strong, armed men. Nineteenth-century zamindars could cause havoc with claims on land; thus, the nattar had reason to ask for protection of the established order.

presence of village headmen or the presentation of *uluppai* to the zamindar. Several informants discussed both. It appears that offerings of uluppai – vegetables, sheep and implements – were collected in non-devastanam zamindari villages. Representatives of groups of villages, such as the most powerful headmen, would come to the Navaratri, accompanying the uluppai offerings, which were taken to the palace. These offerings were obligatory symbols of acceptance of the raja's authoritative claim on resources. The *uluppaikkar* was the person who had the right to send the produce to the palace, indicating his superior status in the village. For example the lease between a zamindari and his lessee, indicating the lessee's new authority in the village, might mention that he was the uluppaikkar: 'You and you alone shall collect uluppais &c. which are to be sent to the Zemin for Navaratri', from Madras High Court, documents in Appeal No. 57 of 1894, p. 2. See also documents in Appeal No. 14 in 1898 and Documents in Regular Appeal No. 35 of 1873, pp. 73 and 83. Rengasamy, interview in Sivagangai, 10 May 1975, reported that uluppai came only from wet lands, *pannai* lands, controlled directly by the royal house.

[52] Jakob Rösel and V. Narayana Rao (personal communication).

[53] Subbiah, of the family of the first Zamindar of Devakkottai, reported that the betel nut, *tambuli*, would be taken back to the domains of durbari recipients and distributed there, according to status, thus extending the relationship established in the durbar into the smaller governing units and associating the authority of the nattar of village lord with that of the zamindari. Interview in Devakkottai, 4 March 1979. Mangalanatha Dorai and Kasinath Dorai relate a similar report concerning royal tambuli, interview in Ramnad, 26 April 1979.

Even though the territorial integrity of the samastanams was not militarily threatened in the nineteenth century, from the point of view of the title-holder, the durbar could serve as an arena for the public affirmation of personal support. Securing pledges of loyalty from royal relations played a part in attempts at political integration, given that royal houses were plagued, next to extinction, by litigating kin throughout the nineteenth century. The participation of samastanam administrators could also have been a reference to another threat to the existence of Maravar country zamindaris: the inability to collect full revenue, held back in collusions among estate officials and village heads. Another kind of problem of loyalty and subordination lay in the violence and independence of a few remaining old-style Maravar chiefs in the zamindaris. Baskara Setupati described two relatives as 'Dick Turpins', after a famous British highwayman, and remarked that imperial forces were not strong enough to control their activities.[54]

A badly attended durbar indicated political irrelevance and diminishing social status. Poor attendance involved loss of prestige; thus we understand Baskara Setupati's pleasure with his 1893 vijaya dasami durbar and the significance of his diary notation, 'The number of processions at the Durbar especially of relatives was larger than usual.'[55]

Settings for royal ritual

The association of the zamindari rulers of Maravar country with divine figures and qualities had a complicated figuration. The rajas and ranis of Sivagangai and Ramnad worshipped daily at the temples of their tutelary goddess. However, coming from a royal house which associated itself with all-Indian ideas of legitimate kingship, the Raja of Ramnad was, formally, a Vaishnavite.[56] Precolonial kings were widely believed to be incarnations of Vishnu, the god of wealth, guarding and maintenance. Seeing a king was akin to seeing Vishnu.[57] Representing prosperity, Vishnu and his consort Lakshmi, were important in the iconographic representation of Ramnad kingship. Gajalakshmi, the aspect of Lakshmi with particular suggestions of wealth, was sculpted over major doorways in the palace grounds – in one place, with 'Long Live our King' painted in English below. The eight aspects of Lakshmi were painted, each figure approximately five feet high, surrounding two verandas on either side of a major passageway in the palace compound. Lotus blossoms, symbols of fertility and representing Lakshmi, formed a

---

[54] Baskara Setupati, Diary for 1893, entries 29 and 30 September 1893.
[55] *Ibid.*, 20 October 1893.
[56] Kasinath Dorai, interview in Ramnad, 7 October 1978.
[57] *Ibid.*, and personal communication from Venkatachari, visiting scholar of Tamil literature and religion, Berkeley, 1977.

Plate 5   A major doorway in the grounds of the Ramnad Palace, mentioned in
Navaratri description by Venkatarama Aiyangar in 1892

protective decoration on the massive door of the formal palace entrance,
built in 1829.[58]

Vishnu appears in sculpture and, on zenana walls, in paintings with his
wives. Both Hanuman and Garuda, Vaishnavite royal insignia, stand as
large figures painted near the Sivagangai and Ramnad palace entrances.
The dating of these wall paintings and doorway sculptures is problematic,
as is the dating of the buildings upon which they appear. At Ramnad the
date of the formal palace entrance, 1829, is confirmed by an inscription; the
other buildings are certainly nineteenth century if not, as in the case of the
zenana and the durbar hall, older.

In Ramalinga Vilasam, the durbar hall of Ramnad, the association of
Maravar rule with the great gods of Brahminical worship was clear. The
Archaelogical Survey of India has dated the painting on the walls of the hall
from about 1725 to very early in the nineteenth century.[59] While various
forms of Siva are prominent, the main iconographic painting is Vaishnavite.
Panels tell stories of Krishna as a child and as a king and the Rama story
fills an entire room. This room, which is directly behind and leads from the
platform where the king sat in durbar, is said to have once contained a

---

[58]   This decoration was called *Lakshmikkaram*, blessed by Lakshmi. Kasinath Dorai, interview
   in Ramnad, 20 October 1978.
[59]   R. Nagasamy, 'Irāmanātapurattu Cētupati Ōviyaṅkaḷ', in *Tamiḻaracu*, 6 June 1978,
   pp. 37–40.

Plate 6 The durbar hall at Ramnad Palace

shrine to Rama. The incorporation of the Rama story into the mythic history and symbolism of Maravar kingship in Ramnad had occurred at least by the fifteenth century, when major building, funded by Maravar kings, began on Rameswaram temple.[60]

The thin line between divine and human protection of both dharma and the kingdom is seen in another set of decorations in the durbar hall. On the left, as durbaris entered, there was a series of extraordinary illustrations of eighteenth-century battles between Ramnad and Tanjore. Elephants, cannons, European mercenaries, Maravar soldiers, the king in durbar, with a queen and his child – these scenes vividly celebrate Ramnad at war and the Setupati as martial leader, ruler and, in the early nineteenth-century drawings, negotiator with the East India Company.

Behind the Rama shrine was another room in the hall containing simple, lively wall drawings of the daily life of a king. Clearly identified in writing on the walls, Raja Muttu Vijaya Ragunatha Setupati,[61] who reigned from 1710 to 1720, is portrayed engaging in a series of playful as well as serious activities: travelling in a palanquin surrounded by ladies of his court, meeting a sage, being crowned by the King of Madurai, receiving Europeans. These human depictions were executed in a light, casual style,

---

[60] A recent discussion of the Ram story in representations of kingship is by Sheldon Pollack, 'Ramayana and Political Imagination in India', in the *Journal of Asian Studies*, vol. 52, no. 2, 1993, pp. 261–96.

[61] Nagasamy, 'Iramanatapurattu', p. 38.

without heavy coloration, which is in striking contrast to the densely
coloured, formulaic representations of the Krishna and Rama panels. It is
almost as if the ruling house were not willing to give its public hall
completely to the more abstract and transcendent demands of sacred kingship, as defined by Brahminical orthodoxy: temporal achievements and the
king as an immediate personality deserved space with the gods.[62]

In the nineteenth century, large portraits of the male zamindars and of
two managers, including Ponnusami Tevar, lined the durbar corridor,
hanging from pillars which led up to the throne. The choice of a European
medium – realistic portraits in separate frames – reflected innovational
qualities in Ramnad kingship under colonial rule. The eighteenth-century
murals of battle were relatively continuous with portrayals of the exploits of
Krishna, Vishnu and Rama. In the nineteenth century, artistic representation no longer showed rajas, unmediated, in the same visual setting as
Vishnu and Rama.

At the same time as the rajas of Ramnad associated themselves with royal
Vaishnavite motifs, they acted as major patrons of Siva worship. In building
the enormous Siva temple at Rameswaram and in promoting the legend
that Rama worshipped Siva there, Maravar kings succeeded in incorpor-
ating the model king securely into local Saivite practice. In both Sivagangai
and Ramnad, Siva lived in a great temple, at Kaliarkoil and Rameswaram,
respectively, and lent his distant and transcendent protection to the welfare
of the kingdoms.[63] The characteristics of Siva were less temporal than those
of Vishnu.[64] Siva represented eternal grace and release into the One. The
common people of the kingdoms did not visit these temples.[65] Too remote
to act in individual cases, say, of smallpox or the infertility of a wife, in the
manner of a great king, Siva lived in a fine palace (another meaning for
kōyil), surrounded by his retinue of officials and ritual officiants, and
attended to generalised problems of the expiation of sin and the liberation
of the soul.[66]

Under colonial rule the special relationship between Siva at Rameswaram
and the royal house was regularly enacted in temple ritual. Every Friday
night, as Siva made his way to bed with his priestly retinue, the palanquin
holding the icon stopped before two statues.[67] These were the statues of
Tirumalai Setupati, who won special titles and privileges for the ruling
house of Ramnad, and his son, Ragunatha Tirumalai Setupati. Temple
servants garlanded the statues and gave offerings of betel nut and flowers. If

[62] These are qualities one finds in ideological innovations of the Nayaka period according to
Narayana Rao, Shulman and Subrahmanyam, *Symbols of Substance.*
[63] Kasinath Dorai, interview in Ramnad, 7 October 1978.
[64] *Ibid.*
[65] James Burgess, 'The Ritual of Rameswaram', p. 315.
[66] Raj Gopal Sharma, 'Dakshinamaya Sri Sringeri Jagadgurus and Rameswaram Temple and
Sethupathis', in Somalay (ed.), *The Saga of Rameswaram Temple,* p. 183.
[67] James Burgess, 'The Ritual of Rameswaram', pp. 316 and 326.

servants of the zamindar were present, they then received these items for their lord.[68]

Association with Saivism was also found in the institution of the *kulaguru*, the spiritual preceptor of the royal family. The kulagurus for the Sivagangai and Ramnad families were heads of maths. Often referred to as Hindu monasteries, maths supported the worship of their saintly founders, served as repositories of sacred knowledge, administered a variety of religious institutions and supplied religious teachers for high-status families.[69]

As an old and prestigious ruling family, Ramnad royalty had secured for its kulagarus the services of one of the most honoured spiritual lineages in India, that of the Dakshinamaya Sri Sringeri Jagatgurus. Better known as the Jagatgurus of Sringeri, the lineage was in direct spiritual descent from the famous Saivite philosopher and teacher, Sankaracharya. The math at Sringeri provided a priest for the Rajarajeswari temple in the Ramnad palace and initiated, trained and blessed ritual specialists at Rameswaram.[70] Sringeri priests performed the installation rituals of the Ramnad zamindar. The arrival of the Jagatguru in Ramnad or Sivagangai was an occasion for formal public welcomings and celebration, organised by the palace. A major function of the kulaguru was to provide solutions for problems of worship that arose among royal kin.

Kingly innovations

Baskara Setupati, more than others of his class, was deeply touched by major issues of urban-based public opinion. He earned the title of 'Maharaja' – given by the Government of Madras – for his enlightened activities; however, as we shall see, his interests were more in the area of political culture than political economy. One profound interest was religious revivalism. Examination of the Raja's activites in this area reveals that religious revivalism, commonly associated with the development of Tamil nationalism and the non-Brahmin movement, was closely related to the interests of zamindari rule. Baskara Setupati's efforts at religious reform foreshadowed zamindari financing and leadership of the anti-Brahmin Justice Party, established in 1916. Unable to exert legal control over temple domains in their localities, zamindari politicians sought leadership in a socio-religious movement in the public sphere, a movement which became associated with a wider challenge to Brahmin cultural and political influence in Madras Presidency.

Baskara followed his uncle Ponnusami in patronising activities initiated

---

[68] There is no evidence that this ritual was discontinued during the periods of greatest hostility between the temple administrators and the royal house.

[69] Richard Devitt (personal communication).

[70] Raj Gopal Sharma, 'Dakshinamaya Sri Sringeri Jagadgurus', p. 185, and Ramanata Setupati, Raja of Ramnad, interview at Rameswaram, 27 February 1975.

to a great extent by Arumukam Navalar (1822–79), a Sri Lankan Tamil from Jaffna who travelled much in south India and published widely. Arumukam Navalar had translated the Bible into Tamil and was influenced in his conception of religion by early contacts with Christian missionaries in Sri Lanka.[71] The intention of his own missionary activity was to establish Saiva Siddhanta as a distinct religion purified of accommodation with the corrupt practices of 'low caste' usages. Precolonial Saiva Siddhanta was the doctrinal base of ritual practice in the great temples of Tamil country and included tantric elements which had created openings for the inclusion of devadasis in ritual practice.

According to Armukam Navalar, Brahmins of the day were ignorant of pure Saivite ritual practice, as it should have been according to the *agamas*, the orthodox texts directing temple ritual. He opposed low-caste Shaivite Bhakti worship, the worship of Murugan (a popular Tamil god), influences from Vaishnaviam, and other forms of syncretism, including blood sacrifice.[72] Hellmann-Rajanayagam relates a major theme in Navalar's writing:

'bad' Brahmins and especially depraved temple trustees try to justify their sins and excesses by a literal reading of the *Kantapuranam* [a text on Murugan] and indulge in the same activity as Murukuan allegedly indulged: such as temple dancing by Devadasis, adultery, etc. in the sacred precincts of the temple.[73]

Associated with a ruling house engaged in a humiliating struggle against temple administrators and their priestly minions, Ponnusami Tevar had been an important patron of Navalar. Caring deeply about retrieving the position of Dharmakartha of Rameswaram, Baskara Setupati was receptive to the revivalist zeal of Navalar's movement. In the following years the movement found powerful adherents among other presidency zamindars as Saiva Siddhanta became part of the anti-Brahmin offensive of the Justice Party.[74]

As revealed by articles and letters in the *Madurai Mail*, Navalar's attitude toward devadasis and his other notions concerning reform of temple practice were shared among English-language public opinion in Madurai.[75] For example, 5 May 1894 was a day heavy with references to the association of the Ramnad samastanam and 'nautch', the practice of hiring devadasis to dance at major occasions. The editors included under the heading, 'News & Notes', a complaint about the Diwan (Manager) of Ramnad:

[71] Dagmar Hellmann-Rajanayagam, 'Arumukam Navalar: Religious Reformer or National Leader of Eelam', *The Indian Economic and Social History Review*, vol. 26, no. 2, 1989, pp. 235–57.
[72] *Ibid.*, p. 237.
[73] *Ibid.*, p. 242.
[74] Irschick, *Politics and Social Conflict in South India*, p. 252.
[75] See, for example, *Madurai Mail*, 27 January, 1894; 5 May 1894; 17 May 1894; 26 May 1894; 2 June 1894; 17 March 1894. I am grateful to Richard Devitt for making this material available to me.

It is with deep regret that we learn that dancing girls were permitted to mar the sacredness of marital proceedings in the house of Dewan Bahadur T. Venkasami Row, Dewan of Ramnad. Our bigwigs are thus wantonly hurting the feelings of those who would set up before society a higher ideal of purity, setting a bad example for the youngsters and lowering themselves in the eyes of all people who have the morals of the people at heart.[76]

In a letter to the *Madurai Mail* published the same day, Baskara Setupati revealed his sensitivity to reform opinion in Madurai. His explanation of an incident involving devadasis was laboured:

Dear Mr Editor
I have been asked by a few friends about the entertainment given me by Mr Virasamy Naidu on the night of the day before yesterday and about a nautch there and I therefore consider it necessary to write to you all that happened in order to avoid unwarranted news spreading about.

Mr Virasamy Naidu invited me to a dinner at his new house and I accepted it on the condition that I was not to be entertained with a nautch. When I got to the house, I saw a nautch was going on in the hall and hence I stopped outside refusing to enter the room. Messrs [Robert?] Fischer and N. Sundram Iyer who were the only persons in the hall came out and shook hands with me, learning that I refused to go into the hall. I was next taken upstairs where I dined while the nautch was kept up in the hall below. After dinner, I was again asked to enter the hall, and on my refusing to do so, the nautch was stopped. I then went into the hall and was entertained by a fiddler and my own sangster. When I left the house, the nautch was again commenced. These statements of mine will be borne out by my host and Messrs Fischer and N. Sundaram Iyer.
        M. Baskara Setupati[77]

With this background in mind we can examine Baskara's actions with regard to the purification of ritual practice in his samastanam in 1894. He decided that year that he wanted to alter the ferocious aspect of Rajarajeswari, known as *ukkiram*. Her puja up to this time was the *vamamarga* puja, animal sacrifice, done to Durga. In order to change the character of the Goddess, so that she would appear calm and benevolent like Parvati or Sarasvati, it was necessary to redesign the ritual of worship. The Raja asked several Brahmins on the estate to undertake the task, but all refused, thinking that they did not have the personal power to ward off the potentially dreadful effects of the anger of the ferocious Goddess.[78] It was decided that only the Jagatguru of Sringeri was powerful enough to change the *pali* (sacrifice). Baskara approached the Jagatguru while he visited the zamindari in 1894 and the latter agreed to redesign the pali:

That night, special pujas and prayers were performed and it is stated that the deity appeared in the dream of His Highness [the Jagatguru] first in the form of

[76] *Ibid.*, 5 May 1894.
[77] *Ibid.*
[78] Kasinath Dorai, interview in Ramnad, 7 October 1978.

Mahakali and subsequently as Rajarajeswari and gave her approval to the change.[79]

The chakra was redrawn; the motion of the priest's hands as he offered camphor was redirected; meat was eliminated. The old nature of Rajarajeswari was not, however, completely obliterated. The new puja substances were selected and sacrificed in such a way that some of her ferocious nature could remain. The goddess became 'Durga Pacified'.[80] The Navaratri festival that year contained other innovations. The banishment of dancing girls from the proceedings was striking and duly noted by the reformist *Madurai Mail*.[81] Sent from temples throughout the zamindari, the dancers and their trains of musicians had played a highly visible role in the festivities in previous years in Sivagangai and Ramnad, accompanying the rajas in their processions and giving performances to palace guests. Baskara's move was a radical one in terms of its implications for the meaning of kingship in Maravar country. As explained earlier, association with devadasis was traditionally highly auspicious for south Indian kings and the women had occasionally served as *de facto* wives and concubines for the king/zamindars and chiefs. In common conceptualisations the king/zamindar was appropriately fine-figured, a fine-looking man with a prodigious procreative capacity. Supporting devadasi concubines and their royal bastard offspring was an element of the symbolic drama which Maravar kings, like their counterparts elsewhere in south India, enacted for their subjects.

Perhaps because Baskara excluded the dancers and their musicians from the festival, he felt constrained to provide a form of replacement in the vijaya dasami procession. This year, the paper reported, there was:

A coloured boat mounted on a carriage with two boatmen seated therein, a beautifully decorated chariot, the figure of two girls facing each other with their feet fixed on a pivot over a cart and making rapid circles.[82]

Boatmen in a boat was a motif found in Saiva processions at this time. The vijaya dasami procession had become a vehicle for the Raja's religious reforms. In the midst of reform Baskara, himself, appeared:

in his most comely dress on an elephant ... [and] drew no small attention of the public as he went on returning the salutations of the numerous persons who came near to pay their respects to him. [83]

Another Navaratri innovation was a public lecture by the Raja, on the seventh day of the festival, entitled 'The Necessity for Religious Studies'.[84] Baskara quoted sacred texts from a number of world religions and argued

---

[79] Raj Gopal Sharma, 'Dakshinamaya Sri Sringeri Jagadgurus', p. 185.
[80] Kasinath Dorai, interview in Ramnad, 7 October 1978.
[81] *Madurai Mail*, 13 October 1894.
[82] *Ibid.*
[83] *Ibid.*
[84] *Ibid.*

that every person could achieve 'salvation' in his own religion. In the course of the talk he discussed the rationale for 'idolatry' in Hinduism and the expansion of the Theosophical movement 'in the cause of the spiritual regeneration of India'. Speaking for nearly two hours, Baskara fulfilled the role of protector of the dharma of his subjects in a modern mode, infusing his performance with the aims and values of a movement for 'religious' reform which was part of public discourse. As he sought to justify the 'idolatrous' pageant he lavishly patronised, Baskara talked of the importance of *atma*, a concept from classical writing prominent in the westernised discourse on the nature of Hinduism. Intellectual products of the colonial encounter received front-stage display in this royal festival for the Goddess.

Other elements of the 1894 festival followed the patterns we discussed earlier. The newspaper covered the first-day durbar; dispelling devadasis did not imply a more modest role for the zamindar:

[T]he Raja Sethupathy was seated in the state chair and all his male relatives and the palace officials paid their due respects to him, in the manner prescribed to each class. The relatives all prostrated before the Sethupathy; so also did the non-Brahmin officials and servants, while the Brahmin officials wished him with a garland or a lime and the Shastries [wished him] with their coconut besmeared with saffron, and repeating some sloka or sacred word from the Shasters.[85]

According to custom, a priest sent from Rameswaram assisted in the 'usual' Brahminical pujas. On Sarasvati puja day, 'all the implements of war were carried through the streets in two long parallel rows with great pomp and splendour.'[86] Nor did Baskara depart with the arrow-shooting ceremony:

The procession, having reached the place of destination at about 5 P.M., the Sethupathy was taken thrice round the figure of Mount Meru drawn up for the occasion, and the priest of the Goddess and the Rajah went through the programme of aiming the arrows at the Vanni tree to represent the slaying of the demon 'Mahishadura', who had transformed himself into the shape of that tree.[87]

There is no mention of sheep being sacrificed on the maidan and it is likely that Baskara had ordered an end to that practice along the lines of his other reforms. In the next year the Raja declared war on animal sacrifice in general in his samastanam.

By 1893, Baskara shared the belief of other Saivite revivalists that Hindu priesthood had, in general, suffered a deterioration of morals and training. 'Those in this Zamindary', he wrote in his diary, 'are all of them utterly unworthy to pose as Gurus or poojakas [priests] to the deities in the temples.'[88] He was angered by the ignorance of the officiants at minor Siva

---

[85] *Ibid.*
[86] *Ibid.*
[87] *Ibid.*
[88] Baskara Setupati, Diary for 1893, entry on 18 November 1893.

temples on the estate. In 1895, Baskara struck out at worship at the temples of the smaller guardian dieties, delivering a lecture on sacrifice in which he opposed meat offerings. He argued that Kali, Karuppan and 'like deities' should become 'purely Saivite', i.e. purely vegetarian.[89] The zamindar passed orders on his estate that those priests who had been doing puja in temples of guardian dieties as well as at temples of vegetarian gods were to undergo purification rituals. They had polluted themselves by performing puja in temples properly classed as Kali temples. If the officiants did not obey the zamindar's orders, he argued, all the temples in Ramnad were better closed, than pujas be made by 'unholy men'.[90] He also ordered that all icons of Kali, Karuppan and similar kaval tevam should be removed. Opposition formed in response to these radical orders; however, the conflict did not develop substantially further because Baskara was forced to relinquish his office of zamindar as a result of his indebtedness.

Conclusion

Kathama Nachiar's use of a ducal crown in her coronation ritual was probably orientated towards official opinion in Madras Presidency, toward influence with the colonial regime. Thirty years later, however, a public sphere had emerged with groups who sought control over the state. The ritual innovations of Baskara Setupati in 1894 were orientated towards public opinion. The protection of royal authority in Ramnad Zamindari had become dependent on influence in this new type of political domain.

Kathama Nachiar accepted that she was a sort of 'aristocrat', subordinate, as it were, to the empress in London. Baskara made a more ambitious display, trying out new possibilities for kingly dharma at the same time as he made a radical departure from the cultural roots of kingship in Maravar country. The sakti of Baskara's Navaratri of 1894, as far as the symbolism specifically organised by the king was concerned, was the bloodless sakti of a new category in the consciousness of participants in the civic arena: a 'Hinduism' which was a distinct 'religion' and, as such, conceptually separated from monarchical ideology in, among other places, Maravar country.

The Navaratri had previously been a political ritual organised by men and women who would articulate the cosmic range of their personal rule, relating themselves to the multivalent meanings of the Goddess in the minds of their subjects, elite and common. Here sakti was a concept which resonated powerfully with associations of the necesary impurity of shedding blood in the maintenance of life, the blood of warriors in defence against enemies and the blood of women in processes of reproduction.[91]

---

[89] *Madurai Mail*, 14 December 1895.
[90] *Ibid.*
[91] Warfare as sacrifice is a theme of Alf Hiltebeitel, *The Ritual of Battle*, pp. 292, 296, 317, 326

Baskara altered the representative range of his lordship locally by barring the participation of devadasis in the Navaratri of 1894. Devadasis were emblems of sexuality in their resonance with themes of fertility and abundance. Like animal sacrifice, their sakti symbolism spoke in a direct, if less dramatic, way to the vital concerns of a wide range of royal subjects. Animal sacrifice to Durga and the participation of devadasis had been important elements in the conduct of Navaratri festivals as instruments of broad social communication. Baskara's ritual choices were orientated away from the daily dramas of his rural samastanam subjects and towards the spiritual preoccupations of the makers of public opinion.[92]

Baskara ordered the showing of arms and soldiers on vijaya dasami, the customary time for martial display during Navatratri; however, the meaning of this symbolism had changed. This show of arms was not a reference to an active military intent on the part of Baskara. It was a demonstration of Baskara's 'aristocratic' pedigree, a statement of his inherited right to his title as the scion of a wealthy family. Navaratri was a time when worshippers of the goddess traditionally brought their tools to be blessed, that they might be effective in their tasks. However, only a family tradition allowed Baskara Setupati the right to display arms. His association with the sacrifice of battle had thus been objectified. It was no longer a part of contemporary kingly praxis, but had become a historic experience, the memory of which Baskara would impress upon both local observers and readers of the elite, English-language press.

The Navaratri of 1894 was still an affair of sacred kingship, a dressing of the zamindari in dharmic clothes, but Baskara's innovations were a part of his participation in the cultural change among Indian elites which set religion off from concerns which were of a 'secular' nature. One force for change was the grounding of imperial legitimacy in the abstract rule of law. Baskara's support for Saiva Siddhanta and its bitter denunciation of the desecrated practice of ignoramuses was the result, however, of more than acquaintance with European learning or the ideological structure of imperial rule. Litigation between royal houses and institutions of worship in

and *passim*; the necessity of the pollution of violence in the maintenance of human society, including warfare, is the theme of Shulman, *The King and the Clown*, pp. 28–9, 36–7, 149, 278, 285 and *passim*.

[92] C. J. Fuller and Penny Logan, 'The Navaratri Festival in Madurai', *Bulletin of the School of Oriental and African Studies, University of London*, vol. 48, pt. 1, 1985, pp. 103–5 argues that the Navaratri in Madurai 'cannot celebrate sovereignty, or serve to link the community (or kingdom) to the world of the gods, like the annual goddess festivals or Navaratri elsewhere in India', because today there is no sacrifice to represent the destruction of the demon by the Goddess. She destroys him (in a bloody, polluting struggle) in her shrine without the usual sacrifice – the customary object of the patronage of a king or other community head. Fuller and Logan do not accept accounts which suggest the existence of sacrifice in the Vijayanagar and Nayak periods of the history of Madurai. Our data suggest that the ritual at Minakshi may have been redesigned, eliminating all reference to sacrifice – animal or vegetarian – as a result of revivalist and reform movements in nineteenth and twentieth century Madurai district.

Maravar country had undermined the relationship of complementarity between priests and rajas and set them up as competitors. This relationship of formal antagonism would seem to have made Baskara, as well as other zamindars in a similar position, receptive to an objectifying view of worship which contested the status and authority of contemporary priests. Baskara's son would become active in Justice Party non-Brahminism in the 1920s, urging for religious practice which was less dependent, in general, on Brahmins as priests.[93]

It is striking that, in the late nineteenth century at least, a zamindar interested in religious reform would support the Sanskritic-derived Hinduism of the Theosophical Society and (as we shall see) Swami Vivekananda, at the same time as he was a fervent advocate of Saiva Siddhanta, a movement associated with anti-Brahmin feeling. This evidence suggests that, on the level of political practice, the movement for religious reform had not become polarised. Baskara appears to have been caught up in enthusiasm for new approaches to worship in general, rather than the finer points of reform doctrine. Late nineteenth-century Saiva Siddhanta was anti-Brahmin but, again, on the level of political practice, Baskara made a distinction between degenerate Brahmins and those worthy of his patronage.

Anti-Brahminism, at least in its virulent forms, appears to have receded from the political agenda in Tamil Nadu at the end of the twentieth century. The current Chief Minister is a Brahmin. What she and other politicians seem to have retained from the early history of Tamil nationalism is the concept of the special nature of the ruler. The next chapter continues the examination of Baskara Setupati's blending of motifs from monarchical cosmology with the preoccupations of public opinion.

[93] Irschick, *Politics and Social Conflict*, pp. 248 and 252.

6

Raja Baskara Setupati and the emergence of a new political style

It was the accomplishment of Baskara Setupati, the last Raja of Ramnad in the nineteenth century, to seize the possibilities that existed in the medium of print to present a new image of royalty, one which could reach beyond the observers of palace ritual to the amorphous domain of public opinion, a new political resource in Madras Presidency. The publication of at least one diary, which he wrote before reaching his majority, indicates Baskara's interest in engaging the attention of the English-reading south Indian public.[1] The diary itself shows Baskara as an avid reader of newspapers and intensely sensitive to the intellectual and moral tastes of urban elites in Madras Presidency.

Baskara was educated by Britons under the supervision of the Court of Wards. He did not, however, fulfil the hopes of the Court of producing a financially responsible estate administrator. First in Baskara's concerns was his kingship, but the requirements of brilliant kingship on his terms turned out to be incompatible with financial responsibility. What felled Baskara was not debilitating litigation expenses, but his own political creativity, fitting the particularistic model of the king as vallal (showing largess) to universal political and social visions found in civic arenas in Madras Presidency.

He tried to play the king and succeeded in that in an abundant measure, though he was subject to the authority of the Madras government ... The Setupati became a byword for benevolence, charity and phenomenal generosity.[2]

Unlike Muthu Chella Tevar or his uncle Ponnusami Tevar, Baskara did not attempt to burrow, more or less secretly, into the governing apparatus of the state and influence the operation of its procedures. Perhaps because of his education and early exposure to social, intellectual and political institutions and discourses in Madras, Baskara seems to have decided that the future of the most important ruling house in Tamil country – Ramnad – lay in the mobilisation of respect for his person in the public sphere. In the late nineteenth century the power of public opinion had developed to the point

---

[1] Baskara Setupati, *My Trip to India's Utmost Isle* (Madras: G. W. Taylor, 1890). Another printed diary is reported, but was unavailable.
[2] S. Tiruvenkatachari, *Sethupatis of Ramnad*, pp. 76 and 78.

that colonial governments in India were forced to give grudging recognition to specific spokesmen and to negotiate over points of disagreement. Baskara used techniques usually directed towards the achievement of legitimacy in a local domain to develop a following among those who would transcend local issues of honour and rank to engage in a universalised competition for control over the imperial state. He found new uses for the royal tool of largess and tied his 'phenomenal generosity' to promotion of the great causes of public concern. He appears to have tried to bridge the gap between the metropolitan issues of social welfare, political progress and 'religious' reform on the one hand, and the presentation of a man of ruling status in terms of dharmic order and cosmic energy on the other.

In the sixth year of his reign, however, at the age of twenty-six, he was forced by the pressure of his creditors to relinquish financial control over the zamindari and to put the estate in trust for his minor son. One year later, a Nattukkottai Chettiar merchant-banker family picked up the lease to Ramnad Zamindari, which it was to hold for nineteen years. Completing his humiliation was the loss of the cherished Managership of Rameswaram.

In the meantime, in his diaries and in newspaper reportage, Baskara left a rare portrait of a political innovator, combining old and new symbols for the creation of a modern Tamil political style.

The education of a royal aristocrat

Baskara Setupati's father died when he was four years old. His younger brother, Dinakaraswami, was aged one. The Court of Wards, which administered Ramnad Zamindari during Baskara's minority, took responsibility for the education of both boys. Muthu Ramalingam's sons were not brought up in the zenana, under the supervision of their mother and male relatives, but were moved to Madras, where they received instruction from British tutors and attended Government schools. Baskara mixed with other zamindari sons at a school for minors at Landon's Gardens and went on to pass the First in Arts examination with a second class degree, the result of a weakness in mathematics.[3] Raja Ram Rao, the Agent of the Court of Wards preceding Baskara's majority, commented on the non-academic aspect of his charge's education:

[Baskara and his brother] have learnt to move in good society and are well behaved. Under the orders of the Court of Wards they made tours in Northern India and Ceylon with their European Tutor, visited many Native States and persons in authority and position and have benefited themselves much by learning the manners and customs obtaining there.[4]

---

[3]   Baskara Setupati, *My Trip*, p. 82. The diary begins at 5 January 1888, and ends at 24 February 1888. It covers a trip to Sri Lanka which Baskara took with one of his tutors, Mr Creighton, the latter's wife, and Dinakaraswami. Baskara was about twenty years of age at the time.

[4]   T. Raja Ram Rao, *Ramnad Manual*, pp. 505–6.

Plate 7   Royal emblem painted next to a major doorway in Ramnad Palace

The intent of the Court of Wards in this close attention to its charges is seen in the Agent's further prediction:

The [new] Zemindar with his present education and training and with the best example of the Court of Wards in the management of the Estate before him can hardly fail to keep his own Estate solvent and the tenants prosperous and to introduce further improvements tending to the prosperity of both.[5]

With intense involvement in western ideas and manners on the part of the Zamindar, financial insolvency, the curse of the zamindari system, might be avoided.

The Minor Zamindar of Ramnad was a willing student. He learned to play the piano and studied English translations of Latin masters.[6] For his pleasure, he read the novels of Sir Walter Scott, and had a particular affection for *Ivanhoe*. For the improvement of his mind, there was Mill on Natural Religion. And, when Baskara went to a book store on his trip to Sri Lanka, he bought Bacon's *Essays*, Scott's *Demonology and Witchcraft*, and Coleridge's *Table Talk*. Mindful of Dinakaraswami's development, he purchased *Waverly* and the *Arabian Nights*. At the age of nineteen, Baskara made wishful plans to visit England where, he explained, he might see *East Lynne* better acted.[7] His taste in sheet music ran to 'God Abide with Me' and 'Nearer My God to Thee', and one hobby was the collection of Jubilee memorabilia, including the *Life of Her Majesty the Queen* by one Valentine.

Young Baskara appeared to have learned his lessons very well and appeared to appreciate the reasons for the close monitoring of his development. He wrote one year before his majority:

If he considers and feels that his subjects are not created to be the instruments of his pleasure, that he is a responsible being, responsible for his own actions and for the weal or woe of his people, that it is the loyal duty of the aristocrats to aid the Paramount Power by their enlightened view, and if he will but look to his exchequer and do credit to the education he has received, administering his estates in an enlightened manner, he will have amply repaid the kind care of the Court of Wards and their agents who brought him to Madras, had him educated and have now set him up, let us hope, to be a model zamindar.[8]

The young Raja was not, however, a *tabula rasa* upon which the imperial government could write a code for the behaviour of the model zamindar. Baskara's diary from his minority shows that his transportation from Ramnad at a young age did not mean a completely successful separation from the practices, old and new, of his native place. As befitted a young man whose favourite novelist was Sir Walter Scott, he felt keenly the lost glory of the ruling dynasties. When referring to the Sub-Division Zamindar

---

[5] *Ibid.*, 506.
[6] Baskara Setupati, *My Trip*, pp. 4 and 36.
[7] *Ibid.*, p. 94.
[8] *Ibid.*, p. 69.

of Palavanattam, his cousin Pandit Thorai Tevar, he wrote of the 'Marava Chief of the West'. Another relative was the 'Marava Chief of the East'. The 'ancient warcry of the Maravas', he remembered was 'Ram, Ram, Rama Jayam'.[9] When Baskara invited his British tutor and his wife to Ramnad following the educational tour to Sri Lanka, he arranged a durbar:

> The entrance to the palace was lined by elephants, horses, swordsmen and spearsmen and a salute was fired as the party entered the Durbar Hall which was lined by all the ancient insignia of Ramnad.[10]

With a prophetic weakness for mathematics and a love of historical romance, the young man experienced conflicts regarding the 'enlightenment' of British rule versus the prestige of his dynasty. He wrote in English, but expressed fondness for the precolonial warrior past, citing his older male relations as military chiefs and imagining his realm in categories that were derived more from martial terminology than the *taluks* and sub-divisions of revenue administration. Baskara made his youthful aim clear, even before he was installed:

> Ramnad, Shevagunga, Vizeanagaram, and such other ancient states have been put on a par with quite modern zemindaries, and it remains in the future, as I have always declared, for them to rise from their fallen state aided by enlightened administration, and win back their name and fame from the Paramount Power.[11]

Baskara's vision of enlightened administration was not unaffected by his expensive education; however, as we shall see, he made a selection from what was offered to him and mixed it with elements of the strategies for royal reproduction developed by his nineteenth-century forebears. Baskara's was a mixed idiom.

According to a former tutor of a Sivagangai zamindar, Rengasamy Iyer, a zamindar did not need a facility in mathematics.[12] A zamindar was supposed to be trained in oral skills, and in mixing with people and presenting himself to others.[13] *Vijayam*, the presence of a powerful, authoritative person, was an important element in the definition of Tamil kingship. The presence of the king had to be a fine one; presenting himself appropriately, making vijayam, the king brought success to a function. The sight of the king's vijayam, his dignified magnificence, filled lesser men and women, theoretically, with enjoyment and satisfaction.[14] Ronald Inden,

---

[9] *Ibid.*, pp. 103 and 106.
[10] *Ibid.*, p. 112.
[11] *Ibid.*, p. 41.
[12] J. Rengasamy Iyer, interview in Sivagangai, 8 May 1975.
[13] *Ibid.*
[14] *Sri Setu Samstanam Virotikirutu Maha Navarattiri Mahotasvattil vittuvankal patiyapatilkal* (Maturai, 1912), p. 4. This introduction to a collection of poems from the 1912 Navaratri celebration in Ramnad palace has many suggestions of the joyous importance of the king's presence. My thanks to M. Anjali Anna Bai for her assistance in translation and her comments on the text.

following J. Gonda, writes of the importance of the sight of the king in early medieval sources:

The body or person of the king was the symbolic linchpin of the medieval Hindu kingdom, the cultural feature which gave a kingdom its unity and prosperity ... A view of the king, handsome, in good health, bathed, anointed, crowned, decked with ornaments, and seated in state was believed to be auspicious and to please ... the people. It ... brought about prosperity for the persons who had contact with the king in this way.[15]

Baskara would lend his presence to a range of formal contexts undreamed of by his predecessors. As the previous discussion of the Navaratri celebrations indicated, however, he maintained the desire that was both Tamil and royal of providing a gorgeous spectacle. Giving lectures and speaking splendidly in English or Tamil, announcing lavish donations to worthy causes, organising innovational festivals, Baskara was a rare public figure. In transcending the customary particularism of royal arenas, he presaged the glamorous gift-givers in electoral politics in twentieth-century Tamil Nadu.

Baskara as a gentleman Zamindar

'[He] bids fair to turn out a gentleman, if his company be good', Baskara wrote, commenting on the progress of his second brother-in-law.[16] In 1893, at the age of twenty-five, Baskara Setupati kept a diary in which he detailed his thoughts and impressions, as well as his activities. From this work, notions emerge of what it could mean to be a gentleman zamindar, a late nineteenth-century aristocrat. We also derive impressions of what Baskara's royal existence meant to him, in his urban context and, sometimes unhappily, back in Ramnad Zamindari. First we present the English-trained, gentleman zamindar, a figure of antastu status; in the following section, the dharmic Raja appears more strongly. This dichotomy is not meant to suggest that Baskara had two separate existences. He hints at difficulty in facing the tangled world of samastanam politics and quotes a Briton as saying, 'Who is there in Ramnad that can appreciate your talents? There are snakes and scorpions there.'[17] He appears, however, to have developed a unified sense of his political role within his spheres of action and influence, a

[15] Ronald Inden, 'Ritual, Authority and Cyclic Time in Hindu Kingship', in J. F. Richards (ed.), *Kingship and Authority in South Asia* (Madison: South Asian Studies, University of Wisconsin, 1978), p. 54.
[16] Baskara Setupati, 'Diary' (Inscribed in Lett's Colonial Rough Diary and Almanac for 1893), entry for 18 September 1893. I am grateful to Nicholas Dirks for making his transcription available to me and to S. Kamal and Mangalanatha Dorai for providing a Ramnad palace transcription of the 'Diary'. The diary is found in the Regional Committee for Survey of Historical Records, the Tamilnad Archives.
[17] *Ibid.*, undated entry.

sense which enabled him to integrate the varying influences in his life for the creation of a widely popular persona.

The young Zamindar of Ramnad felt very much at home in Madras, where he spent the first four months of 1893. He played tennis and took riding lessons. He rode a tricycle in the evenings, meeting and chatting on the cycle path with luminaries of the capital scene. Baskara met with other 'landed aristocrats', keeping careful score of the exchanges of social time, noting whose turn it was to receive or to be received.[18] He was himself received by British officials and shared some of their social life, remarking at one point on the 'fashionable' wedding of one Miss Firth: 'the elite of Madras European Society being present in the Cathedral including Lady Wenlock [the Governor's wife]'.

In keeping, however, with his notions of what it meant to be an exemplary zamindar, Baskara did not dribble his time frivolously away. Not of the 'old school', he attended various clubs and societies for social improvement. He presided at a meeting of the Total Abstainers and attended a session of the Society for the Prevention of Cruelty to Animals. He went to meetings of the Carnatic Masonic Lodge and fretted over the sincerity of its members. He listened intently and critically to lectures on both Hinduism and Christianity. Regarding a speaker on 'Regeneration' in Christianity, Baskara wrote: 'He is an enthusiast and very eloquent though bigoted.'[19] Taking part in the political life open to a zamindar in the capital city, he heard a debate on the caste system in the Progressive Union and joined discussions on fund-raising for a statue to William Miller, one of the most talented and beloved British teachers of nineteenth-century Madras. In the absence of the Raja of Venkatagiri, Baskara presided at a meeting of the Landholders' Association. He found the meeting disappointing, as the members did 'not take sufficient interest'.[20] The Zamindar was granted a private interview with the Governor at Government House and successfully lobbied for relief works in Ramnad. Among the prominent Indians he met with was V. Bhashyam Iyengar, a great figure of the Madras bar and an important participant in public life. Baskara observed the proceedings of the Legislative Council at Fort St George and remarked, 'I was struck with the independent spirit of Mr Sankaran Nair and the thoroughly yielding nature to Government of the Maharajah of Vizianagaram.'[21] (Sankaran Nair was an important figure in nationalist politics in the Presidency.)

For Baskara Setupati, his activities in Madras had the character of taking part in the great changes of the times: lectures and debates on caste, on female education and on abstinance, meeting with city worthies and observing the mild drama of the Legislative Council. The significance of

---

18 *Ibid.*, entries for 3 February 1893 and 27 January 1893.
19 *Ibid.*, entry for 3 March 1893.
20 *Ibid.*, entry for 21 February 1893.
21 *Ibid.*, entry for 12 April 1893.

these occasions to the zamindar is found in a comment about P. Sreenavasa Rao, Chief Judge of the City Civil Court, who called on him one morning:

He is a good old man and one of the old school set. Men of these days lose conservatism and very often become out and out Radicals. It is a blessing to have a few conservatives in our midst to now and then pull us back when we advance with a headlong speed.[22]

Baskara was a young man in something of a hurry. At the age of twenty-five, after listening to a Chettiar's daughter in Madras playing the piano 'beautifully', he bemoaned that he was not still a bachelor and confided, 'My life is one that has lost a large and fair number of opportunities.'[23] He was impatient with his fellow zamindars in the Landholders' Association, a place where he might have expected to find progressive peers.[24]

On the birthday of his son, he wished that the child would grow into both a 'loyal subject' of the Queen Empress and a 'patriotic citizen'.[25] Part of Baskara's 'radicalism' was his own patriotism, nuanced as it was by the particular values of elite political engagement in the nineteenth century. Discomfort with racial discrimination was one element. Soon after reaching Ramnad, coming back from Madras, he commented on the performance of a Malayali gymnast:

Had he been English, he would have advertised his arrival in the papers, brought a mammoth tent with him, arranged first, second, and third class charges for tickets, etc. – But the poor humble native, however equal he may be to his European brother, he is destined to be looked down on![26]

A major element of Baskara's patriotism was his leading role in the financing of projects for the improvement of Indian society. We have no record of Baskara's activities before 1893 in this sphere; however, following his trip to Madras, the record shows that the Raja gave generously of his presence and money to projects of (westernised) improvement.

A special focus of Baskara's patriotic action was, as discussed earlier, the reform of 'Hindu' practice. He also attempted to publicise the contribution which he believed Hinduism could make as a world religion. He financed Swami Vivekananda's successful trip to the Chicago Parliament of Religions in 1896[27] and lectured widely himself.

When Baskara returned to Madurai and to Ramnad, his engagement in the activities of public life continued. In Madurai, for example, he attended a party honouring Rama Subbier upon his election as a Madras Legislative

22 *Ibid.*, entry for 31 March 1895.
23 *Ibid.*, entry for 18 April 1893.
24 S. Srinvasa Raghavaiyangar, *Memorandum on the Progress*, p. 248.
25 Baskara Setupati, 'Diary', entry for 21 May 1893.
26 *Ibid.*, entry for 17 May 1893.
27 Swami Vivekananda, *Lectures from Colombo to Almora* (Calcutta: Advaita Ashrama 1963) shows that Ramnad was the Swami's first stop in India upon returning from the United States.

Council member for the Southern Municipalities. He presided at a meeting at the 'town club' in Madurai where a local lawyer lectured on 'foreign travels'. The latter, he complained, 'was a bad lecturer in every way and I am sorry I had to snub him quietly'.[28] The laying of the foundation stone for a new Masonic Lodge was the occasion for another visit to Madurai, where he attended a banquet followed by a dance that lasted until 3.30 in the morning. He frequently visited the home of an official British couple where there would be singing and playing on the piano:

Mr Eury's recitation of that well known poem – 'the dream of Eugene Aram' was simply imposing. The Rev. Mr Johnston read with feeling and expression a piece from *Pickwick Papers*. The glee was well sung.[29]

A significant difference existed between the Raja's role among the westernised elite of Madurai and that he took in Madras. In the Presidency capital, he presided occasionally at meetings but was mainly a keen observer. In Madurai, Baskara was a substantial force in public activities, becoming well-known for his extraordinary liberality. In 1893 he gave 1,000 rupees to the American Mission Women's hospital;[30] the following year he promised 6,000 to the American Mission towards a new hospital for men.[31] To the Union Club he earmarked 5,000 rupees for a Library Hall in his name; another 4,000 rupees were pledged for the new Masonic Lodge Pandyan.[32] He gave 40,000 to Madras Christian College for a hostel and started a High School.[33] He agreed to endow a Native College, to be amalgamated with his High School, with land yielding an income of 3,000 rupees. Among the conditions of the endowment were stipulations that a quarter of the grant would pay poor students' fees and that another quarter would pay the charges of the College, with a special subsidy for instruction in 'Hindu religion'.[34] The zamindar borrowed from his devastanam endowments for these projects. He promised that he would endow Madura College from a chattiram endowment at Rameswaram which was, he said, in excess of that chattiram's needs.[35]

Baskara followed up his appreciation of Sankaran Nair with a donation of 10,000 rupees to the Indian National Congress.[36] He shared in the emerging nationalist vision which saw India as a single country, affected by the successes and failures of its constituent parts. Upon the death of Kasinath Telang, a major figure in early nationalist politics from Bombay Presidency, the Raja wrote in his diary of his deep regret and lamented,

[28] Baskara Setupati, 'Diary', entry for 26 August, 1893.
[29] *Ibid.*, entry for 25 August 1893.
[30] *Ibid.*, entry for 26 August 1893.
[31] *Madurai Mail*, 25 August 1894.
[32] *Ibid.*, 19 May 1894.
[33] *Ibid.*, 9 March 1895.
[34] *Ibid.*, 5 May 1894.
[35] *Ibid.*
[36] *Ibid.*, 9 April 1895.

'What a loss to India! What a loss to learning!'[37] When he heard of the death of Sir T. Muthusamy Aiyer, the first Indian Justice of the Madras High Court, Baskara wired his agents in Benaras, Chidambaram and Rameswaram to make arrangements for ritual observances. He further directed that five Brahmins should bathe in the Ganges to obtain salvation for Muthusawmy Aiyer and that one cow should be left in the Annupuri temple in Benaras. He gave 3,000 of almost 6,000 rupees collected for a memorial for the Justice.[38]

Besides supporting clubs, schools and hospitals, Baskara led an active life of debates and speeches on religious topics. So familiar a speaker did he become that one of his journalistic detractors took well-placed aim:

Our titular Rajahs are taking to speechifying. Our own Rajah of Ramnad, as everybody knows, has a special knack that way, and if he could only be induced to act with a tithe of the wisdom that characterises his utterances, he and his magnificent estate would not be what they are.[39]

A more generous view came from a newspaper correspondent in Chidambaram, who noted that Baskara had quoted in a lecture there from well-known European and Indian writers and philosophers, giving 'ample proof of the Rajah's vast and varied learning of English, Tamil and Sanskrit'.[40] He went on to advise:

All the great cities in India should in my humble opinion earnestly invite the Raja to enlighten them on the hidden truths of the Hindu Philosophy and religious institutions.[41]

Other praise came for the high standards of discourse Baskara tried to maintain in Ramnad itself. In the evenings he and his cousin Pandit Thorai Tevar, a son of Ponnusami Tevar and a well-known patron of Tamil studies and poetry, met in the palace with local 'gentry, official and non-official'.[42] The assembled engaged themselves:

in a variety of pleasant amusements, highly edifying debates and discussions, calculated to promote the healthy development of the physical, intellectual and moral faculties of all concerned.[43]

Rural magnates during the early decades of the Indian National Congress have recently come into focus as manipulators of patron-client networks with minimal ideological orientation.[44] Baskara does not fit this description.

[37] Baskara Setupati, 'Diary', entry for 2 September 1893.
[38] *Madurai Mail*, 2 February 1895.
[39] *Ibid.*, 27 October 1894.
[40] *Ibid.*, 19 January 1895.
[41] *Ibid.*
[42] *Ibid.*, 20 January 1894.
[43] *Ibid.*
[44] David Washbrook, 'Country Politics: Madras 1880 to 1930', in *Modern Asian Studies*, vol. 7, pt. 3, 1973, pp. 501–8.

He was one of what would appear to have been a small group of 'radical' zamindari magnates who sympathised with Congress and with nationalist stirrings, even as they waited upon officials of the empire and looked to them for continued support of their estates and status. These two activities were not contradictory, as evidence points to the desires of zamindars to be more significant in Presidency politics towards the beginning of the twentieth century.

A cousin of Baskara, Sivasubramania Tevar, Zamindar of Singampatti, was Chairman of the Reception Committee of the Fourteenth Madras Provincial Conference in 1906. In a speech in this capacity he called for greater attention to the Native States (independent kingdoms within the empire) as presenting 'object lessons of efficient administration' and for the formation of Maravar and Kallar regiments in the Indian army.[45] Pointing to the Native States as examples of sound administrations led by Indians was not uncommon in the early years of the nationalist movement; however, the focus of discussion was usually on the non-royal *diwans* of rajas, rather than the leadership of the latter.[46] Presenting themselves as understanding the requirements of national improvement and pointing to the example of contemporary royal regimes was an indication of a developing public awareness among Presidency zamindars.

We saw earlier that young Baskara hoped to win back the 'name and fame' of the 'ancient' royal dynasties. One strategy he appears to have followed with respect to his own political interests was to become an enlightened ruler who could measure up to standards sets by imperial lords. We find the articulation of this desire, together with the theme of enlightened rule in the Native States, in a speech which the Raja gave in 1895.[47] He called lawyers, samastanam officials, learned Brahmins and his brother to a meeting in Ramnad town at which he announced the establishment of a school for untouchables. Baskara would lay out capital worth 15,000 rupees to supply the school with 100 rupees per month interest. Speaking in Tamil, he began by saying that he intended to do a dharmic act, though he realised that some people might call his act 'adarmam', against dharma. But Baskara was not looking to traditional models in this matter:

Her Most Gracious Majesty looks on all subjects equally and makes no distinction in governing them. So also I, being blessed with a large estate, feel it a duty to treat all the subjects of this Samastanam also alike and without distinction.[48]

---

[45] A. Vadivelu, *The Aristocracy of Southern India*, vol. II, p. 168.
[46] For example, in his collection of biographical sketches, *Representative Men of South India* (Madras: Price Current Press, 1896), 'G. P'. describes the careers of one raja of a Native State (Rama Varma of Travancore), one zamindar (Vizia Rama of Vizianagram) and four former dewans of Native States, all Brahmins (T. Madava Row, V. Ramiengar, C. V. Runga Charlu and A. Seshia Sastri), out of a total of twelve entries.
[47] *Madurai Mail*, 29 June 1895.
[48] *Ibid.*

He related that he had much compassion for the 'backward class of humanity' and realised that untouchables in past eras had 'boldly represented Hinduism in all branches'. The Raja of Ramnad would not do anything not sanctioned by the Sastras, but he would open his school, 'an idea which has been in my mind for two years'. There was, furthermore, precedent for his action in a Native State: 'I am only doing something on the lines pointed out by the late Maharaja of Mysore under whose administration such schools have been started in Mysore, Bangalore and other places.'[49] Baskara hastened to allay fears that he was initiating a social revolution and told his audience that they need not fear that there would no longer be anyone available to do the 'Pariah's' work because of his school: 'Only a few [would] succeed.'[50]

Baskara was spending money very quickly during the first five years of his titleship, not only on improving charities, but also on projects in the practice of worship, as we shall see below. He was in a frenzy of promises and support, and was not always able to follow through on his plans. By November, 1894, grumblings began to appear in the local press: while the Zamindar continued with promises of gifts, he had not completed earlier donations.[51] Nine months later a correspondent commented that the palace in Ramnad 'swarm[ed] with hopeful seekers of presents', warning that some came away disappointed.[52] The Headmaster of the National High School in Trichinopoly, having travelled to Ramnad to collect a promised 2,000 rupees for the construction of a school building, was among the disappointed.[53]

Baskara Setupati's lavish expenditure, requiring deeper and deeper dependency on Nattukottai Chettiar bankers, finally reached the point of threatening his position as a bright protegé of imperial rule. The Government in Madras had conferred the title of Maharaja on Baskara in 1891, two years after his installation as Zamindar. By early 1895, however, the Governor was rumoured to have lost patience and to be considering revoking the title. The Zamindar still had strong supporters in Madras and, as the local newspaper groused, 'The usual backstairs influence is at work in the Rajah's favour'.[54] Eventually Baskara involved himself to a position where even his powerful friends could not save him from financial ruin.

Baskara as a reforming raja

In Madras, even while he engaged in the Anglicised, gentlemanly pastimes of tennis and the appreciation of fine piano-playing, Baskara paid attention

[49] *Ibid.*
[50] *Ibid.*
[51] *Ibid.*, 3 November 1894.
[52] *Ibid.*, 17 August 1895.
[53] *Ibid.*
[54] *Ibid.*, 9 March 1895.

to the requirements of worship befitting his vision of a dharmic ruler. The entire night of Miss Firth's fashionable cathedral wedding he stayed awake and fasted for Sivaratri. Two days later he delivered a lecture on the Saivite saint, Gnanasambanda Swamikal, for the Young Men's Hindu Association; and that night he attended the 'Floating Festival' in a tank in the Triplicane section of Madras.[55] Baskara organised domestic worship, sometimes on a lavish scale, in his Madras home. For his father's 'Annual Ceremony Day', he spent 1,000 rupees.[56] The Zamindar took side trips from Madras to important temples, where he worshipped deities and met with temple authorities. At Conjeevaram, after watching a car festival and doing puja, he read aloud a poem he had composed for the major female deity of the town, Kamakshi, at her shrine.[57] Baskara was on royal tour of the major temples of Tamil country, inspecting administrations, commenting on the manner of conducting festivals and presenting himself in a grand style. On Rama Navami Day at Conjeevarm he distributed nearly 400 rupees to Brahmins who had recited the Vedas during a major procession. With his reforming attention to 'religious' practice, he noted, 'The repetition of the Vedas is very well conducted here and gives the [worshippers?] a solemn idea.' Influenced, it would seem, by the sober ambience of the religious observances of his British mentors, Baskara lamented the relative chaos and noisy confusion of Hindu festivals. A comment regarding a festival in Trivellor was one often repeated in his diary: 'It is a pity festivities are not more solemn and less crowded.'[58] Back in Ramnad, the Raja organized festivals and ceremonies with the aim of inducing more order into the proceedings. This urge to solemnity was a major aspect of Baskara's reforming mission in 'Hinduism'.

Baskara's trips were not simply displays of personal piety, though nothing suggests that he was not a sincere devotee. Important officials from the Collectorates, temple administrators and trustees, and local officials of the judiciary would meet him at his stops. At Tiruvellor he was received with high honours: 'The temple authorities accompanied as usual by musicians, etc., received me and conducted me to the residence prepared for me in a procession of paraphernalia.'[59] Returning south, he attended with remarkable energy and enthusiasm to the role of organising, conducting and observing the rituals and festivals of his people. Amid his goals of religious reform and of the maintenance of his duty of dharmic protection through attention to ritual, Baskara emphasised the royal spectacle.

Rudyard Kipling was cited recently as observing that 'Providence' created the Maharajas of India to provide the world with 'a spectacle, a

---

[55] Baskara Setupati, 'Diary', entry for 16 February 1893.
[56] *Ibid.*, entries for 11 March and 1 April in 1893.
[57] *Ibid.*, entry for 24 March 1893.
[58] *Ibid.*, entry for 28 February 1893, is an example.
[59] *Ibid.*, entry for 1 March 1893.

dazzling vision of marble palaces, tigers, elephants and jewels'.[60] In Tamil culture, not only the vijayam of the king – the presence of his own auspicious and splendid form – but the wonderful sight (*kāṭci*) which his wealth and largess supported was a component of his royal responsibility. Over and over again, in the palace propaganda of Baskara's son's reign, the happiness, the speechless enjoyment and pleasure which a fine display gave the festival crowd were emphasised.[61] A procession (*pavani*) was described as a *pavanikāṭci*, a sight so stupendous as to be put on the scale of a world event and one not to be missed.[62] The durbar which followed the pavani-katci was called the *tarparkāṭci*. In the durbar, the *taricanam* (sight) of the Setupati was likened to the sight of Siva himself. Tamils use a special word to suggest the special nature of the king's sitting in durbar: *vīrriru*, to sit majestically. The propagandist said that the sight of the deities in the royal procession on vijaya dasami gave *manam paravacam* or 'ecstacy and transports of joy' to the minds of those who witnessed the event.[63]

Baskara Setupati was conscious of the royal spectacle as having a special significance; however, one finds little reverberation of cosmic meaning in unofficial reports or his diary. A local story about the raja is typical.[64] Baskara was taking a tour of his domain, travelling in a palanquin. During the tour one day he exchanged clothes with a palanquin bearer, giving him his jewels to wear, while he himself walked along dressed as a palanquin bearer. In the streets of the villages through which the entourage passed, villagers continued to raise their folded palms in obeisance to the figure in the palanquin, moving the zamindar to whisper in the ears of his bearers that when people judged a raja, his jewellery and dress weighed the most in their estimation. An 1893 entry suggests further his objectification of his position. At Rameswaram, where he had joined in celebrating a car festival, he remarked, 'On the car reaching its usual place, I amused myself by throwing plantains and sweetmeats in the midst of the crowd'[65] (throwing food and money to a crowd was a traditional royal practice.)[66] Shortly later, Baskara took part in another procession: 'The procession at night was most grand – the God on an elephant and the Goddess on the golden palanquin. I appeared in full Oriental Costume'.[67] He was, however, touched by the presentation of a small girl:

[60] Larry Collins and Dominique Lapierre, *Freedom at Midnight* (New York, 1975), p. 168.
[61] *Sri Setu Samstanam*, (Madurai, 1910), p. 2 and *Sri Setu Samstanam* (1912), p. 4; and *Sri Setu Samstanam* (1913), p. 4. These are a collection of pamphlets containing songs and poems composed for the Navaratri celebrations at Ramnad during 1910, 1912 and 1913. The introductions to the poems describe the events of the festival.
[62] *Sri Setu Samstanam* (1910), p. 2.
[63] *Ibid.*, pp. 3–4.
[64] K. Seshadri, 'The Setupatis of Ramnad', unpublished doctoral dissertation, Madurai College, Madurai, 1976, p. 173.
[65] Baskara Setupati, 'Diary', entry for 12 August 1893.
[66] Inden, 'Ritual, Authority and Cyclic Time', p. 55.
[67] Baskara Setupati, 'Diary', entry for 16 August 1893.

A small Ahambadiya girl about nine years old presented me with a lime and when asked why she did so pertinently remarked, I hear you are the Rajah of our Caste ... and therefore I present this to you.[68]

The young zamindar revelled in the orderly procession, the well-ornamented idol, the dazzling vehicles of the gods. He wrote of a procession at Rameswaram:

I rode by the side of the procession and it was a warm walk to be sure. The Thapas seva was grand and solemn. It was a pity I had no camera to photograph the splendid view of the site, the vahanams, the orderly crowd, and the sepoys ... The Goddess's procession at night was very grand.[69]

Innovational in his practice and support of worship, Baskara did not break with the precedents of zamindari rule in Maravar country and establish an effective revenue-collecting administration. Ramnad Zamindari in the 1890s experienced chaotic management which undid the work of sixteen years of attempts by the Court of Wards to establish regular and strict collections. The Court had not succeeded in repressing the heterogeneous, segmented character of the zamindari collection procedures. In a relatively decentralised system of this nature, the head was obliged to make a show of his specialness and to establish continually that he was the first among domain lords. Part of the strategy to cajole subordinate land-controllers into honouring him and accepting his authority lay in a dazzling display of material accumulation which marked the ruler as one apart. The right to organise such a display was *paramparai urimai*, the dynastic right. At the same time, the king/zamindar theoretically shared with the people of his samastanam, in acts of dress and feats of festival organisation, the fruits of his power to mobilise resources.

In January, 1893, Baskara made up a list of his life ambitions. First and in some detail came his concern for the renovation of the palace temple of Rajarajeswari.[70] Second, Baskara wished to learn and practice sakti tantra, the practice associated with the worship of Devi. Low on this list of thirty-three items, at item twenty-two, came redemption of the estate from debt. Certainly in 1893, the Raja's family goddess was, when he was on the estate, a major focus of his attention. Upon his return from Madras, he went straight to her temple in the palace and a week later he presented her with a jewelled cup and a gold sari which he had purchased in Madras. From June until the last week of October, Baskara was involved with details of the renovation of the palace temple and of the 'great event', the kumbabishekam or purification ceremony of the temple.[71]

The daily ritual of the royal family evolved importantly around the worship of Rajarajeswari. Her ornamentation was a concern of the Raja,

[68] *Ibid.*, entry for 23 May 1893.
[69] *Ibid.*, entry for 14 August 1893.
[70] *Ibid.*, entry for 13 January 1893.
[71] *Ibid.*, entry for 16 June 1893.

who noted how she was decorated on special occasions – like Sarasvati (goddess of skills and learning), like a 'Rajah' in honour of the marriage of the Prince of Wales, like Nataraj (dancing Siva) – 'Sree Rajarajeswari was decorated like Nataraja and my most respected mother visited the temple at 4 pm to see this alangaram [decoration].'[72] Baskara studied the Devi Mahatmya Rahasya in his pursuit of sakti tantra. He believed that the good that came to him, the birth of a son, success in an important lawsuit, was due to the grace of Rajarajeswari: 'It is all Her Grace. By that Divine Grace we live and by that Divine Grace we move. All is in Her Power. She in Her Wisdom has so far blessed all proceedings with success.'[73] The proceedings in this case were the kumbabishekam for the renovated temple – for which occasion Baskara had caused to be made a great gilt lion vehicle at a cost of nearly 8,000 rupees.[74] His pleasure over the events of the ceremony, which he described in his diary in red ink, is clear:

This is a red letter day in the annals of Ramnad. The vimanam [dome] of Sree Rajarajeswari's Temple was partially covered with gold plate and great Kumbabhi-sekam was performed early in the morning. All my blood relations were present besides other relatives and friends. The number of people who came to worship was very large. At 9 p.m. the goddess started in procession through the principle streets which had never had the immense fortune of having the Goddess's procession. The whole route was decorated and all the residents naturally decorated their houses and offered poojah to the Great Goddess [Devi] who for the first time passed through their streets in this form. The procession itself was unique and most grand.[75]

While some of Baskara's patronage of worship was traditional – for example, his purchase of a new temple car for the Minakshi-Sundaresvarar temple in Madurai in 1894[76] – in keeping with his attraction to the Saiva Siddhantha reform movement, other activities were innovational.

Baskara's diary from his twentieth year shows the early influence of Christian and Christian-influenced criticism of low-status religious prac-tices. He wrote at some length about the 'devil-dancers' of Sri Lanka:

Those who worship devils hold of course that the chief of the devils, whoever that being may be, is really the God of the Universe. This will look very wicked to a person with any idea of an all-holy God, but it must be remembered that among the majority of devil-worshippers there is no idea whatever of purity or sacredness ... [B]lood-thirsty revenge and cruelty are encouraged between man and man who forget that they are all the children of one kind Father who brooks no discord in His family, and that they are all responsible for their actions in this temporary life on the records of which depend their happiness or misery in the life to come.[77]

---

[72] *Ibid.*, entry for 27 June 1893.
[73] *Ibid.*, entry for 1 November 1893.
[74] *Madurai Mail*, 13 October 1894.
[75] Baskara Setupati, 'Diary', entry for 29 October 1893.
[76] *Madurai Mail*, 28 April 1894.
[77] Baskara Setupati, *My Trip*, pp. 11 and 14.

Baskara described as 'devil-god', a female deity with some of the same characteristics of the terrifying goddess worshipped by the majority of Maravar clansmen and, for that matter, the majority of the people on his estate:

Kola Sannyaka ... is depicted as a hideous monster with two men hanging from her mouth, one man hanging from her breast and two men trampled under her feet.[78]

The Zamindar issued directives to zamindari priests to reform their practices, supported the temples of men he believed competent and oversaw changes in arrangements for worship. Much of his aim appears to have been to make available to ordinary people a type of worship which reformers considered pure and undiluted by low-status practice. The reforms show traces of a universalistic social ethic, not unrelated, perhaps, to that expressed in the establishment of a school for untouchable children. As we saw above, he brought Rajarajeswari out in an innovational tour of the samastanam capital following her kumbabishekam; usually she came out once a year on vijaya dasami. At Rameswaram, it appears that Baskara arranged that idols from the temple be brought to the site of the pilgrims' purifying ocean bath during a festival, so that they would not have to walk eighteen miles back for *darshanan* (a view) of the gods:

People say that such an arrangement was never made during their life-time and that they never heard of such a thing being done. The Rajah of Ramnad and his cousin ... who were here for the mela had occasion to see and feel for the thousands of pilgrims that congregated here. This may be one of the sacred reforms that the Rajah is intending to effect in the Devastanam affairs.[79]

Besides the Navaratri innovations discussed in the previous chapter, Baskara initiated new festivals on the zamindari; in line with his interest in Saiva Siddhanta these were for the most part guru pujas, the worship of a great Saiva saint on his death day. One occurred in June 1893, the guru puja of Gnanasambanda Swamikal, the saint who was the topic of Baskara's lecture to the Young Men's Hindu Association earlier in Madras. The Raja ordered a full day of processions and worship in Ramnad town and played an active part in the observances. He rose before daylight and joined priests in the conduct of rituals on the banks of a sacred tank. After the worship, he rode in a procession through the town. He fasted until the 'celestial unification with God took place', around midday, and spent the afternoon reading in the *puranas*.[80] In the evening he observed a temple procession honouring the guru which ended after midnight. Later that month, for the first time in Ramnad, the guru puja of Manikkavacakar took place with a

[78] *Ibid.*, p. 14.
[79] *Madurai Mail*, 24 February 1894.
[80] Baskara Setupati, 'Diary', entry for 5 June 1893.

procession at the major Siva temple in the capital town, and with a 'solemn ceremony ... impressively performed'.[81]

An 1895 festival for Manikkavacakar indicates the attention that Baskara gave to his reform effort and the money with which he parted in its service. The festival was conducted at a zamindari temple – for the first time – according to procedures set down by the head of the famous Saiva math at Tiruvaduthorai.[82] To aid in a dramatic representation of a well-known incident from the life of the saint, the zamindar ordered oxen and horses from his own stable to be brought to the village. His own 'attenders' carried the idol of the local Siva deity in procession. Baskara joined Saivite singers and musicians, sent from the math at his request, in singing passages from the poetic canon of the Saiva saints. He presented the Siva idol with a belt set with diamonds, emeralds and rubies worth nearly 50,000 rupees and gave other presents worth thousands of rupees.[83]

With his characteristic enthusiasm and in keeping with his vision of raja-dharma, Baskara performed the actions of largess to individuals, as well as to establishments of worship. As already noted, the palace at Ramnad 'swarmed' with seekers after the zamindar's generosity. After his mother's death, faced with the insult to her memory which Rameswaram priests had delivered, Baskara engaged in extraordinary measures, periodically feeding thousands of poor people, distributing clothing and paying for medical aid. The *Madurai Mail* noted:

Ever since [the Senior Ranee died], he has been with unflinching liberality giving away presents as Danams [religious charity] and feeding all people freely and well. The other day a tom-tom was beaten all round the town calling on all people who may be desirous to go to Rameswaram, Benaras and other Holy Hindu places of pilgrimage and all people of the Mussalman, Christian and other communities who may be desirous of going to their holy places ... to go into his presence and there to take presents which he will be pleased to award. People are going everyday in throngs ... [though some return empty-handed].[84]

The Raja's liberality extended in a direction which had plagued other zamindars of the Madras Presidency since the onset of the Permanent Settlement, namely, towards palace 'hangers-on'. Early nineteenth-century lists of royal dependants suggest that, before the establishment of British sovereignty, Maravar kings had supported people in their palace establishments who served generalised functions. A continuous line of British administrators and, later, of more conscientious zamindars, bemoaned this Presidency-wide phenomenon, seeing these palace clients as a drain on resources and a degenerate influence in zamindari affairs. Collector Lushington, who made the first settlements in Sivagangai and Ramnad, had

---

[81] *Ibid.*, entry for 19 June 1893.
[82] *Madurai Mail*, 13 July 1895.
[83] *Ibid.*
[84] *Madurai Mail*, 1 June 1895. See also. *Ibid.*, 8 June 1895.

found the palace associates of the first Zamindar of Sivagangai to be even less qualified for administering an estate under zamindari tenure than the Zamindar, whom he had judged 'unacquainted with the habits of business'.[85] The Zamindar's refusal to dismiss these dependants – 'ill-qualified by their education and acquirements for the arduous trust of governing a country ...' – had seemed sufficient reason, in Lushington's mind, for the Government to take over the administration of the estate.[86]

Approximately one hundred years later, the Zamindar of Vadagarai sent a letter of advice to another, younger zamindar, listing the four main vices which he believed to result in the 'wreck' of the reputation of the ancient ruling houses and of the 'stability and integrity' of their estates.[87] First on the list, which was later published as a pamphlet and sent on wider circulation, was the 'admission of bad characters as our menial servants and dependants round our person'.[88]

Baskara Setupati was unable to depart from the royal responsibility of showing generosity towards people maintained as palace dependants, characterised in the *Madurai Mail* as 'useless hangers-on who [did] nothing but fleece him'.[89] The practice of supporting men who were ostensibly in one's personal service was a requirement in the representation of oneself as a man of wealth and influence. In this regard the zamindar was, to a certain extent, trapped by his own desire for wide recognition. He did not dare go against certain kinds of conventional expectations. Baskara resented these drones and complained bitterly into his diary that while he was lavish with presents, his largess resulted neither in his clients' loyalty nor in their gratitude: '[F]ew are grateful. How few appreciate the gifts ! ... I have within the last four years [spent] forty lakhs and though I have thus been foolishly extravagant, the leeches that drunk my blood are not a whit more grateful to me'.[90]

Baskara's comments concerning two musicians who were in the pay of the samastanam provide an example of his discontent with this obligation of lordship:

They are not by any means celebrated singers as they lack the first condition of good singing – a good voice. The father is out-spoken ... Both are highly avaracious and a discontented lot altogether. They have a bad habit of speaking ill of others in their absence and praising those whom they speak ill of in their presence. They are not to be trusted. But they dance attendance on me constantly and thus curry favour with me.[91]

85 High Court of Madras. Documents in Appeal Suit No. 21 of 1887. Exhibit Z, Letter to William Petrie, President and Member of the Special Commission, from S. K. Lushington, Collector, p. 68.
86 *Ibid.*, p. 69.
87 A. Vadivelu, *The Aristocrats*, vol. II, p. 242.
88 *Ibid.*
89 *Madurai Mail*, 6 January 1894.
90 Baskara Setupati, 'Diary', entry for 27 June 1893.
91 *Ibid.*, entry for 12 December 1893.

Over the next two years Baskara attempted to find loyal servants and supporters among the Ahambadiyas, a caste lower in political status than the Maravars which had traditionally provided servants in Maravar palaces. He favoured several Ahambadiyas with extraordinary presents, bringing them into prominence in his staff. One Arumugam Servai received 15,000 rupees in cash, 6,000 rupees for the construction of a house, jewels and two villages on kaul lease.[92] Arumugam was in charge of the zamindar's food and drink and his confidential papers during a period of heavy litigation, when Baskara had suspected 'foul play'.[93] Arumugam had been a poor man when he first came into palace service.

During his years as zamindar Baskara carried on the struggle of his predecessors to retrieve the management of Rameswaram temple. Like zamindars and zamindarnis before him, he believed intensely in the significance of this dynastic privilege for the maintenance of its superior status. The third item in his list of life ambitions was to regain the Managership of the temple administration back from the Pandarams who, he believed, had usurped control in the late eighteenth century. Upon hearing that he had been appointed Manager, in May 1893, Baskara wrote:

This intimation has been very acceptable to me and to all who care for the prestige of Ramnad. Everything connected with Ramnad is closely interwoven with Rameswaram. It was really the misfortune of the Setupathies to have remained for the past century and a half mere *Sethupathies* [his emphasis] in name only. May the great Ramanatha [Siva] so grant that ere long the Sethupathies may become the hereditary trustees ... of this Devasthanam and may it be granted to me to have that privilege accorded in my days.[94]

The young zamindar had to struggle fiercely with various factions of the temple administration to maintain and strengthen his connection. He brought to the fray his general contempt for temple administration in south India. Upon taking temporary charge of the managership, he went to Rameswaram and made an inspection of temple affairs. There he found, 'a good many irregularities in the temple ... too numerous to allow specification', and added to his observations, 'I don't think much can be made of these fellows as they are all an uncouth, selfish, weak and foolish set of men, and most of them are of low birth.'[95] In his reform fashion, he remarked: 'the Pandarams of these days are a set of iniquitous men and trust property in their hands suffers considerably.'[96] A 'demi-official' report to the Madurai Collector followed.

The Ramnad diary entries of the young raja show that his metropolitan tastes and interests did not interfere with an intense preoccupation with the

---

[92] *Madurai Mail*, 22 September 1894.
[93] *Ibid.*
[94] Baskara Setupati, 'Diary', entry for 20 May 1893.
[95] Baskara Setupati, 'Diary', entries for 5 and 6 August 1893.
[96] *Ibid.*, entry for 9 August 1893.

royal status and privileges he had inherited. The Saiva Siddhanta reform movement, with its standardisation of practices of worship, represented, perhaps, the universalisation of worship in the context of modern structures of a centralised state.[97] Universalisation does not necessarily imply democratisation, of course. Baskara's almost passionate attachment to the worship of the tutelary deity of his royal house synchronised with his desire to introduce religious reforms on his estate. The reforms were not conceived of as democratic in nature. The aim was to introduce high-status, elite, somewhat westernised practices of worship. Baskara's diary entries illustrate how the processes of ideological universalisation which ushered in Tamil nationalism and the non-Brahmin movement encompassed ideas of status and dominance which would compete with egalitarian values and notions of public service in the twentieth century.

As noticed earlier, through his extravagance the hapless zamindar had given his opposition at Rameswaram temple dangerous ammunition to fire against his control, and over the next few years their own charges rang out in newspapers and in the law courts of imperial administration. His 'imprudence and extravagance' were cited:[98] he had gone deeply into debt and, worse, he had given devastanam and chattiram villages on lease for long periods to cover these debts. Even under his own administration, it was alleged, irregularities continued in temple management. Using material alleged in other cases against the Raja, temple officials accused him of bribery and of keeping the police in his pay. The attackers from the temple accused the reforming zamindar of being 'a party to filthy and obscene doings and [forfeiting] ... all respect and deference even from his own servants'.[99] Stanikars of the temple presented a petition to the Madurai district Judge charging Baskara's unfitness on several grounds, focusing on the financial administration of his zamindari as 'not ... altogether a success'.[100]

In the third year of his proud managership of the temple, Baskara was ruined. Fifteen gun salutes and torchlit parades of zamindari sepoys were inadequate protection of legal status, as the Raja proved vulnerable to the pitfalls of imprudent estate management. Baskara eventually resigned his Managership in 1901 and the major creditor of the royal family, the Nattukkottai Chettiar Zamindar of Devakkottai, took the office.

The finances of the realm

Late in 1895, the *Madurai Mail* reported the continuation of evenings of elevated discourse in the Ramnad royal palace. Baskara Setupati would

[97] David Gilmartin (personal communication).
[98] *Madurai Mail*, 4 August 1894.
[99] *Ibid.*
[100] *Ibid.*

lecture or ask his pandits to lecture on 'important questions of the day'.[101]
Occasionally when the Raja lectured:

> [O]ne peculiar feature may be noticed; the Raja shows himself to feel regretted and
> to be touched on account of some acts of his own which he would not have
> committed if proper thought had been bestowed previously upon the subject ...
> [T]he results are gloomy and unhappy. In whom or in what does the fault consist is a
> question which troubles and vexes the sympathetic mind of a few interested in the
> affairs of the Raja and of the Samastanam.[102]

Gloom and unhappiness had resulted from Baskara's wide-ranging liberality: he suffered the loss of control over Ramnad Zamindari. The previous
July Baskara had signed all financial responsibility to a dewan trustee who
was in the process of negotiating a loan from creditors in Britain.[103] These
were desperate and necessary manœuvres to save the estate from being
carved up by its various local creditors. The estate had been put in trust for
the Zamindar's son, and the Zamindar and his relations paid an allowance.
A. L. A. R. Ramasami Chettiar and his partners, major creditors of
Baskara, took the estate on lease, in 1896, and kept it for the next nineteen
years.[104] In Ramnad in the 1880s and 1890s, A. L. A. R. Ramasami Chettiar
and his rival L. A. R. R. N. Ramanadhan Chettiar became intimately
involved in the personal and political affairs of the royal family. Baskara's
public displays had taken their unstable rooting in negotiations and
relations with bankers and agents.

The Raja's initial involvement with Ramasami Chettiar was a product of
his minority. The Senior Rani, his mother, had refused to accept the
confines of the family allowance from the Court of Wards and borrowed
heavily from the banker. The latter, taking the advantage at hand, made
himself useful to the family in a variety of ways, including helping the Rani
to outwit the government on the issue of Baskara's marriage. With the
financial help of Ramasami, she was able to carry though two marriages.[105]
The Rani then borrowed approximately 47,000 rupees for her son's Rendition ceremony – when he reached his majority and received the estate from
the Government – and for his installation ceremonies. Again, the banker
performed services for the family in the celebration arrangements. Other
loans went for Navaratri celebrations, household expenses, jewels and
furniture, and for the young Raja's obligatory tours within his samastanam
previous to his installation. By the time Baskara assumed financial control
of Ramnad, the debts had accumulated to 350,000 rupees[106] (the total

[101] *Ibid.*, 21 September 1895.
[102] *Ibid.*
[103] *Indian Law Reports: Madras Series*, vol. 44, 1921, January–December, p. 278.
[104] K. Seshadri, 'The Setupatis', p. 162.
[105] P. V. N. Iyengar, 'Ramnad Supplement', unpublished manuscript, p. 5. I am grateful to the
Ramnad Samastanam staff for making this manuscript available to me. K. Seshadri
identified the author of the manuscript.
[106] *Ibid.*, pp. 21–2.

government demand for a year was approximately 317,000 rupees). Agents of the Court of Wards, after paying off the debts accumulated by Raja Muthu Ramalingam Setupati and by Ponnusami Tevar, had, with careful management, produced a 351,261 rupee balance with which the new Zamindar could start his rule. Among his first acts, however, Baskara repaid 200,000 rupees to Ramasami and issued a pronote for another 150,000 rupees in his favour: 'The Rajah also began to have cash dealings on a large scale with Mr Chettiyar.'[107]

Ramasami Chettiar had carefully prepared the ground during Baskara's minority to move into the position of chief creditor to the Zamindar. The fact that his family had been Ramnad creditors for two previous generations placed him in an advantageous position for his efforts. Not only did the banker give the Senior Rani advances of money and other articles which she required, but he played a leading role in the marriage and Rendition arrangements. Further, 'he is said to have employed all means to secure the goodwill of the Rajah in furtherance of objects of his [desire?].'[108] Ramasami's various 'helps and services' to young Baskara reached fruition in an intimate dependency and friendship which lasted throughout their lives.[109] Occasionally periods of hostility separated them; however, more common was amiability as Baskara socialised with Ramasami, consulted with him regarding legal and administrative matters, borrowed money from him and gave him zamindari leases. Three days after the rendition, Baskara gave the banker two *mahanams* (divisions of land) for a total of twenty-four villages on a fifty-year lease with a light revenue demand. Four years and thousands of rupees of debt later, the term lease was made into a permanent one.[110]

By August 1890, within his first year of title, Baskara had borrowed 486,000 rupees from Ramasami. He had purchased two houses in Madura and a house in Ramnad for a total of 67,000 rupees. He had spent over 100,000 of rupees on vessels, jewels and vehicles for Rajarajeswari, and had acquired jewels for himself and his wives worth over 300,000 rupees.[111] To discharge these and other debts, the Zamindar took a loan of 750,000 rupees in 1891 from the Commercial and Land Mortgage Bank of Madurai at 8 per cent a year on the security of his estate. Ramasami Chettiar received 200,000 rupees from that loan and 18,000 rupees were set apart for the Navaratri festival that year.[112] The Raja used the remainder to finance his philanthropic projects as well as acts of largess to individuals. One of these acts was 13,000 rupees for the wedding expenses of a daughter of Venkataswami Nayudu, a local man of influence who was later to become his Agent.[113]

---

[107] *Ibid.*, p. 10.
[108] *Ibid.*, p. 11.
[109] *Ibid.*
[110] *Ibid.*, pp. 11–12.
[111] *Ibid.*, pp. 22–3.
[112] *Ibid.*, p. 23.
[113] *Ibid.*, pp. 23–4.

Upon his Rendition in 1889, Baskara presented the former Manager of
Ramnad under the Court of Wards, T. Raja Ram Rao, with a purse of
100,000 rupees, a fifty-year kaul for a village and made him his Estate
Manager. Shortly thereafter, however, he dismissed the Diwan (as the
Manager was now known) and became his own Manager.[114] Until June,
1893, there was no autonomous diwan on the samastanam; the Zamindar
made all the major financial decisions. He eventually promoted the Head
Clerk of the revenue establishment, Kesavaswami Ayyar, to *Simai Peshkar*,
a title suggesting major accounting discretion; Kesavaswami, however, held
only routine responsibility and carried out Baskara's orders. With the
assistance of Venkataswami Nayudu, Baskara negotiated another major
transaction in 1891, leasing most of Hanmananthagudy taluk to
S. R. M. M. R. M. Muthia Chettiar and V. A. R. V. Arunachalam Chettiar
for 800,000 rupees. Baskara immediately gave 680,000 rupees of the sum to
the Commercial and Land Bank, 99,000 rupees to Ramasami Chettiar and
kept 20,000 rupees for himself.[115] He ceased to have important dealings
with banking institutions like the Commercial and Land Bank, after this
last transaction, but secured his loans by leasing zamindari villages in
batches to individuals. By July, 1895, the month of the formation of the
Zamindari Trust, Baskara had given 306 villages on permanent leases and
294 term leases.[116] The number of *amani* villages (those paying revenue
directly to the estate revenue establishment) had gradually decreased from
1,011 villages to 439 villages. Ramasami Chettiar was the major recipient of
these villages leases. In 1892 alone the banker received 255 villages.[117] At
one time he had possession of over 800 samastanam amani and devastanam
villages, while relatives of the banker held approximately another 80
villages.[118] In June, 1893, Baskara appointed retired Government official,
T. Venkataswami Rao, Diwan and the rate of leasing diminished.

In singling out one Chettiar as the preponderant influence in his financial
affairs, Baskara made himself vulnerable to the jealousy which other
powerful and wealthy men felt for the banker. L. A. R. R. M. Ramanadhan Chettiar so resented Ramasami's influence at the Ramnad court
that he attempted to destroy the samastanam as a single unit.[119] Within ten
weeks of the Rendition, Ramanadhan induced Dinakaraswami, Baskara's
eighteen-year-old brother, to file a suit against the Raja claiming half of the
zamindari assets as his inheritance.

The lawyers of Dinakaraswami and Ramanadhan argued unsuccessfully,

[114] *Ibid.*, p. 19.
[115] *Ibid.*, p. 34.
[116] *Ibid.*, pp. 35–6. P. V. N. Iyengar has difficulty in deciding on the correct figures. These
figures are in his range. He does not use the word 'kaul' in describing these leases; however,
this leasing appears to follow the same pattern as that described in Chapter 3.
[117] *Ibid.*, p. 41. Others may have been leased, p. 43.
[118] *Ibid.*, p. 44.
[119] *Ibid.*, p. 12.

first in the District Court and then at the High Court in Madras, that the brothers were members of an 'undivided Hindu family subject to the law of partition'.[120] The samastanam, they argued, was 'ordinary coparcenary property' and, as thus, was not subject to the rules of primogeniture.[121] Justice Muthusami Aiyar, however, defended the royal nature of Ramnad in a long decision. Discussing the history of the area, he concluded that Ramnad had been a 'real Kingdom'.[122] He then presented contemporary evidence in trying to reach a decision concerning the continuing nature of the zamindari under the Permanent Settlement. Muthusami Aiyar found that the British had not destroyed the 'original incidents' of Ramnad in making the Permanent Settlement; Ramnad still possessed the 'character' of a raj or principality.[123] The decision of Muthusami Aiyar, the first Indian judge of the High Court of Madras, was perhaps among the strongest judicial statements in support of Ramnad or Sivagangai as royal polities which had come down from that bench. Rather than appealing the case to the Privy Council, Dinakaraswami came to a compromise agreement with his elder brother.

The entire incident however, proved expensive for the Zamindar. Baskara agreed to a monthly 2,000-rupee allowance for Dinakaraswami and to a payment of 250,000 rupees for past allowances.[124] He also agreed to provide separate lodging for Dinakaraswami. Ramanadhan Chettiar met Dinakaraswami's legal expenses, which came to approximately 127,000 rupees. Baskara probably spent a similar amount.[125]

In the meantime, Ramanadhan had become further involved in royal family politics. As soon as Baskara discovered that Dinakaraswami had filed his case, the Raja cut off the palace allowance to Dorai Raja Nachiar, Dinakaraswami's mother and Baskara's stepmother.[126] Ramanadhan Chettiar had been Dorai Raja's major Chettiar creditor during the minority and, before the rendition, Baskara had entered into an agreement with the banker and his stepmother to pay the debts of the Rani's daughter. When he heard of Ramanadhan's treacherous alliance with Dinakaraswami, Baskara refused to pay the debts and new litigation, also reaching the High Court, ensued.[127]

The ambitious Venkataswami Nayudu, 'a gentleman of tact and considerable influence in high circles', succeeded in exploiting Baskara's dismissal of Diwan Raja Ram Row to create conflict between Ramasami Chettiar and the young Zamindar.[128] His success was such that, in 1890 and 1891,

[120] *Indian Law Reports: Madras Series*, vol. 24, 1901, p. 614.
[121] *Ibid.*, p. 616.
[122] High Court of Madras. Judgement in Appeal Suit No. 89 of 1891, p. 8.
[123] *Ibid.*, p. 18.
[124] P. V. N. Iyengar, 'Ramnad Supplement', p. 16.
[125] *Ibid.*, p. 17.
[126] *Madurai Mail*, 17 March 1894.
[127] High Court of Madras. Documents in Appeal No. 149 of 1894.
[128] P.V.N. Iyengar, 'Ramnad Supplement', p. 25.

lawsuits against the banker were planned and, on occasion, filed.[129] Baskara opened an account with another Chettiar banker and repaid 300,000 rupees to Ramasami, as an indication of intention to sever relations. Venkataswami Nayudu became Baskara's adviser on legal and financial matters. Venkataswami took the responsibility for organising the second major loan of 1891, setting up two Chettiar factions to bid for the Hamananthagudy Taluk lease. However, the Nayudu himself became a spokesman for one faction; and the leader of the other called in Ramasami Chettiar to aid with the negotiations. In a dramatic meeting at Rameswaram, Baskara and Ramasami resolved their differences. Baskara promised to refrain from further court action against the banker and Ramasami issued the Raja a cheque for an additional 10,000 rupees for a lease they had quarrelled over.[130] Venkataswami's period of influence had passed. Dissatisfied with the turn of events, he plagued Baskara with a suit claiming a larger commission. In an out-of-court settlement, the Zamindar gave the former Agent 60,000 rupees.

The leasing of large numbers of samastanam villages and the granting of others either rent-free or on low rents had disadvantageous effects on Ramnad finances. There were recurrent deficits in the revenue. By 1893, Baskara's total debts had accumulated to approximately 763,000 rupees.[131] By 1894 he owed Ramasami alone 837,035 rupees.[132] That sum represented money borrowed for peshkash payments, for litigation expenses, for charges of the estate revenue establishment and for the expenses of the Raja's household.[133] From 1893, the estate was jeopardised by creditors filing suits for payment and pressing for execution proceedings. Ramasami Chettiar joined the other creditors in pressing for settlement of Baskara's debts. The latter secured a mortgage deed in 1894 for the sum he owed Ramasami on security of the Zamindari.[134] By mid-1895, Baskara's total debt reached 2,000,000 rupees, owed to fifteen creditors. Attempts to raise the money at reasonable rates of interest failed.[135]

As early as 1893 Baskara had written to the Governor of Madras suggesting that a trust committee might be formed to protect the estate for his son. The Government found the idea agreeable, but only on condition that the Zamindar limit his annual personal expenses to 100,000 rupees and that he put 100,000 rupees aside annually for the settling of his debts.[136] Baskara postponed the scheme, hiring instead T. Venkataswami Rao as his Diwan. However, he resisted heeding Venkataswami Rao's advice and it

[129] *Ibid.*, pp. 28–30.
[130] *Ibid.*, p. 33.
[131] *Ibid.*, p. 45.
[132] *Ibid.*, p. 48.
[133] *Ibid.*
[134] *Ibid.*
[135] *Ibid.*
[136] *Ibid.*, pp. 57–8.

was finally necessary, in 1895, to form a trust committee with rules which allowed the Zamindar stringently limited access to zamindari resources.

Baskara Setupati did not descend into oblivion after 1895. He retained his Managership of Rameswaram until 1901 and he continued such acts of largess and religious reform as he could support. His piety and brilliance, and the memory of his past generosity, helped to maintain a good reputation for the Raja amid the 'abuse' and 'vilification' of his detractors.[137] His supporters believed, along with the Raja, that he would someday regain control over the estate. However, in 1903, at the age of thirty-five, Baskara Setupati died suddenly. In attempting to integrate values of the new public life with those of aristocratic kingly rule, he had paved the way for a Chettiar *raj* in Maravar country. A. L. A. R. Ramasami Chettiar became the Zamindar of Devakkottai in 1896 with a domain from the twenty-four villages granted to him in 1889. In the same year, he and his partners gained possession of the entire Ramnad Zamindari on lease.

In reviewing the narrative of Baskara's financial dealings, one is likely to wonder why he was not more protective of his holdings. This question belongs in a set which includes the financially suicidal litigation behaviour of his forebears and royal relations: why did they engage in political behaviour which, as in the extreme case of Sivagangai, completely undermined their financial base? Part of the answer lies in the notion of appropriate training for royal kin. I quoted earlier the former tutor of a Sivagangai zamindar in saying that a raja was not expected to learn to deal with numbers. The focus on his training was on skill in verbal exchange: a ruler should be able to talk easily with a wide range of people. This observation, however, points to a wider one: the ideological context in which political competition took place. Because honour and royal status were independent elements as objects of competition, not simply reflections of power, the desire to achieve or to protect honour took on a priority in political calculations which is difficult for late twentieth-century rationalists to comprehend. The dynamic of competition for honour had the power to overwhelm other political considerations, such as protection of the financial base. Indeed, if one of Baskara Setupati's goals with his largess was long-lasting respect, at the same time as some disparaging voices appeared in the *Madurai Mail*, indications are that he was widely admired as long as he lived. Recollections of his career have lived on in Madurai city and Ramnad district throughout the twentieth century. In 1984 Chief Minister M. G. Ramachandran and other state politicians took part in a function in which, during the presentation of plans to create three districts out of Ramnad district, the Chairman of the Legislative Council, M. P. Sivagnanam, unveiled a new portrait of the Raja. One of his descendants, identified as Rani Indira Devi Nachiar, presented 25,000 rupees towards

---

[137] Ramanatha Sivasankara Pandiyaji, 'H. H. Rajah Bhaskara Setupati avl. Maharaja of Ramnad', in Pandiyaji and Venkatarama Aiyangar, 'Celebration', p. 21.

the development the new district headquarters. The news reporter added, 'She was honoured on the occasion.'[138]

Conclusion

Baskara Setupati's meeting with the print media showed that he was heir to a repository of symbolic action which had the capacity attract a new kind of attention and admiration in public life.[139] He linked kingly behaviour to issues of public concern, creating a special notice for himself in the civic arena of Madurai town. Baskara proved that one could rework the criteria for honour and high status to create a charismatic presence in the public realm. The ruler of a segmented polity properly oversaw processes of redistribution which affirmed the lordships of minor figures in the domain, settling issues of disputed status. In Baskara Setupati the redistributive ruler chose objects for his generosity which had universal meaning, ostensibly beyond particularistic issues of local dominance, for participants in the public sphere. Schools, hospitals, the Congress Party – in the rhetoric of public opinion these should serve the needs of Indians at large. The target community of Barkara's largess was theoretically undifferentiated, sharing a common status vis-à-vis the state. This ruler was to be seen meeting the needs of broad-based social and political welfare. At base Baskara's generosity was only lightly touched by an ethic of universal rights: it remained kingly, in that the context of the generous act focused attention on the person who gave. Government officials who tried to introduce revenue reforms in Ramnad soon found out that, in effect, if the betterment of Baskara's subjects could not be seen as coming personally from his hand, he was not interested.[140]

Under electoral democracy in the Tamil Nadu of Independent India, a movie star politician, rumoured to have a fabulous fortune, would show the further development of this redistributive model, his most flamboyant gestures aimed at the poor. Baskara lent his charisma to elite symbols of universal progress in the public sphere. Populist politicians in postcolonial Tamil Nadu would spread largess thinly to poor voters as symbols of the protective potential of state government under their leadership.

---

[138] *The Hindu*, 18 July 1984.

[139] As yet no evidence has appeared to show that Baskara patronised poets to sing his praises or publicists to advertise his cause.

[140] See, regarding Lee Warner's efforts, BP August, no. 2060, enclosure no. 1, From Lee Warner, 10 May 1874, p. 5963 (TNA). Two articles in the *Madurai Mail* – 29 September 1894 and 13 October 1894 – told of Baskara's opposition to revenue reforms. At one point he filed more than a thousand cases against farmers in a drought-prone taluk.

Conclusion

This study has two trajectories. One trajectory covers approximately 100 years (from around 1800 to around 1900), focusing on the fate of elite institutions of rule – little kingdoms – during the British colonial regime in an area of southern Tamil country. The second trajectory follows briefly the presence of monarchical symbols and values in political practice in the twentieth century.

A major focus has been on conflicts within kingly domains, over succession to the title in two ruling houses and between the ruling houses and institutions of worship. These processes of conflict in politically particularistic localities played a role in ideological development in universalistic public spheres as they emerged in Madras Presidency. Conflict management in the Anglo-Indian legal system gave these political engagements social and political significance beyond issues of local ranking and access to resources. The process of conflict management altered the meaning of the conflicts, as it redefined the relationship of participants to one another and exposed them to public view in new ways. The process contributed to the fragmentation of precolonial political visions in civic arenas as relationships which had previously been perceived as complementary became antagonistic and royal symbols were discussed in new contexts, altering in meaning. The representation of royalty in legal processes contributed to the reconceptualisation of Indian society in the emerging public sphere. Social categories received new definitions and were universalised through application in litigation. These definitions acquired legitimacy in a time of accelerated cultural and political flux. The credibility of sacred kingship dissolved in public opinion, the amorphous domain of articulate and mobile men of Anglicised civic arenas.

Centralised conflict management supported the novel forms of imperial integration of the colonial government, blocking native political institutions from sharing in the ruling authority of the colonial state. Through the procedures and rhetoric of the legal system the colonial state articulated its separateness from smaller local realms, drawing lines of political authority, protecting its sovereignty. The new legal position of royal elites contributed to processes of cultural change which redefined them ambiguously as the 'native aristocracy'.

Attempts at the reproduction of royal status in the context of the colonial legal system undermined a major prop of sacred kingship, the complementary relationship between royal houses and ritual practitioners. The paradigmatic shift in the relationship between rajas and priestly establishments contributed to the conceptualisation of the realm of the 'religious' as separate from that of the 'political'. Antagonism between zamindari rulers and the administrators of temples and maths became intensified in the course of the nineteenth century, laying the groundwork for royal support of ethnic antagonism on the part of non-Brahmins towards Brahmins in the twentieth century. Nineteenth-century royal Maravars reacted to their own delegitimisation in the (Brahmin-dominated) public sphere by supporting activities which would 'reform Hinduism' and undermine the special status and sacred nature of contemporary priests.

The loss (or alteration) of symbolic props of sacred kingship in the public sphere did not destroy preoccupation with the honour and status of a ruling person in the zamindari localities. Documentation of zamindari politics and ritual performances indicates that a major goal of political reproduction was to protect the notion of the special qualities of a person of high ruling status. Innovative political strategies also aimed at this end. Zamindars and their managers relied on merchant-bankers to acquire cash which they used to develop different kinds of domains of royal influence, penetrating lower levels of the local colonial bureaucracy and attempting to control processes of colonial dispute management. In the process, dharmic morality and cosmic energy (sakti) came to play less of a role as constituents of royal honour and the possession of cash and access to important officials and non-officials expanded in importance in defining the nature of a zamindar's status. This change took place slowly while royal kin struggled to protect their privileges of high honours in temple worship and continued to support the presence of Brahmins in palace rituals.

Baskara Setupati succeeded in applying the particularistic concept of the special nature of a domain ruler to fit the demands of universalistic symbolism in the civic arena of Madurai. He drew mainly on the model of the high-status ruler as a vallal, a man of dharmic largess as he supported projects of social and political progress. Baskara played on the image of the king as supporter of dharma, paradoxically, by taking the lead (in part through his patronage of the famous Swami Vivekananda) in portraying Hinduism, 'reformed', as a (world) 'religion'. Baskara sought the dharmic honour of temple and palace ritual, at the same time as he drew on the relatively amoral notion of high status as the product of the influence of wealth.

The case of Baskara Setupati leads to a line of documentation and reasoning which takes issue with recent argumentation to the effect that public discourse in India developed differentiated from the idioms of local practice. Douglas Haynes concludes his study of public culture in Gujarat with the assertion that 'bilingual politics' eventually emerged under colonialism, with the idiom of the civic arena separate from the one 'addressing ordinary city dwellers'.[1] The result is that, today, 'the language of progress, civic duties and representation offer limited scope for the cultivation of truly popular support'.[2] Haynes argues that characteristic aspects of postcolonial political practice in non-European societies generally are primarily the product of colonial hegemony: 'products of the rhetorical and practical adaptations of indigenous leadership to the needs of representative systems they have been "granted" by their colonizers'.[3] The evidence of this study suggests the capacity of ideologies and practices of the public sphere in India to translate and encompass symbols and institutions of political segmentation. Work on post-independence Africa points to the same conclusion.[4]

Because centralising, universalising tendencies in the colonial state were not powerful enough to erase local, segmented structures and particularistic practices, as we have seen in the case of the Permanent Settlement, the most prominent of these structures became embedded in the structures of the state. For this reason, one might argue that the colonial state, paradoxically, played a vital role in the reproduction of ideologies of particularism.[5] The exploration of this argument is beyond the scope of this work. My argument is that major forces for the reproduction of ideologies of particularism came from political dynamics within segmented domains, dynamics which the colonial state could mould, but not control.

By the end of the nineteenth century, influence in the zamindari locality required influence in civic arenas, and figures in zamindari politics began to enter into novel political contexts. On the other hand, the introduction of electoral processes under colonial rule eventually came to mean that influence in public spheres, with the possibility of gaining control of the government, required influence in localities. Baskara Setupati was perhaps the first populist Tamil politician, as he personalised the universal value of progress with widespread gifting. As a strategy for legitimacy and electoral support in the last quarter of the twentieth century, public largess has come to symbolise the proclaimed intention of the modern state to work for the benefit of all.

A study of the evolution of monarchical symbolism in two little kingdoms in the nineteenth century is only part of the story of the fate of monarchical cosmology in modern Tamil country. In focusing on the royal houses of

---

[1] Haynes, *Rhetoric and Ritual in Colonial India*, p. 293.
[2] *Ibid.*, p. 293.
[3] *Ibid.*, p. 295.
[4] See, for example, Robert H. Jackson and Carol G. Rosenberg, *Personal Rule in Black Africa: Prince, Autocrat, Prophet, Tyrant* (Berkeley: University of California Press, 1982).
[5] David Gilmartin (personal communication).

zamindaris, I offer them as important sites of both change in monarchical symbolism and ideology and its reproduction. In the course of this study I have referred to writing on temples and village practice, in particular, to suggest that aspects of monarchical political culture continue to play a role in social and political exchanges in both urban and village settings. When late twentieth-century Tamil politicians use monarchical symbols and gestures in their public representations, it is not because of long-lasting influence from zamindari practice in particular. Zamindari politics contributed to processes of cultural and political reproduction which had their basis in a variety of institutions of social and political segmentation. It appears that there was a dialectical relationship between zamindars and members of their constituencies, with zamindars responding to what they assumed to be local canons of political legitimacy and honour.

Below is a quick review of some of the evidence for the continuing salience of monarchical values and symbols in Tamil politics in the twentieth century.

The public sphere expanded in the course of Indian nationalist mobilisation in Madras Presidency. In the context of the idealism of nationalist discourse, the particularistic practices of the zamindari politicians of the anti-Brahmin, loyalist Justice Party became discredited as corruption.[6] As the ascetic Gandhi and the notion of sacrifice for the national community became popular, the image of a ruler as appropriately a man of wealth became discredited. This much was conveyed by the song about Gandhi which novelist Raja Rao had his villagers sing:

Our King, he was born on a wattle-mat,
He's not the King of the velvet bed.
He's small and he's round and he's bright and he's
    sacred.[7]

Here the ruler is poor, but he is still a person of divine qualities.

Evidence of the application of the notion of royal qualities adhering to a leader who leads a simple life comes from Maravar politics, specifically in the career of Muthuramalinga Tevar, founder of the Forward Bloc party. Muthuramalinga Tevar was, like Baskara Setupati, radical in his context. He also benefited from the recognition of ruling status for one who was generous, though the scope of his giving was less comprehensive.

Born of a noted warrior line and heir to the Pasumpom domain of thirty-two villages in Ramnad Zamindari, Pasumpom Muthuramalinga Tevar (1908–63) entered the Congress movement at the age of nineteen.[8]

[6] Christopher John Baker, *The Politics of South India, 1920–1937* (Cambridge: Cambridge University Press, 1976), pp. 306–10.

[7] Raja Rao, *Kanthapura*, p. 203.

[8] 'Thevar, Pasumpon Muthuramalinga (1908–1963)', (Emmanuel Divien) [research fellow] and P. K. Mookiah Thevar [writing contributor], in S. P. Sen, *Dictionary of National Biography, Vol. IV, (S–Z)*, (Calcutta, 1974), pp. 345–6.

Revolutionary and emotional, he opposed Gandhi's policies of non-violence and associated himself with Subhas Chandra Bose and his Forward Bloc party. Muthuramalinga eventually left Congress and organised the Forward Bloc in Tamil country in 1939. He became involved in the labour movement in south India and worked as a labour organiser in the Mahalakshmi Textile Mills from 1936 to 1937, becoming president of the TVS Workers' Union. Muthuramalinga was first arrested for labour agitation in 1938.[9]

From 1937 Muthuramalinga was a member of the Legislative Assembly at Madras, to which he was returned by his constituents in East Ramnad while he was in jail. The British imprisoned him from 1939 to 1945 because of his association with Bose.[10] After Independence he was elected to the national parliament three times, in 1952, 1957 and 1962. Muthuramalinga campaigned actively for the repeal of the Criminal Tribes Act (which discriminated against Maravars), speaking at hundreds of meetings.

P. K. Mookiah Tevar, Maravar and leader of the Forward Bloc Party after the death of Muthuramalinga in 1963 wrote this about the party founder:

Being born in a family of a local chieftain, Thevar was almost a royal personage minus the arrogance, selfish ambition and other associated vices. His parentage had imbued in him a sense of honour, generosity, benevolence and kindness. It is said that even today his house is almost like a *choultry* [chattiram], feeding the depressed and the poor, wayfarers and others ...

Amassing wealth had never been a passion with Thevar and, as such, his lands were extensively let out on lease ... not even a single case of rent extracted in the manner of the traditional bailiff. His status in the society was more like that of a royal personage. But there was nothing royal about his costume or bearing – so simple was he in dress and appearance and so easily accessible both to the poor and the rich ...

The fact that the Maravars of Ramanathapuram adored him as a god did not go to show that Thevar was a communal leader ... His followers took inspiration from him in many ways. The populace found in him a moral force to rise against oppression and dishonesty.[11]

The theme of simplicity and superior morality in the special status of a great leader continued in the decades following Independence in the Tamil nationalist movement of the Dravida Munnetra Kazhagam (DMK). C. N. Annadurai, a brilliant orator and the founder of the DMK, emphasised values of collective leadership during the movement phase of the party (1949–69).[12] Party propagandists wrote and talked about the politician as

---

[9] *Ibid.*, p. 346.
[10] *Ibid.*
[11] *Ibid.*, pp. 345–6.
[12] The DMK came to power in 1967, the first non-Congress party to do so in Independent India. Annadurai died two years later, his term as Chief Minister cut short by illness.

'the Gandhi of south India' and discussed him as an honest man of simple habits. As party leader, he shied away from expansive, transactional gestures, but this did not prevent party adherents and supporters from developing powerful feelings of attachment to his person. For some people Annadurai's charisma held qualities of divinity. As a former DMK propagandist, M. R. Ganesan, explained, Annadurai was not seen as *kaṭavuḷ* or supreme creator. To ordinary people, after his death, Annadurai was a *teyvam*, a person who had been so superior morally, so capable of great deeds, that he deserved the respect due a god.[13] The year Annadurai died, Ganesan wrote the play *Anna is Our God* in which he had Gandhi and Tiruvalluvar and Bharathi, two of the greatest figures in the Tamil nationalist pantheon, appear before Annadurai, telling him that he is their god and that they bow to him and honour him above all others.[14]

M. Karunanidhi succeeded Annadurai to party leadership and became the next Chief Minister of Tamil Nadu. He broke quickly with the policy of collective leadership and the simple style of his mentor. The shift to control of the government under electoral processes had brought new transactional elements into the politics of cultural nationalism and resulted in the emphasis of culturally conservative elements in its practice.[15] The idealistic, movement phase of party development came to an end as DMK politicians consolidated their hold on sources of patronage in the governing apparatus. Critics of the DMK charge that the regime was unprecedented in its activities of corruption. The DMK reverted from the relatively universalistic principles of both British imperial rule and the leadership of the Indian nationalist movement and engaged in particularistic practices of highly personalised leadership in small domains. Karunanidhi initiated political ritual in which acts of redistribution played an important role. This ritual would appear to legitimise personal discretion in the implementation of government policies.

Celebrating the birthday of a zamindar with a durbar had become regular practice in twentieth-century Tamil country. Karunanidhi's birthday celebrations in the 1970s used ritual practices of zamindari kingship in the articulation of ideological themes of the DMK, Karunanidhi's party, and included concern for 'the little man'.[16] The birthday activities of the Chief Minister customarily presented him as a distributor of funds to the poor. From 1971 to 1974 Karunanidhi asked that money be collected on that day

---

[13] M. R. Ganesan, interview, 20 August 1991.

[14] *Anna is Our God*, was performed about 100 times. It was never published.

[15] Pamela Price, 'Revolution and Rank in Tamil Nationalism', forthcoming.

[16] Probably Karunanidhi was not consciously copying zamindari practice. It appears that today zamindars are more associated in popular awareness with economic exploitation than Tamil monarchical traditions. Jayalalitha organised a birthday celebration in 1993 to celebrate her forty-fifth birthday. As she took a ritual bath at a major temple at Kumbakonam in Tanjore district, the crowd pressed forward and forty-five people were killed: Bruno Philip, 'The "Iron Lady" of Madras Politics', in *Guardian Weekly*, 16 January 1994.

for projects of social welfare.[17] In 1975, however, he asked that money which his well-wishers might have spent on a garland or on travel to come and greet him be given to an election fund for the DMK. People wishing to donate to a drought relief fund or to a fund for state-run orphanages should still do so. The focus on vulnerable groups in society was embedded in an overall celebration of the personal influence of Karunanidhi. The man of antastu was shown mariyatai.

On 3 June, from 7 am the Chief Minister began to receive visitors in a hall in his house. A large hundi (container) stood in the hall to receive contributions of money from the people who came.[18] Among those to honour Karunanidhi were government officials and leaders of political parties in Tamil Nadu, including members of the Muslim League and the Communist Party. K. K. Shah, the Governor of Tamil Nadu, came bearing a garland and fruit. One man presented a poem wishing Karunanidhi a long life. Prasadam from a Siva temple, a Vishnu temple and a Vinayaka temple were presented to the Chief Minister. Fifty-two youths in relay – one for each year of his life – brought a torch from his birthplace 210 miles away and an inter-caste marriage was celebrated in his presence. The president of the NGGO, an association of Tamil Nadu government servants, greeted the Chief Minister on their behalf and asked for raises in pay that would put Tamil Nadu (state) salaries on a par with those of Central Government workers. First copies of a new DMK daily and a monthly magazine to support the interests of government servants were presented to Karunanidhi. An ornamental arch across a wide street was opened. The day's collections totalled: 256,884 rupees for the election fund; 1,100,000 rupees for the drought relief fund; and 54,000 rupees for the orphanage.

Karunanidhi's borrowing from royal symbolism took place as he celebrated his positions as party leader and chief executive of a state which was bureaucratised. The organisation of the birthday performance spoke not to the principles of centralisation which lie formally in the structure of the state in Tamil Nadu, but to the particularism of informal administrative practice.[19] Karunanidhi's post-Independence birthday durbar pointed to the significance of personal domains in the all-important informal structures of dominance in the government. The focus on Karunanidhi would seem to reflect the major significance of the personal discretion of government officials and bureaucrats as they implemented government policy, taking in

---

[17] *Indian Express*, 4 June 1975, gives the following details.
[18] In the major temples of Tamil Nadu, people place their money offerings to support temple upkeep in hundis.
[19] Hans Blomkvist, 'The Soft State: Making Policy in a Different Context', in Douglas Ashford (ed.), *History and Context in Comparative Public Policy* (Pittsburgh: University of Pittsburgh Press, 1992), pp. 117–50, and Blomkvist, 'The Soft State: Housing Reform and State Capacity in Urban India', PhD dissertation, Department of Government, University of Uppsala, 1988.

a wide range of social and political considerations when processing individual cases.[20]

It is with the career of the movie star and founder of the AIADMK, M. G. Ramachandran (MGR), however, that the political possibilities of monarchical populism found fuller development. The actor, who made a great fortune playing the roles of brave and good 'little men', became famous for his acts of largess towards poor people, including rickshaw drivers, slum dwellers and old women.[21] His fans saw him as divine even before he started his own political party.[22] After MGR became Chief Minister in 1977 and started his activities of expanded subsidies (including 'free' lunches for school children), adoration of him spread.

The enormous popularity of MGR appeared to result from the widespread perception of him as a generous man, and acts of public largess became a common strategy of succeeding Chief Ministers as they sought ruling legitimacy and electoral support. When Karunanidhi returned to power as Chief Minister in 1989, after the death of MGR, he continued the subsidy schemes, financially ruinous for the state, as monarchical populism became a major dynamic in electoral politics in Tamil Nadu.[23] Free rice was now distributed to poor people as part of Karunanidhi's birthday celebration.[24]

Karunanidhi has associated himself with kingship (not divinity), while MGR was widely characterised as a god. With Jayalalitha the themes of kingship and divinity have clearly been joined in the representation of her rulership. T. S. Subramaniam of *Frontline* pointed out the 'single-person focus' and royal elements, in particular, in the two-day party conference organised by Jayalalitha in Madurai to celebrate the anniversary of her first year in power.[25]

Even the formal trappings of a coronation were not missing, P. V. Rajendran, a devout young craftsman, led a team of 58 carpenters to create a 'Raja Simhasanam' (or should it rather be a 'queen's throne'?) for Jayalalitha ... With folded hands, holy ash and kumkum on his forehead and 'rudraksh malas' about his neck

---

[20] *Ibid.*

[21] Recent discussions of the career of MGR are Pandian, *The Image Trap* and Sara Dickey, 'The Politics of Adulation: Cinema and the Production of Politicians in South India', in *The Journal of Asian Studies*, vol. 52, no. 2, 1993, pp. 340–72.

[22] Robert Hardgrave, 'The Celluloid God: MGR and the Tamil Film', *South Asia Review*, vol. 4, no. 4, 1971, pp. 307–14. Another south Indian film actor who made a successful career in politics is N. T. Rama Rao from Andhra Pradesh. He built his political persona around his roles as a god in films in which he starred.

[23] Madras Institute of Development Studies, *Tamil Nadu Economy: Performance and Issues* (New Delhi: Oxford University Press and IBH, 1988), p. 333. The authors of this study refer to the subsidy schemes as 'competitive populism'.

[24] K. P. Sunil, 'The Theatre of the Absurd', in *The Illustrated Weekly of India*, May 4–5 1991, p. 21.

[25] T. S. Subramanian, 'A Famous "Victory"?: Jayalalitha and the Madurai Conference', in *Frontline*, 31 July 1992, pp. 106–10. I am grateful to Sumathi Ramaswami for making this article available to me.

Rajendran told his story thus: 'Ninety-nine kg of pure silver has gone into the making of this throne for *amma*: fifty-eight *acharis* worked day and night from June 18 to June 27 to finish making this throne. We scoured the drama props of R.S. Manohar to get the correct design for the *simhasanam*. But we were not satisfied. Then this design appeared to me in my dream. I quickly aroused myself from sleep and drew up the design ... I performed a puja to the throne and breathed life into it.' He could not contain his pride when it came to the comfort of the product. 'How wonderful it will be to relax on it ... it has an eight-inch foam cushion supported by spring action.'[26]

Slogans praised the Chief Minister; Ministers, Members of the Legislative Council and party functionaries competed to give speeches honouring her courage and intelligence and then prostrated themselves at her feet. Jayalalitha gave two long speeches which told of her 'valiant' struggle to reach what Subramanian describes as the 'Tamil Nadu *gaddi*' (throne).[27] A thousand cooks prepared food packets which were distributed to 'several lakhs of people'.[28]

V. Geetha and S. V. Rajadurai explain the royal style in Tamil politics thus:

Praise and panegyric are not new to Tamil political culture, for had not the DMK introduced into public life pseudo-bardic conventions and arcane feudal practices in their attempts to reconstitute political space in the state to stimulate an imagined Tamil feudal order?[29]

Evidence produced in this study should serve to suggest that monarchical populism is more than a product of the strategies of DMK politicians and their propagandists. In speaking succinctly to the question of Geetha and Rajadurai, however, reference to some abstract notion of the 'weight' of monarchical traditions begs the question. It is more useful to begin with a consideration of the contemporary role of royal symbolism and values in rural and urban worship.[30] The distribution of honours in the ritual of worship, however, is only one aspect of the continuing significance of honour in political relations in the twentieth century. Historical research into the mobilisation of the DMK in Madurai district in the 1950s and 1960s suggests ways in which the conception of honour in the small domains of rural and urban life was transformed in the DMK's formulation of the larger, encompassing domain of the Tamil nation.[31] It is important to ask first why the DMK's propaganda strategies succeeded and, then, why they have continued to bear fruit.

[26] *Ibid.*, p. 107.
[27] *Ibid.*, p. 106.
[28] *Ibid.*, p. 110.
[29] V. Geetha and S. V. Rajadurai, '"Off with Their Heads": Suppression of Dissent in Tamil Nadu', in the *Economic and Political Weekly*, 6 June 1992, p. 1184.
[30] For example, Hiltebeitel, *The Cult of Draupadi*, vol. 2, and Mosse, 'Caste, Christianity and Hinduism'.
[31] Price, 'Revolution and Rank'.

Under the leadership of E. V. Ramaswamy Naicker (1879–1973) in the 1930s a radical dimension developed in Tamil cultural nationalism. At the same time as EVR (as he was known) condemned priestly influence and derided Hindu 'superstition', he remained preoccupied with honour, with mariyatai. He appears to have decided that an overwhelming, revolutionary change in Tamil society depended on Tamils developing new conceptions of personal worth and evaluation in their relations with one another. EVR promoted a new conception of personal honour which he called *suya-mariyātai*, self-honour. In the popular conception of EVR's ethic, one gained suya-mariyatai through a refusal to subordinate oneself to the authority of a person because of his higher-caste status. One developed suya-mariyatai through treating all men and women as equal in caste status. Suya-mariyatai involved a conception of an absolute, not relative, status which was based on the inner qualities of a person, his cultivation of, among other things, a rational and moral mode of thinking and behaving.[32] Suya-mariyatai translated in English as 'self-respect': one acquired a respect for oneself which was not dependent on the honour which others showed you. The importance of the suya-mariyatai in EVR's movement is seen in its attribution as the Self-Respect Movement.

Interviews with about forty former activists in the DMK movement which broke from EVR's leadership confirm that honour was a major preoccupation in the DMK mobilisation in Madurai district in the 1950s and 1960s.[33] Activists conceived of honour in terms of both mariyatai and suya-mariyatai. They preferred, however, to use the words *mānam* and *tān-mānam*, which they considered more approximate to 'pure Tamil' than 'mariyatai'.

The major propagandists of the DMK, travelling widely and delivering eloquent speeches, created a Tamil nationalist cosmology, with frequent reference to an imagined pre-Aryan Tamil community without the distinctions of caste. Cultivating tan-manam, Tamil men would create a homogeneous national domain without the debilitating disunity and demoralisation of hierarchies based on caste. Since the Tamil nation would be peopled by men of tan-manam, it would be superior to the domains of north Indians, which were constituted of men and women without honour. Tamil men of tan-manam would constitute a national community which would be superior to others, having superior (collective) honour.

At the same time as DMK propagandists used EVR's definition of personal honour, expanding on suya-mariyatai as an appropriate political identity in a domain, they transformed the concept of the domain to which the individual related. The domain became universalised as the Tamil nation, a nation which would be ranked against other nations in the world, not just

---

[32] *Ibid.*
[33] *Ibid.* Along with Velraj P., my research assistant, I took these interviews in 1991; he, in villages to the south-west and west of Madurai city, and I, in Madurai city.

the communities of north India. Hierarchies ranked according to considerations of honour played an implicit role in the nationalist cosmology.

In the 1950s and 1960s the DMK departed from the austere moral exhortations of EVR in an attempt to encourage young men to take steps of active social and political rebellion against the elders of their villages, who generally belonged to the Congress Party. The DMK popularised their appeal in order to achieve greater political effectiveness, aiming for control of the state government. There came into DMK rhetoric a reliance on conceptions of humiliation and insult which were associated with living without honour. This mariyatai mitigated the revolutionary impact of a focus on self-respect. DMK rhetoric painted various actions of Congress politicians and the central goverment as insulting to Tamil honour. With the *vīram*, or courage, of the heroic Tamils of the pre-Aryan age, followers of the DMK would shrug off the humiliation of various kinds of subordination and win back honour for themselves and the Tamil country. They would be the heroic protectors of Mother Tamil, the chaste goddess which was the Tamil language.[34]

When the DMK won the state elections in 1967, the self-discipline of suya-mariyatai lost its appeal as part of a heroic struggle. Suya-mariyati had been popular, for the most part, among young men. For most of the rest of the rural and urban population, 'self-respect' had never seriously threatened conceptions of mariyatai as relative honour and status which had to be confirmed and defended continuously, not only in ritual, but in the manifold transactions of daily life.[35]

As the DMK popularised and widened its appeal for the purposes of electoral advantage, it had diluted the universalism in its ideological code. Annadurai held firm to the 'principles' (as they were called) of the movement of cultural revolution, but DMK members of the Legislative Assembly set about building up their domains of personal influence, earning the subordination of people who would flatter them with displays of mariyatai, in order to acquire their protection as men of antastu.

The story of DMK mobilisation in Madurai district demonstrates clearly how issues of honour have played a significant role in political conceptions of leadership and appropriate political practice well into the twentieth century. This example suggests, however, that it is insufficient to argue that royal honour – the conception of the ruler as a person of royal and divine

---

[34] A recent discussion of Mother Tamil is Sumathi Ramaswamy, 'Battling the Demoness Hindi: The Culture of Language Protest in Tamilnadu, 1938–1965', in Sandria B. Freitag (ed.), *Culture as Contested Site: Popular Participation and the State in the Indian Subcontinent* (forthcoming). See also, Ramáswamy, 'En/gendering Language: The Poetics of Tamil Identity', in *Comparative Studies in Society and History*, 1993, pp. 683–725.

[35] See Frank Heidemann, 'Respekt als Ausdruck sozialer Beziehungen bei den Badagas in Süd-Indiens', in Matthias S. Laubscher (ed.), *Beiträge zur Ethnologie Mittel- und Süd-Indiens* (Munich: Anacon, 1991), pp. 29–44. I am grateful to Dr Heidemann for providing an English synopsis of his article.

qualities – is salient in Tamil politics mainly as a function of the continuing significance of the symbolism in temple worship. It seems more fruitful to see royal models and the focus on the special status of a ruler as a function of widely distributed ideas of personal value in a society of profound social and political segmentation. DMK rhetoric focused on manam and tan-manam because, for most people, the institutional structure of their daily experience was in small domains of personal administration. The Tamil nation constituted an encompassing domain which was made familiar to potential voters with references to honour in political relations.

Another way to phrase the issue is to say that a focus on personal honour is a function of comprehensive segmentation in social and political organisation. These units (from clan and sub-caste organisation to the political networks of members of the Legislative Assembly) support administration based on personal relations, where the development and maintenance of personal authority is a major political feature. A continuing focus on the person of the ruler is a function of administration of the affairs of the multitude of domains which constitute life in Tamil Nadu. From this point of view what we call Hinduism today can be seen as an informal ideology of personalised administration, on both a local and state level.

The co-existence of symbols and values of worship and rule in religio-political ideologies is not particular to the Tamil country in India. A special focus on the person of the ruler is common in modern Indian politics.[36] I have written elsewhere of the role of royal models in political behaviour generally, particularly with reference to leadership in factions.[37] Perhaps because Tamil country did not experience long-term Muslim rule, the role of royal symbolism in ideologies of worship and administration has been stronger here than, for example, in much of north India.[38] The Tamil experience may bring to our attention processes of political development that have been less obvious in other parts of the subcontinent.[39] That aspects of monarchical political culture play a role in state politics in north India is suggested by the career of Haryana populist Devi Lal who, in 1991, boasted to news reporters that his rural supporters presented him with gold crowns, silver staffs and swords and garlands of currency

---

[36] A recent analysis of increasing tendencies towards both populism and the personal power of leaders is Atul Kohli, *Democracy and Discontent: India's Growing Crisis of Governability* (Cambridge: Cambridge University Press, 1990).

[37] Price, 'Kingly Models in Indian Political Behavior: Culture as a Medium of History', in *Asian Survey*, vol. 29, no. 6, 1989, pp. 559–72.

[38] This is suggested by the relative absence of discussions of royal symbolism in works on ritual practice in the Gangetic valley. On the other hand, Davis' study of political competition in a village in West Bengal in the 1970s finds issues of domination and rule expressed with reference to kingly models: Marvin Davis, *Rank and Rivalry: The Politics of Inequality in Rural West Bengal* (Cambridge: Cambridge University Press, 1983).

[39] I discuss parallels between late precolonial patterns of political competition in Tamil country and patterns in the emergence of political careers organised around the mobilisation of ethnic identities in 'Democracy and Ethnic Conflict in India: Precolonial Legacies in Tamil Nadu', in *Asian Survey*, vol. 33, no. 5, 1993, pp. 493–506.

notes.[40] In the absence of the obvious use of royal symbolism, observers sometimes discuss political behaviour vaguely in terms of style of governance. Journalists have referred to the Nehru-Gandhi 'dynasty' in the central goverment,[41] commenting on, for example, Indira Gandhi's 'reign', the 'raja cult' surrounding Rajiv,[42] Rajiv's use of 'largess'[43] and Congress Party 'durbars' and 'dubaris'.[44]

This study suggests that the adoption of royal styles reflects the existence of political values in which focus on the development and protection of domains of personal influence and control is of the utmost importance. Morris-Jones appears to have shared in this formulation when he commented on Indira Gandhi's policies regarding the Congress Party and the central administration:

In politics, style is often substance and Mrs Gandhi's style has transformed these relations from ones of political bargaining to ones akin to feudal tutelage. Or rather, that is what was attempted ...[45] The steady erosion of two such key institutions inevitably creates a vacuum that feudal-style fealty cannot fill.[46]

The royal style of the Gandhi family at the centre reflected processes of particularisation which Atul Kohli's research indicates to have been taking place in Indian party politics since the 1970s.[47] The disjuncture between the formal codes and models which organise the state and popular perceptions of authoritative rule appears to have created distructive political tensions. Kohli also uses the term 'vacuum' – 'authority vacuum' and 'organizational vacuum' – to describe the impact of processes of particularisation.[48] Political parties as institutions have been disintegrating while organisations built on networks of influence and control have increasingly come to dominate democracy in India. Politicians focus on building personal support among voters with populist appeals and evade or otherwise undermine formal party organisation. Jackson and Rosenberg describe 'de-institutionalisation' thus:

[40] 'Devi Lal Harps on Coalition Govt', in *Indian Express*, 19 February 1991 and Ritu Sarin, 'Go for Gold: Devi Lal Adopts Cheap Gimmicks to Flaunt his Popularity', in *Sunday*, vol. 28, no. 6, 10–16 February 1991, p. 26.
[41] See, for example, 'Congress(I)'s Existential Conundrum', during the 'draft Sonia' campaign after the death of Rajiv Gandhi, *The Hindu*, 9 August 1991 and 'In High Orbit', in *India Today*, 15 June 1994, p. 10.
[42] In Edward Behr, 'The Problems of Being Rajiv', in *Encounter*, January, 1988, pp. 57 and 58.
[43] BM, 'Making the Plan Irrelevant', in *The Economic and Political Weekly*, 11 January 1986, p. 60.
[44] 'The Congress After Rajiv: In Search of a New Identity', in the *Indian Express*, 18 August 1991.
[45] W. H. Morris-Jones, 'India – More Questions than Answers', in *Asian Survey*, vol. 24, no. 8, 1984, p. 811.
[46] *Ibid.*, p. 814. Atul Kohli has written on the vacuum in Indian party politics in his *Democracy and Discontent*.
[47] Kohli, *Democracy and Discontent*.
[48] *Ibid.*, p. 384 and *passim*.

... where persons take precedence over [formal] rules, where the officeholder is not effectively bound by his office and is able to change its authority and powers to suit his own personal or political needs.[49]

Paradoxically, the deinstitutionalisation of Indian parties is in part the result of changes in the public sphere which have accompanied the increasing mobilisation of the Indian population to take part in electoral processes. As mentioned in connection with the development of the political practice of DMK politicians in power, electoral politics emphasises transactional elements in governance. These in turn encourage the penetration of the public sphere in India by the values of personal authority which inform the ideology of administration in segmented domains.

In the meantime, what has happened to the royal house of Baskara Setupati? Back in Ramnad district in the 1970s royalty survived much reduced in scale and appeared not to awaken much interest in the hearts and minds of the inhabitants of Ramnad town. Ramanata Setupati, who died in 1979, was not a man of ostentatiously substantial means (though Zamindari abolition probably left him and his kin with important holdings in land). He looked to the theme of the protection of worship in demonstrating his special heritage. Ramanata, quiet and pious, devoted much of his attention to his responsibilities as trustee for temples of the former samastanam, including the great temple at Rameswaram. There he was chairman of the Board of Trustees and of the Renovation Committee for the grand Kumbhabishekam of 1975. Ramanata prayed every day at the palace temple of Rajarajeswari. The vijaya dasami procession which he organised in her honour in 1978 attracted a considerable crowd.

After Ramanata's death his heir, an adolescent male relative, underwent an installation ceremony and an installation durbar, the latter in front of Ramalingam Vilasa. The durbar must have been a disappointment for the remaining brothers of the last Zamindar of Ramnad: few people other than royal relatives attended. Afterwards the young man in question, the new Setupati, seemed unaffected by what he had been through and relaxed outside the old durbar hall playing ball with his many cousins. In Tamil democracy the glamour of semi-divine, high-status rule had, again, become a quality which was earned.

[49] Jackson and Rosenberg, *Personal Rule in Black Africa*, p. 10.

BIBLIOGRAPHY

Primary sources

Records of administration

Board of Revenue: Boards of Consultations (BC); Proceedings of the Board of
    Revenue (BP). Tamilnadu Archives
District Court Records. Tamilnadu Archives and Madurai district Collectorate
'Letters sent regarding Ramnad Zamindary while under attachment, from the
years 1842–1846'. Tamilnadu Archives
Madurai District Records. Tamilnadu Archives
Military Country Correspondence. Tamilnadu Archives
Miscellaneous Correspondence for Madura District. Tamilnadu Archives
Revenue Department: Government Orders (GO); Miscellaneous Series; Numbers of
    the Revenue Department. Tamilnadu Archives
'The Report of the Commissioners G. D. Drury and W. A. Moorehead'. Tamilnadu
    Archives

Records of litigation

The following were consulted at the Record Room, Appellate Side, High Court of
    Judicature at Madras:
Special Appeal no. 569 of 1870
Regular Appeal no. 35 of 1873
Regular Appeal no. 36 of 1874
Regular Appeal no. 43 of 1874 and Regular Appeal no. 46 of 1874
Regular Appeal no. 42 of 1874
Regular Appeal no. 80 of 1876
Appeal Nos. 13 and 23 of 1878
Appeal no. 22 of 1879
Appeal no. 21 of 1887
Appeal no. 118 of 1890
Appeal no. 7 of 1894
Appeal no. 149 of 1894
Appeal no. 215 of 1895
Appeal no. 65 of 1908

The following were consulted at the Judicial Committee of the Privy Council in London:
The Collector of Madura vs. Muttu Vijaya Raghunatha Muttu Ramalinga Sathupathi, 1868
Ramamani Ammal vs. Kulanthai Nachiar, 1871

Published decisions came from the following series:
Indian Decisions. New Series (Indian Law Reports) (Ind. Dec., N.S.I.L.R.)
Indian Decisions. New Series (Madras High Court Reports)(Ind. Dec., N.S.M.H.C.R.)
Indian Law Review: Madras Series
The Law Reports: Indian Appeals (IA)
The Law Reports: Madras Series
Annasawmy Ayer, R. (compiler) *The Sivaganga Zamindary, Its Origin and Its Litigation, 1730–1899*, Madras, Hoe and Company, 1899
Mills, J. M. C. *Reports of Cases Decided in the High Court of Madras in 1871–1874 (MHCR)*
Moore, Edmund F. *Reports of Cases Heard and Determined by the Judicial Committee and the Lords of Her Majesty's Most Honorable Privy Council*

Newspapers and magazines

The Hindu, 1842–3
The Hindu, 1980s and early 1990s
Indian Express, 1975, 1991
India Today, early 1990s
Madurai Mail, 1894–5

Inscriptions

Burgess, James and S. M. Natesa Sastri, *Tamil and Sanskrit Inscriptions*
Archaeological Survey of Southern India, vol. 4, Madras: The Government Press, 1886, pp. 56–65
Plate Number 30, Rameswaram Copper Plate in possession of the Raja Sahib of Ramnad
Rangacharya, V. *A Topographical List of the Inscriptions of the Madras Presidency*, vol. 2, Madras: The Government Press, 1919

Reports, unpublished manuscripts, manuals, accounts, poems, diaries and legal decisions

Baskara Setupati 'Diary'. 1893, Tamilnadu Archives
Baskara Setupati *My Trip to India's Utmost Isle*. Madras: G. W. Taylor, 1890
Bobbili, Maharaja of *Advice to the Indian Aristocracy*. Madras: Addison, 1905
Chandrasekharan, T. (ed.) *Śivagaṅgaic Carittirak Kummiyum Ammāṉaiyum*. Madras: Government Press, 1954
Holloway, William 'Notes on the Madras Judicial Administration'. Madras: 1853
Iyengar, P. V. N. 'Ramnad Supplement'. Manuscript, n.d.

Nelson, J. H. *The Madura Country: A Manual.* Madras: William Thomas, 1868
Paes, Domingos and Fernao Nuniz. Vasundhara Filliozat, (ed.). Translated by Robert Sewell. *The Vijayanagar Empire.* New Delhi: National Book Trust, 1977
Pandiyaji, Ramanatha Sivasankara. 'H. H. Rajah Bhaskara Setupati Avl. Maharajah of Ramnad'. In *The Miniature Hindu Excelsior Series,* English Number IV, pp. 18–22
Pandiyaji, Ramanatha Sivasankara and S. A. Venkatarama Aiyangar 'Celebration of the Navaratri Festival at Ramnad in 1892'. In *The Miniature Hindu Excelsior Series,* English Number IV
Raja Ram Rao, T. *Ramnad Manual,* title page missing, 1889?
Shortt, John. 'Habits and Manners of Maravar Tribes of India'. In *Memoirs Read Before the Anthropological Society of London,* vol. III, 1867–70, pp. 201–15
Śrī Sētu Samstānam Virōtikirutu Mahā Navarāttiri Mahōtasvattil vittuvānkaḷ pātiyapātalkaḷ. Madurai: 1910, 1912 and 1913
Srinivasa Raghavaiyangar, S. *Memorandum on the Progress of the Madras Presidency During the Last Forty Years of British Administration.* Madras: The Government Press, 1893
Tanippātal tirattu uraik kurippukkalutan. vol. II. Tirunelvēli: Tirunelvēli Tennintiyā Saivasittānta Nūrpatippak Kalakam, 1964
Taylor, William. 'Marava-jatha-Vernanam'. In *Madras Journal of Literature and Science,* vol. 4, 1836, pp. 350–60
Vaiyapuri Pillai, S. (ed.) *Rāmappaiyan Ammānai.* Madras: University of Madras, 1951

Interviews
R. Baskaran, Ramnad, 1975
K. Chandrasekharan, Madras, 1974
Kasinath Dorai, Ramnad, 1975, 1978 and 1979
Mangalanatha Dorai, Ramnad, 1975, 1978 and 1979
K. Muttusamy, Madurai, 1978 and 1979
The Raja Sahib of Sivagangai, Sivagangai, 1975
Raja Ramanata Setupati, Ramnad and Rameswaram, 1975
Subiah Chettiar, Devakkottai, 1979
J. Rengasamy Iyer, Sivagangai, 1975 and Madurai, 1978
Velu Dorai, Sivagangai, 1975

Secondary works

Articles and Books

Amin, Shahid. 'Gandhi as Mahatma: Gorakhpur District, Eastern UP, 1921–2'. In Ranajit Guha (ed.) *Subaltern Studies III: Writings on South Asian History and Society.* Delhi: Oxford University Press, 1984, pp. 1–61
Anderson, Benedict. 'The Idea of Power in Javanese Culture'. In Claire Holt, (ed.) with Anderson, B. and Siegel, J. *Culture and Politics in Indonesia.* Ithaca: Cornell University Press, 1972, pp. 1–69
Imagined Communities: Reflections on the Origin and Spread of Nationalism. London: Verso, 1983
Appadurai, Arjun. 'King, Sects and Temples in South India, 1250–1700'. In Burton

Stein (ed.) *South Indian Temples: An Analytic Reconsideration*. New Delhi: Vikas Publishing House, 1978, pp. 47–73
'Right and Left Hand Castes in South India'. In *The Indian Economic and Social History Review*, vol. 11, nos. 2–3, 1974, pp. 216–59
Worship and Conflict under Colonial Rule: A South Indian Case. Cambridge: Cambridge University Press, 1981
Appadurai, Arjun and Breckenridge, Carol Appadurai. 'The South Indian Temple: Authority, Honor and Redistribution'. In *Contributions to Indian Sociology (NS)*, vol. 10, no. 2, 1976, pp. 187–211
Apter, Andrew. *Black Critics and Kings: The Hermeneutics of Power in Yoruba Society*. Chicago: University of Chicago Press, 1992
Arasaratnam, S. 'A Note on Periathamby Marikkar – a 17th Century Commercial Magnate'. In *Tamil Culture*, vol. 2, no. l, 1964, pp. 51–7
'Commercial Policies of the Sethupathis of Ramanathapuram: 1660–1690'. In *Proceedings of the Second International Conference Seminar of Tamil Studies*. Madras: International Association of Tamil Research, 1967, p. 251
'The Dutch East India Company and the Kingdom of Madurai, 1650–1700'. In *Tamil Culture*, vol. 10, no. l, 1963, pp. 48–74
'The Politics of Commerce in the Coastal Kingdoms of Tamil Nad, 1650–1700'. In *South Asia*, no. 1, 1971. pp. 1–19
Arbuthnot, Alexander J. (ed.) *Major General Sir Thomas Munro, Bart., K.C.P., Governor of Madras: Selections from his Minutes and Other Official Writings*. London: Kegan Paul & Co., 1881
BM. 'Making the Plan Irrelevant'. In *Economic and Political Weekly*. 11 January 1986, pp. 60–61
Baker, Christopher John. *An Indian Rural Economy, 1880–1955: The Tamilnad Countryside*. Delhi: Oxford University Press, 1984
The Politics of South India, 1920–1937. Cambridge: Cambridge University Press, 1976
'Tamilnad Estates in the Twentieth Century'. In *Indian Economic and Social History Review*, vol. 13, no. 1, 1975, pp. 1–44
Basu, Aparna. 'A Century's Journey: Women's Education in Western India, 1820–1920'. In Karuna Chanana (ed.) *Socialization, Education and Women: Explorations in Gender Identity*. New Delhi: Orient Longman, 1988, pp. 65–95
Bayart, Jean-François. 'Finishing With the Idea of the Third World: The Concept of the Political Trajectory'. In James Manor (ed.) *Rethinking Third World Politics*. London: Longman, 1991, pp. 51–71
Bayly, Susan. *Saints, Goddesses and Kings: Muslims and Christians in South Indian Society, 1700–1900*. Cambridge: Cambridge University Press, 1989
Beck, Brenda E. F. 'The Goddess and the Demon: A Local South Indian Festival and its Wider Context'. In *Autour de La Déesse Hindoue: Études Réunies par Madeleine Biardeau. Puruṣārtha*. no. 5. Paris: Éditions de l'École des Hautes Études en Science Sociales, 1981, pp. 83–136
Behr, Edward. 'The Problems of Being Rajiv'. In *Encounter*, January, 1988, pp. 56–61
Bhat, M. Mariappa, (ed.) *Kittel's Kannada-English Dictionary*. Madras: University of Madras. 1969

Blomkvist, Hans. 'The Soft State: Making Policy in a Different Context'. In Douglas Ashford, (ed.) *History and Context in Comparative Public Policy*. Pittsburgh: University of Pittsburgh Press, 1992, pp. 117–50

Bourdieu, Pierre. *Outline of a Theory of Practice*. Cambridge: Cambridge University Press, 1977

Breckenridge, Carol Appadurai. 'From Protector to Litigant – Changing Relations Between Hindu Temples and the Raja of Ramnad'. In Burton Stein (ed.) *South Indian Temples: An Analytic Reconsideration*. New Delhi: Vikas Publishing House, 1978, pp. 75–106

Burgess, James. 'The Ritual of Rameswaram'. In James Burgess, (ed.) *The Indian Antiquary, a Journal of Oriental Research*, vol. XII, December, 1883, pp. 315–26

Cañcīvi, N. *Marutiruvar*. Madras: Pāri Nilaiyam, 1968. Third Edition

Chandavarkar, Rajnarayan. 'Industrialization in India before 1947: Conventional Approaches and Alternative Perspectives'. In *Modern Asian Studies*, vol. 19, no. 3, 1985, pp. 623–68

Chakrabarthy, Dipesh. 'Postcoloniality and the Artifice of History: Who Speaks for "Indian" Pasts'. In *Representations*. no. 37, 1992, pp. 1–26

Chanana, Karuna, (ed.) *Socialisation, Education and Women: Explorations in Gender Identity*. New Delhi: Orient Longman, 1988

Cohn, Bernard S. 'Notes on the History of the Study of Indian Society and Culture', in Milton Singer and Bernard S. Cohn (eds.) *Structure and Change in Indian Society*. Chicago: Aldine Publishing Company, 1968, pp. 3–28

'Recruitment of Elites in India under British Rule'. In Leonard Plotnicov and Arthur Tuden, (eds.) *Essays in Comparative Social Stratification*. Pittsburgh: University of Pittsburgh, 1970, pp. 121–47

'Representing Authority in Victorian India'. In Eric Hobsbawm and Terence Ranger, (eds.) *The Invention of Tradition*. Cambridge: Cambridge University Press, 1983, pp. 165–209

Davis, Marvin. *Rank and Rivalry: The Politics of Inequality in Rural West Bengal*. Cambridge: Cambridge University Press, 1983

Derrett, J. Duncan M. 'The Administration of Hindu Law by the British'. In his *Religion, Law and the State in India*. London: Faber and Faber, 1968, pp. 274–320

'The British as Patrons of the Sastra'. In his *Religion, Law and the State in India*. London: Faber and Faber, 1968, pp. 225–73

'The History of the Juridical Framework of the Joint Hindu Family'. In *Contributions to Indian Sociology*, no. 6, 1962, pp. 17–47

Devitt, Richard. 'Succession Struggles and the State: The Development of Strategies in Tamil *Maths*'. Paper presented to the Association for Asian Studies annual meeting, 1981

Dickey, Sara. 'The Politics of Adulation: Cinema and the Production of Politicians in South India'. In *Journal of Asian Studies*, vol. 52, no. 2, 1993, pp. 340–72

Dirks, Nicholas. 'From Little King to Landlord: Property, Law, and the Gift under the Madras Permanent Settlement'. In *Comparative Studies in Society and History*, vol. 28, no. 2, 1986, pp. 307–33

The Hollow Crown: The Ethnohistory of an Indian Kingdom. Cambridge: Cambridge University Press, 1987

'The Pasts of a Pāḷaiyakārar: The Ethnohistory of a South Indian Little King'. In *Journal of Asian Studies*, vol. 41, no. 4, 1982, pp. 655–83

'Political Authority and Structural Change in Early South Indian History'. In *Indian Economic and Social History Review*, vol. 13, no. 2, 1976, pp. 125–58

'The Structure and Meaning of Political Relations in a South Indian Little Kingdom'. In *Contributions to Indian Sociology (NS)*, vol. 13, no. 2, 1979, pp. 169–206

Dresch, Paul. 'Segmentation: Its roots in Arabia and its flowering elsewhere', in *Cultural Anthropology*, vol. 3, no. 1, 1988, pp. 50–67

Dumont, Louis. 'Hierarchy and Marriage Alliance in South Indian Kinship'. *Occasional Papers of the Royal Anthropological Institute*, no. 12. London, 1957

'Structural Definition of a Folk Deity of Tamil Nad: Aiyanar the Lord'. In *Contributions to Indian Sociology*, no. 3, July, 1959p pp. 75–87

Emeneau, M. B. and Burrow, T. *Dravidian Borrowings from Indo-Aryan*. Berkeley: University of California Press, 1962

Errington, Shelly. *Meaning and Power in a Southeast Asian Realm*. Princeton: Princeton University Press, 1989

Fabricius, J. P. *Tamil and English Dictionary*. Tranquebar, 1972. Fourth Edition. First published in 1779

Francis, W. *Madras District Gazetteers: Madurai*. Madras: Government Press, 1906

Freitag, Sandria B. *Collective Action and Community: Public Arenas and the Emergence of Communalism in North India*. Berkeley: University of California Press, 1989

'Introduction'. In *South Asia. New Series*, vol. 14, no. 1, 1991, pp. 1–13

Frykenberg, Robert Eric. 'The Emergence of Modern "Hinduism" as a Concept and as an Institution: A Reappraisal with Special Reference to South India'. Günther D. Sontheimer and Hermann Kulke (eds.) *Hinduism Reconsidered*. Delhi: Manohar, 1989, pp. 29–50

Guntur District, 1788–1848: A History of Local Influence and Central Authority in South India. Oxford: Clarendon Press, 1965

Fuller, C. J. *Servants of the Goddess: The Priests of a South Indian Temple*. Cambridge: Cambridge University Press, 1984

Fuller, C. J. and Penny Logan. 'The Navaratri Festival in Madurai'. In *Bulletin of the School of Oriental and African Studies*. University of London. vol. 58, pt. 1. 1985, pp. 79–105

'G. P'. *Representative Men of Southern India*. Madras: Price Current Press, 1896

Galanter, Marc. 'The Displacement of Traditional Law in Modern India'. In the *Journal of Social Issues*, vol. 24, 1968, pp. 65–91

'Indian Law as an Indigenous Conceptual System'. In *Social Science Research Council. ITEMS*, vol. 32, nos. 3–4, 1978, pp. 42–46

Ganapathyraman, R. 'The Birth and Growth of Rule of Law in Madurai'. In *Madura Bar Association: Souvenir, Centenary Celebration, 1872–1972*. Madurai: no publisher, n.d. No pagination

Geetha, V. and Rajadurai, S. V. '"Off With Their Heads": Suppression of Dissent in Tamil Nadu'. In *Economic and Political Weekly*. 6 June 1992, pp. 1184–5

Gilmartin, David. *Empire and Islam: Punjab and the Making of Pakistan*. Berkeley: University of California Press, 1988

Gopal Sharma, Raj. 'Dakshinamnaya Sri Sringeri Jagadgurus and Rameswaram Temple and Sethupathis'. In Somalay (ed.) *The Saga of Rameswaram Temple.* Rameswaram: Arulmigu Ramanathaswami Thirukkoil, 1975, pp. 183–6

Gopalratnam, V. C. *A Century Completed (A History of the Madras High Court), 1862–1962.* Madras: Madras Law Journal Office, n.d.

Guha, Ranajit. *A Rule of Property for Bengal: An Essay on the Idea of Permanent Settlement.* Paris: Mouton, 1963

Hardgrave, Robert. L. 'The Celluloid God: MGR and the Tamil Film'. In *South Asia Review*, vol. 4, no. 4. pp. 307–14

Harman, William P. *The Sacred Marriage of a Hindu Goddess.* Bloomington: Indiana University Press, 1989

Haynes, Douglas. *Rhetoric and Ritual in Colonial India: The Shaping of a Public Culture in Surat City, 1852–1928.* Berkeley: University of California Press, 1991

Heesterman, J. C. 'Indian and the Inner Conflict of Tradition'. In his *The Inner Conflict of Tradition: Essays in Indian Ritual, Kingship, and Society.* Chicago: University of Chicago Press, 1985, pp. 10–25

Heidemann, Frank. 'Resepkt als Ausdruck sozialer Beziehungen bei den Badagas in Süd-Indiens'. In Matthias S. Laubscher (ed.) *Beiträge zur Ethnologie Mittel- und Süd-Indiens.* Munich: Anacon, 1991, pp. 29–44

Heifitz, Hank and V. Narayana Rao. (trans.) *For the Lord of the Animals – Poems from the Telugu: The Kāḷahastīśvara Śatakamu of Dhūrjaṭi.* Berkeley: University of California Press, 1987

Heitzman, James. 'State Formation in South India, 850–1280'. In *The Indian Economic and Social History Review*, vol. 24, no. 1, 1987, pp. 35–61

Hellman-Rajanayagam, Dagmar. 'Arumukam Navalar: Religious Reformer or National Leader of Eelam'. In *The Indian Economic and Social History Review*, vol. 26, no. 2, 1989, pp. 235–57

Hemingway, F. R. *Madras District Gazetteers: Trichinopoly.* Madras: Government Press, 1907

Hiltebeitel, Alf. *The Cult of Draupadi.* vol. 1. *Mythologies From Gingee to Kuruksetra.* Chicago: University of Chicago Press, 1988

The Cult of Draupadi. vol. 2. *On Hindu Ritual and the Goddess.* Chicago: University of Chicago Press, 1991

The Ritual of Battle: Krishna in the Mahabharata. Ithaca and London: Cornell University Press, 1976

'Sexuality and Sacrifice: Convergent Subcurrents in the Firewalking Cult of Draupadi'. In Fred W. Clothey (ed.) *Images of Man: Religion and Historical Process in South Asia.* Madras: New Era Publications, 1982, pp. 72–111

Inden, Ronald. 'Orientalist Contructions of India'. In *Modern Asian Studies*, vol. 20, no. 3, 1986, pp. 401–46

'Ritual, Authority and Cyclic Time in Hindu Kingship'. In J. F. Richards (ed.) *Kingship and Authority in South Asia.* Madison: South Asian Studies, University of Wisconsin, 1978, pp. 28–73

Inglis, Stephen Robert. 'Village Arts of Madurai District: Some Notes on Technique and Style'. Unpublished paper, Madurai University Tamil Department, 1975

Irschick, Eugene. *Politics and Social Conflict in South India: The Non-Brahman*

Movement and Tamil Separatism, 1916–1929. Berkeley: University of California Press, 1969
Tamil Revivalism in the 1930s. Madras: Cre-A, 1986
Jackson, Robert H. and Rosenberg, Carl G. *Personal Rule in Black Africa: Prince, Autocrat, Prophet, Tyrant*. Berkeley: University of California Press, 1982
Jouveau-Dubrueil, G. *Iconography of Southern India*. Varanasi, 1978. Trans. by A. C. Martin. Reprinted from 1937 edition. French original printed in 1914
Kadhirvel, S. *A History of the Maravas, 1700–1802*. Madurai: Madurai Publishing House, 1977
Kalaikalañciyam. Madras, 1954–
Kamaliah, K. C. 'Anatomy of *Rāmappaiyan̲ Ammān̲ai*'. In *The Journal of Tamil Studies*, no. 7, 1975, pp. 29–50
Kidder, Robert L. 'Litigation as a Strategy for Personal Mobility: The Cases of Urban Caste Association Leaders'. In the *Journal of Asian Studies*, vol. 33, no. 2, 1974, pp. 177–91
Kersenboom-Story, Saskia C. *Nityasumaṅgalī: Devadasi Tradition in South India*. Delhi: Motilal Banarsidas, 1987
Kohli, Atul. *Democracy and Discontent: India's Growing Crisis of Governability*. Cambridge: Cambridge University Press, 1990
Kolff, Dirk H. A. 'The End of an *Ancien Régime*: Colonial War in India, 1798–1818'. In J. A. Moor and H. L. Wesseling (eds.) *Imperialism and War: Essays on Colonial Wars in Asia and Africa*. Comparative Studies in Overseas History, 6. Leiden: Brill, 1989, pp. 22–49
Naukar, Rajput and Sepoy: The Ethnohistory of the Military Labour Market in Hindustan, 1450–1850. Cambridge: Cambridge University Press, 1990
Konduri Sarojini Devi, *Religion in Vijayanagar Empire*. New Delhi: Sterling Publishers, 1990
Krishna Sastri, H. *South-Indian Images of Gods and Goddesses*. Benaras, 1974. First published in 1916
Leslie, I. Julia. *The Perfect Wife: The Orthodox Hindu Woman According to the Strīdharmapaddhati of Tryambakayajvan*. Delhi: Oxford University Press, 1989
Lingat, Robert. Trans. by J. Duncan Derrett. *The Classical Law of India*. Berkeley: University of California Press, 1973
Ludden, David. *Peasant History in South India*. Princeton: Princeton University Press, 1985
McCormack, William C. 'Caste and the British Administration of Hindu Law'. In *Journal of Asian and African Studies*, no. 1, pt. 1, 1966, pp. 25–32
Madras Institute of Development Studies. *Tamilnadu Economy: Performance and Issues*. New Delhi: Oxford University Press and IBH, 1988
Mahalingam, T. V. (ed.) *Mackenzie Manuscripts*. vol. 1. Madras: University of Madras, 1972
Manor, James (ed.) *Rethinking Third World Politics*. London: Longman, 1991
Marglin, Frédérique Appfel. 'Kings and Wives: The Separation of Status and Royal Power'. In T. N. Madan (ed.) *Way of Life: King, Household, Renouncer – Essays in Honor of Louis Dumont*. Delhi: Motilal Banarsidass Publishers, 1987, pp. 155–81
'Power, Purity and Pollution: Aspects of the Caste System Reconsidered'. In *Contributions to Indian Sociology (N.S.)*, vol. 2, no. 2, 1977, pp. 245–70

Wives of the God-King: The Rituals of the Devadasis of Puri. Delhi: Oxford University Press, 1985

Metcalf, Thomas R. *Land, Landlords and the British Raj: Northern India in the Nineteenth Century.* Berkeley: University of California Press, 1979

Mookia Thevar, P. K. and Emmanuel Divien. 'Thevar, Pasumpom Muthuramalinga (1908–1963)'. In S. P. Sen, (ed.) *Dictionary of National Biography*, vol. 4 (S–Z). Calcutta: Institute of Historical Studies, 1974, pp. 345–7

Moore, Molly. 'Queen Bee: She is India's Most Powerful Woman, Sweet as Honey but with a Sting'. Washington Post Foreign Service, 16 October 1993

Moore, Sally Falk. 'Descent and Legal Position'. In Laura Nader, (ed.) *Law in Culture and Society.* Chicago: Aldine Publishing Company, 1969, pp. 374–400

Morris-Jones, W. H. 'India – More Questions than Answers'. In *Asian Survey*, vol. 24, no. 8, 1984, pp. 809–16

Nadarajan, M. 'Nattukottai Chettiar Community in South East Asia'. In *Proceedings of the First International Conference Seminar of Tamil Studies*, vol. 1. Kuala Lumpur: International Association of Tamil Research, 1968, pp. 251–9

Nagasamy, R. 'Irāmanātapurattu Cētupati Ōviyaṅkal'. In *Tamilaracu*, June 6, 1978, pp. 37–40

Narayanan, Vasudha. 'The Goddess Śrī: Blossoming Lotus and Breast Jewel of Vishnu'. In John Stratton Hawley and Donna Marie Wulff (eds.) *The Divine Consort: Radha and the Goddesses of India.* Delhi: Motilal Banarsidas, 1984, pp. 224–37

Narayana Rao, Velcheru, Shulman, David and Subramanyam, Sanjay. *Symbols of Substance: Court and State in Nayaka Period Tamil Nadu.* Delhi: Oxford University Press, 1992

O'Hanlon, Rosalind. 'Issues of Womenhood: Gender and Resistance in Colonial Western India'. In Douglas Haynes and Gyan Prakash (eds.) *Contesting Power: Resistance and Everyday Social Relations in South Asia.* Delhi: Oxford University Press, 1991, pp. 62–108

Pandian, M. S. S. *The Image Trap: M. G. Ramachandran in Film and Politics.* New Delhi: Sage Publications, 1992

Pfaffenberger, Bryan. *Caste in Tamil Culture: The Religious Foundations of Sudra Domination in Tamil Sri Lanka.* Syracuse: Syracuse University, 1982

Philip, Bruno. 'The "Iron Lady" of Madras Politics'. In *Guardian Weekly.* 16 January 1994, p. 13

Pollack, Sheldon. 'Rāmāyaṇa and Political Imagination in India'. In *Journal of Asian Studies*, vol. 52, no. 2, 1993, pp. 261–96

Price, Pamela G. 'Acting in Public versus Forming a Public: Conflict Processing and Political Mobilization in Nineteenth Century South India'. In *South Asia. New Series.* no. 1, 1991, pp. 91–121

'Competition and Conflict in Hindu Polity, c. 1550–1750: the Integration and Fragmentation of Tamil and Andhra Kingdoms'. Paper delivered to the Eighth European Conference on Modern South Asian Studies. Tällberg, Sweden, 1983

'Democracy and Ethnic Conflict in India: Precolonial Legacies in Tamil Nadu'. In *Asian Survey*, vol. 33, no. 5, 1993, pp. 493–506

'Honor, Disgrace, and the Depoliticization of Women in South India: Changing

Structures of the State under Colonial Rule'. In *Gender and History*, vol. 6, no. 2, 1994, pp. 246–64

'Ideology and Ethnicity under British Imperial Rule: "Brahmins", Lawyers and Kin-Caste Rules'. In *Modern Asian Studies*, vol. 23, pt. l, 1989, pp. 151–78

'Kingly Models in Indian Political Behavior: Culture as a Medium of History'. In *Asian Survey*. vol. 29, no. 6, 1989, pp. 559–72

'Revolution and Rank in Tamil Nationalism'. Forthcoming

'The State and Representations of Femaleness in Late Medieval South India'. In *Historisk tidsskrift* (Oslo), no. 4, 1990, pp. 589–97

'Using Cultural History in Development Studies'. In *Forum for utviklingsstudier*, no. 2, 1989, pp. 147–58

Puttaiya, B. 'A Note on the Mysore Throne'. In *The Quarterly Journal of the Mythic Society*, vol. 9, no. 3, 1921, pp. 261–6

Raheja, Gloria Goodwin. 'India: Caste, Kingship and Dominance Reconsidered'. In *Annual Review of Anthropology*, vol. 17, 1988, pp. 497–522

Raja Rao. *Kanthapura*. Delhi: Orient Paperbacks, 1971

Rajayyan, K. *The Rise and Fall of the Poligars of Tamilnad*. Madras: University of Madras, 1974

South Indian Rebellion: The First War of Independence, 1800–1801. Mysore: Rao and Raghavan, 1971

Ramaswami, A. *Tamil Nadu District Gazetteers: Ramanathapuram*. Gazetter of India. Madras: Government of Tamil Nadu, 1972

Ramaswami Aiyar, L. V. 'Semantic Divergences in Indo-Aryan Loanwords in South Dravidian'. In *Journal of Oriental Research, Madras*, vol. 8, 1943, pp. 252–66

Ramaswamy, Sumathi. 'Battling the Demoness Hindi: The Culture of Language Protest in Tamilnadu, 1938–1965'. In Sandria B. Freitag (ed.) *Culture as Contested Site: Popular Participation and the State in the Indian Subcontinent*. Forthcoming

'En/gendering Language: The Poetics of Tamil Identity', *Comparative Studies in Society and History*. 1993, pp. 683–725

Reiniche, M. L. 'Le Temple dans la Localité: Quatre Exemples au Tamilnad'. In Jean-Claude Galey (ed.) *L'Espace du Temple: Espaces, Itinéraires, Méditations*. *Puruṣārtha* no. 8. Paris: Éditions de l'École des Hautes Études en Sciences Sociales, 1985, pp. 75–119

Rudner, David West. *Caste and Capitalism in Colonial India: the Nattukottai Chettiars*. Berkeley: University of California Press, 1994.

Rudolph, Lloyd I. and Rudolph, Susanne Hoeber. *The Modernity of Tradition: Political Development in India*. Chicago: University of Chicago, 1967

Rudolph, Susanne Hoeber. 'Presidential Address: State Formation in Asia – Prolegomenon to a Comparative Study'. In *Journal of Asian Studies*, vol. 46, no. 4, 1987, pp. 731–46

Sahlins, Marshall. *Islands of History*. Chicago: University of Chicago Press, 1985

'Other Times, Other Customs: The Anthropology of History'. In *American Anthropologist*. vol. 85, no. 3, 1983, pp. 517–44

Sarin, Ritu. 'Go for Gold: Devi Lal Adopts Cheap Gimmicks to Flaunt His Popularity'. In *Sunday*, vol. 18, no. 6, 10–16 February 1991, pp. 26–9

Sastri, Alladi Jagannatha. *A Family History of Venkatagiri Rajas.* Madras: Addison Press, 1922

Sastri, V. L. et al. (eds.) 'Zemindar of Devakottai'. In *Encyclopedia of the Madras Presidency and the Adjacent States.* Madras: Oriental Encyclopaedia Publishing Co., 1921, pp. 478–80

Sayana, V. V. *The Agrarian Problems of Madras Presidency.* Madras: Business Week Press, 1949

Seal, Anil. *The Emergence of Indian Nationalism.* Cambridge: Cambridge University Press, 1968

Shulman, David Dean. 'Battle as Metaphor in Tamil Folk and Classical Traditions'. In Stuart H. Blackburn and A. K. Ramanujan (eds.) *Another Harmony: New Essays on the Folklore of India.* Delhi: Oxford University Press, 1986, pp. 105–30

'The Crossing of the Wilderness: Landscape and Myth in the Tamil Story of Rama'. In *Acta Orientalia,* vol. 42. 1981, pp. 21–54

The King and the Clown in South Indian Myth and Poetry. Princeton: Princeton University Press, 1985

'On South Indian Bandits and Kings'. In *The Indian Economic and Social History Review,* vol. 17, no. 3, 1980, pp. 283–306

Tamil Temple Myths: Sacrifice and Divine Marriage in the South Indian Saiva Tradition. Princeton: Princeton University Press, 1980

Somalay (ed.) *The Saga of Rameswaram Temple: Kumbabishekam Souvenir.* Rameswaram: Arulmigu Ramanathaswami Thirukkoil, 1975

Sinha, Chittaranjan. *The Indian Civil Judiciary in Making, 1800–33.* New Delhi: Munshiram Manoharlal, 1969

Sontheimer, Günther-Dietz. *The Joint Hindu Family: Its Evolution as a Legal Institution.* New Delhi: Munishiram Manoharlal, 1977

Stein, Burton. 'Devi Shrines and Folk Hinduism in Medieval Tamilnad'. In Edwin Gerow and Margery D. Lang (eds.) *Studies in the Language and Culture of South Asia.* Seattle: University of Washington Press, 1973, pp. 75–90

'Integration of the Agrarian System of South India'. In Robert Eric Frykenberg (ed.) *Land Control and Social Structure in Indian History.* Madison: University of Wiconsin Press, 1969, pp. 175–216

'Mahānavami: Medieval and Modern Kingly Ritual in South India'. In his *All the King's Mana: Papers on Medieval South Indian History.* Madras: New Era Publications, 1984, pp. 1–67

Peasant State and Society in Medieval South India. Delhi: Oxford University Press, 1980

'Temples in Tamil Country, 1300–1750'. In Burton Stein (ed.) *South Indian Temples: An Analytic Reconsideration.* Delhi: Vikas Publishing House, 1978, pp. 11–46

Thomas Munro: The Origins of the Colonial State and his Vision of Empire. Delhi: Oxford University Press, 1989

Vijayanagara. The New Cambridge History of India, vol. 1.2. Cambridge: Cambridge University Press, 1989

Subramania Aiyar, A. V. *Tamil Studies.* Tirunelveli: (copies available from S. R. Subramania Pillai), 1969

Tamil Studies. Second Series. Tirunelveli: (copies available from S. R. Subramnia Pillai), 1970

Subramanian, T. S. 'A Famous "Victory"?: Jayalalitha and the Madurai Conference'. In *Frontline*, 31 July 1992, pp. 106–10

Sunil, K. P. 'The Theatre of the Absurd'. In *The Illustrated Weekly of India*, May
4–5, 1991, pp. 20–23

Suntharalingam, Ramanathan. *Politics and Nationalist Awakening in South India,
1852–1891*. Tucson: University of Arizona Press, 1974

Tambiah, S. J. 'The Galactic Polity in Southeast Asia'. In his *Culture, Thought and
Social Action*. Cambridge, Mass.: Harvard University Press, 1985, pp. 253–87

Thananjayarajasingham, S. *A Critical Study of a Seventeenth Century Tamil Document Relating to a Commercial Treaty*. Peradeniya: The Hindu Students' Union,
1968

Thani Nayagam, Xavier S. *Landscapes and Poetry: A Study of Nature in Classical
Tamil Poetry*. London: Asia Publishing House, 1966

Thiruvenkatachari, S. *The Setupatis of Ramnad*. Karaikudi-3, 1959

Thurston, Edgar. *Castes and Tribes of Southern India*. New York: Johnson Reprint
Corporation, 1965. First printed in 1909

Trautman, Thomas R. *Dravidian Kinship*. Cambridge: Cambridge University Press,
1981

Vanamamalai Pillai, N. *The Setu and Rameswaram*. Rameswarm: V. Narayana,
1929

Vadivelu, A. *The Aristocracy of Southern India*. vol. I. Madras: Vest and Co., 1903.
vol. II appeared in 1908. Madras: Vest and Co

Van Den Hoek, A. W. 'The Goddess of the Northern Gate: Cellatamman as the
"Divine Kshatriya" of Madurai'. In Marc Gaborieau and Alice Thorner (eds.)
Asie du Sud. Traditions et Changements. Paris: Édition du Centre National de la
Recherche Scientifique, 1979, pp. 119–31

Swami Vivekananda. *Lectures from Colombo to Almora*. Calcutta: Advaita
Ashrama, 1963

'Village Survey Monographs'. In *Census of India*, vol. IX, 1961, Madras, part VI,
no. 14

Wadley, Susan. 'Power in Hindu Ideology and Practice'. In Kenneth David (ed.) *The
New Wind: Changing Identities and South Asia*. The Hague: Mouton, 1977,
pp. 133–57

Washbrook, David. 'Country Politics: Madras 1880–1930'. In *Modern Asian Studies*,
vol. 7, no. 3, 1973, pp. 475–531
Emergence of Provincial Politics: Madras Presidency, 1870–1920. Cambridge:
Cambridge University Press, 1976
'Law, State and Agrarian Society in Colonial India'. In *Modern Asian Studies*,
vol. 15, no. 3, 1981, pp. 649–721

Whitehead, Henry. *The Village Gods of South India*. New York: Garland Publishing
Inc., 1980. First Published, 1921

Wink, André. *Land and Sovereignty in India: Agrarian Society and Politics under the
Eighteenth-Century Maratha Svarajya*. Cambridge: Cambridge University Press,
1986

Yocum, Glenn. 'Brahman, King, Sannyasi and the Goddess in a Cage: Reflections
on the "Conceptual Order of Hinduism" at a Tamil Saiva Temple'. In *Contributions to Indian Sociology, (N.S.)* vol. 20, no. 1, 1986, pp. 15–39

Zvelibil, Kamil *Tamil Literature*. vol. 10, fasc. 1. In J. Gonda (ed.) *History of Indian Literature*. Weisbaden: Harrassowitz, 1974

Unpublished dissertations

Blomkvist, Hans. 'The Soft State: Housing Reform and State Capacity in Urban India'. University of Uppsala, 1988

Breckenridge, Carol Appadurai. 'The Śrī Minakṣi Sundrēsvarar Temple: Worship and Endowments in South India, 1833–1925'. University of Wisconsin-Madison, 1976

Mosse, C. D. F. 'Caste, Christianity and Hinduism: A Study of Social Organisation and Religion in Rural Ramnad'. University of Oxford, 1986

Price, Pamela G. 'Resources and Rule in Zamindari South India: Ramnad and Sivagangai as Kingdoms under the Raj, 1802–1903'. University of Wisconsin-Madison, 1979

Rudner, David. 'Caste and Commerce in Indian Society: A Case Study of Nattu-kottai Chettiars, 1600–1930'. University of Pennsylvania, 1985

Seshadri, K. 'The Setupatis of Ramnad'. Madura College, University of Madurai, 1976.

INDEX

Ahambadiyas, 26, 175, 180
Anderson, Benedict, 42
Anglo-Indian legal system, *see* colonial legal
   system
Annadurai, C. N., 193–4
antastu see status
Appadurai, Arjun, 43 n.13, n.15, 45 n.23
Arasaratnam, S., 12
aristocracy, zamindari, 41, 73, 127, 141–2,
   158, 159, 189–90
Arunachellam Chettiar, 103
Arumukam Navalar, 92–3, 154
assemblies
   precolonial, 40
   durbar, 142–3, 144, 145, 146–9, 157, 201,
     202

Baskara Setupati, zamindar of Ramnad, 43,
   127–8
   aristocrat, as, 159
   Christian influence on, 176
   debts of, 175, 182–7
   diaries of, 161, 166
   estate administration of, 128, 181
   largess of, 134, 162, 168, 171–2, 187, 188;
     see also public sphere
   manager of Rameswaram temple, as, 127,
     128, 180, 181, 187
   populist, as a, 134, 191
   public sphere, in the, 133, 161–2, 166,
     167–8, 169–70, 188, 190;
   see also largess of
   religious reformer, as, 129, 131, 153–8,
     158–60, 170, 173, 176–8, 190
   ritual performer, as, 143–6, 149, 165,
     174–6, 190
   youth of, 162–5
Blackburn, J., 80, 83, 84
Bobbli, Maharaja of, 41, 79
Brahmins, 128–9, 134, 154, 160; *see also*
   Baskara Setupati, Navaratri, non-
   Brahmin movement, ritual
Breckenridge, Carol, 43 n.13, n.15, 20 n.48

Cadaikkan Setupati, king of Ramnad
   kingdom, 21, 23–4
cash
   replacement for ritual, as, 135
   zamindari politics, in, 98, 100–2
   see also status
caste membership, 42, 60–1
chattirams, 86, 111
Chettiars *see* Nattukkottai Chettiars
Chettinad, 13
civic arenas, 75–6; *see also* public sphere
colonial legal system, 40; *see also* dispute
   processing, litigation
conflict management, *see* dispute processing
cosmologies
   fragmentation in, 37, 75–6, 130–1
   monarchical, 6, 11, 38, 45, 113, 191
   political, 4
   Tamil nationalist, 198–9
   see also ideology
Court of Wards, 88, 115, 161, 162–4, 175
courts of law, 40
   arenas of ranking, as, 40
   ranking in, 130
   representation in, 42, 130
Criminal Tribes Act of 1911, 62, 193

deinstitutionalisation, 201–2
devadasis, 35, 69,143, 154–5, 156, 159
   allegations in court, 66–7
   see also women, royal
Devi Lal, 200
dispute processing
   colonial, 40–41, 159
   precolonial, 40, 45
   ranking in, 130
   rhetoric of, 130–1
   see also litigation
Dirks, Nicholas, 6, 17 n.38, 26 n.78, 29, 100
Dorasinga Tevar, zamindar of Sivagangai,
   54–8
Dravida Munnetra Kazhagam, 193–5
   Madurai District, in, 197–9

women, royal, 35–6, 47, 49, 51, 70–2, 178
  litigation involving, 52, 69–70, 72–3,74–5
  ritual, in, 71–2
Kulanthai, daughter-in-law of Muthu
  Virayi, 68–9
Kunjara, alledged wife of Zamindar
  Annasami Setupati, 66–7

  see also Kathama Nachiar, Mangaleswari
    Nachiar, Muthu Virayi, Parvata
    Vardhani, Sivagamy Nachiar

zamindari kin, *see* royal kin
zamindari system, 8 n.27

University of Cambridge
Oriental publications published for the
Faculty of Oriental Studies

Lightning Source UK Ltd.
Milton Keynes UK
30 March 2010

152126UK00002B/23/A